Pro Perl Parsing

Christopher M. Frenz

Apress®

Pro Perl Parsing

Copyright © 2005 by Christopher M. Frenz

Lead Editors: Jason Gilmore and Matthew Moodie
Technical Reviewer: Teodor Zlatanov
Editorial Board: Steve Anglin, Dan Appleman, Ewan Buckingham, Gary Cornell, Tony Davis,
    Jason Gilmore, Jonathan Hassell, Chris Mills, Dominic Shakeshaft, Jim Sumser
Associate Publisher: Grace Wong
Project Manager: Beth Christmas
Copy Edit Manager: Nicole LeClerc
Copy Editor: Kim Wimpsett
Assistant Production Director: Kari Brooks-Copony
Production Editor: Laura Cheu
Compositor: Linda Weidemann, Wolf Creek Press
Proofreader: Nancy Sixsmith
Indexer: Tim Tate
Artist: Wordstop Technologies Pvt. Ltd., Chennai
Cover Designer: Kurt Krames
Manufacturing Manager: Tom Debolski

Library of Congress Cataloging-in-Publication Data

Frenz, Christopher.
   Pro Perl parsing / Christopher M. Frenz.
      p.   cm.
   Includes index.
   ISBN 1-59059-504-1 (hardcover : alk. paper)
   1. Perl (Computer program language) 2. Natural language processing (Computer science)   I. Title.
QA76.73.P22F72 2005
005.13'3--dc22

                                                                        2005017530

Printed and bound in the United States of America 9 8 7 6 5 4 3 2 1

Distributed to the book trade worldwide by Springer-Verlag New York, Inc., 233 Spring Street, 6th Floor, New York, NY 10013. Phone 1-800-SPRINGER, fax 201-348-4505, e-mail orders-ny@springer-sbm.com, or visit http://www.springeronline.com.

For information on translations, please contact Apress directly at 2560 Ninth Street, Suite 219, Berkeley, CA 94710. Phone 510-549-5930, fax 510-549-5939, e-mail info@apress.com, or visit http://www.apress.com.

The source code for this book is available to readers at http://www.apress.com in the Downloads section.

For Jonathan!
You are the greatest son
any father could ask for.

Contents at a Glance

Contents

■CHAPTER 9   Finding Solutions to Miscellaneous Parsing Problems 201

■CHAPTER 10   Performing Text and Data Mining 217

■INDEX 243

About the Author

CHRISTOPHER M. FRENZ is currently a bioinformaticist at New York Medical College. His research interests include applying artificial neural networks to protein engineering as well using molecular modeling techniques to determine the role that protein structures have on protein function. Frenz uses the Perl programming language to conduct much of his research. Additionally, he is the author of *Visual Basic and Visual Basic .NET for Scientists and Engineers* (Apress, 2002) as well as numerous scientific and computer articles. Frenz has more than ten years of programming experience and, in addition to Perl and VB, is also proficient in the Fortran and C++ languages. Frenz can be contacted at cfrenz@gmail.com.

About the Technical Reviewer

TEODOR ZLATANOV earned his master's degree in computer engineering from Boston University in 1999 and has been happily hacking ever since. He always wonders how it is possible to get paid for something as fun as programming, but tries not to make too much noise about it.

Zlatanov lives with his wife, 15-month-old daughter, and two dogs, Thor and Maple, in lovely Braintree, Massachusetts. He wants to thank his family for their support and for the inspiration they always provide.

Acknowledgments

Bringing this book from a set of ideas to the finished product that you see before you today would not have been possible without the help of others. Jason Gilmore was a great source of ideas for refining the content of the early chapters in this book, and Matthew Moodie provided equally insightful commentary for the later chapters and assisted in ensuring that the final page layouts of the book looked just right. I am also appreciative of Teodor Zlatanov's work as a technical reviewer, since he went beyond the role of simply finding technical inaccuracies and made many valuable suggestions that helped improve the clarity of the points made in the book. Beth Christmas also played a key role as the project manager for the entire process; without her friendly prompting, this book would probably still be in draft form. I would also like to express my appreciation of the work done by Kim Wimpsett and Laura Cheu, who did an excellent job preparing the manuscript and the page layouts, respectively, for publication. Last, but not least, I would like to thank my family for their support on this project, especially my wife, Thao, and son, Jonathan.

Introduction

Over the course of the past decade, we have all been witnesses to an explosion of information, in terms of both the amounts of knowledge that exists within the world and the availability of such information, with the proliferation of the World Wide Web being a prime example. Although these advancements of knowledge have undoubtedly been beneficial, they have also created new challenges in information retrieval, in information processing, and in the extraction of relevant information. This is in part due to a diversity of file formats as well as the proliferation of loosely structured formats, such as HTML. The solution to such information retrieval and extraction problems has been to develop specialized parsers to conduct these tasks. This book will address these tasks, starting with the most basic principles of data parsing.

The book will begin with an introduction to parsing basics using Perl's regular expression engine. Once these regex basic are mastered, the book will introduce the concept of generative grammars and the Chomsky hierarchy of grammars. Such grammars form the base set of rules that parsers will use to try to successfully parse content of interest, such as text or XML files. Once grammars are covered, the book proceeds to explain the two basic types of parsers—those that use a top-down approach and those that use a bottom-up approach to parsing. Coverage of these parser types is designed to facilitate the understanding of more powerful parsing modules such as Yapp (bottom-up) and RecDescent (top-down).

Once these powerful and flexible generalized parsing modules are covered, the book begins to delve into more specialized parsing modules such as parsing modules designed to work with HTML. Within Chapter 6, the book also provides an overview of the LWP modules, which facilitate access to documents posted on the Web. The parsing examples within this chapter will use the LWP modules to parse data that is directly accessed from the Web. Next the book examines the parsing of XML data, which is a markup language that is increasingly growing in popularity. The XML coverage also discusses SOAP and XML-RPC, which are two of the most popular methods for accessing remote XML-formatted data. The book then covers several smaller parsing modules, such as an RSS parser and a date/time parser, as well as some useful parsing tasks, such as the parsing of configuration files. Lastly, the book introduces data mining. *Data mining* provides a means for individuals to work with extracted data (as well as other types of data) so that the data can be used to learn more about a given area or to make predictions about future directions that area of interest may take. This content aims to demonstrate that although parsing is often a critical data extraction and retrieval task, it may just be a component of a larger data mining system.

This book examines all these problems from the perspective of the Perl programming language, which, since its inception in 1987, has always been heralded for its parsing and text processing capabilities. The book takes a practical approach to parsing and is rich in examples that are relevant to real-world parsing tasks. While covering all the basics of parser design to instill understanding in readers, the book highlights numerous CPAN modules that will allow programmers to produce working parser code in an efficient manner.

CHAPTER 1

■ ■ ■

Parsing and Regular Expression Basics

The dawn of a new age is upon us, an information age, in which an ever-increasing and seemingly endless stream of new information is continuously generated. Information discovery and knowledge advancements occur at such rates that an ever-growing number of specialties is appearing, and in many fields it is impossible even for experts to master everything there is to know. Anyone who has ever typed a query into an Internet search engine has been a firsthand witness to this information explosion. Even the most mundane terms will likely return hundreds, if not thousands, of hits. The sciences, especially in the areas of genomics and proteomics, are generating seemingly insurmountable mounds of data.

Yet, one must also consider that this generated data, while not easily accessible to all, is often put to use, resulting in the creation of new ideas to generate even more knowledge or in the creation of more efficient means of data generation. Although the old adage "knowledge is power" holds true, and almost no one will deny that the knowledge gained has been beneficial, the sheer volume of information has created quite a quandary. Finding information that is exactly relevant to your specific needs is often not a simple task. Take a minute to think about how many searches you performed in which all the hits returned were both useful and easily accessible (for example, were among the top matches, were valid links, and so on). More than likely, your search attempts did not run this smoothly, and you needed to either modify your query or buckle down and begin to dig for the resources of interest.

Thus, one of the pressing questions of our time has been how do we deal with all of this data so we can efficiently find the information that is currently of interest to us? The most obvious answer to this question has been to use the power of computers to store these giant catalogs of information (for example, databases) and to facilitate searches through this data. This line of reasoning has led to the birth of various fields of informatics (for example, bioinformatics, health informatics, business informatics, and so on). These fields are geared around the purpose of developing powerful methods for storing and retrieving data as well as analyzing it.

In this book, I will explain one of the most fundamental techniques required to perform this type of data extraction and analysis, the technique of *parsing*. To do this, I will show how to utilize the Perl programming language, which has a rich history as a powerful text processing language. Furthermore, Perl is already widely used in many fields of informatics, and many robust parsing tools are readily available for Perl programmers in the form of CPAN modules. In addition to examining the actual parsing methods themselves, I will also cover many of these modules.

Parsing and Lexing

Before I begin covering how you can use Perl to accomplish your parsing tasks, it is essential to have a clear understanding of exactly what parsing is and how you can utilize it. Therefore, I will define *parsing* as the action of splitting up a data set into smaller, more meaningful units and uncovering some form of meaningful structure from the sequence of these units. To understand this point, consider the structure of a tab-delimited data file. In this type of file, data is stored in columns, and a tab separates consecutive columns (see Figure 1-1).

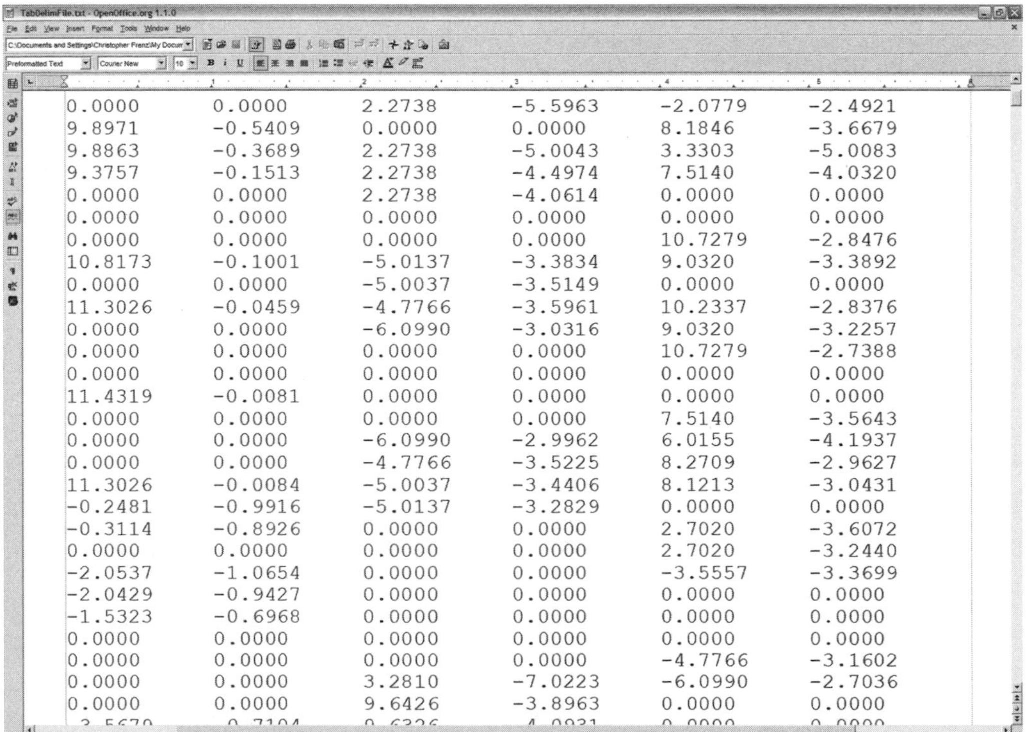

0.0000	0.0000	2.2738	-5.5963	-2.0779	-2.4921
9.8971	-0.5409	0.0000	0.0000	8.1846	-3.6679
9.8863	-0.3689	2.2738	-5.0043	3.3303	-5.0083
9.3757	-0.1513	2.2738	-4.4974	7.5140	-4.0320
0.0000	0.0000	2.2738	-4.0614	0.0000	0.0000
0.0000	0.0000	0.0000	0.0000	0.0000	0.0000
0.0000	0.0000	0.0000	0.0000	10.7279	-2.8476
10.8173	-0.1001	-5.0137	-3.3834	9.0320	-3.3892
0.0000	0.0000	-5.0037	-3.5149	0.0000	0.0000
11.3026	-0.0459	-4.7766	-3.5961	10.2337	-2.8376
0.0000	0.0000	-6.0990	-3.0316	9.0320	-3.2257
0.0000	0.0000	0.0000	0.0000	10.7279	-2.7388
0.0000	0.0000	0.0000	0.0000	0.0000	0.0000
11.4319	-0.0081	0.0000	0.0000	0.0000	0.0000
0.0000	0.0000	0.0000	0.0000	7.5140	-3.5643
0.0000	0.0000	-6.0990	-2.9962	6.0155	-4.1937
0.0000	0.0000	-4.7766	-3.5225	8.2709	-2.9627
11.3026	-0.0084	-5.0037	-3.4406	8.1213	-3.0431
-0.2481	-0.9916	-5.0137	-3.2829	0.0000	0.0000
-0.3114	-0.8926	0.0000	0.0000	2.7020	-3.6072
0.0000	0.0000	0.0000	0.0000	2.7020	-3.2440
-2.0537	-1.0654	0.0000	0.0000	-3.5557	-3.3699
-2.0429	-0.9427	0.0000	0.0000	0.0000	0.0000
-1.5323	-0.6968	0.0000	0.0000	0.0000	0.0000
0.0000	0.0000	0.0000	0.0000	0.0000	0.0000
0.0000	0.0000	0.0000	0.0000	-4.7766	-3.1602
0.0000	0.0000	3.2810	-7.0223	-6.0990	-2.7036
0.0000	0.0000	9.6426	-3.8963	0.0000	0.0000

Figure 1-1. *A tab-delimited file*

Reviewing this file, your eyes most likely focus on the numbers in each column and ignore the whitespace found between the columns. In other words, your eyes perform a parsing task by allowing you to visualize distinct columns of data. Rather than just taking the whole data set as a unit, you are able to break up the data set into columns of numbers that are much more meaningful than a giant string of numbers and tabs. While this example is simplistic, we carry out parsing actions such as this every day. Whenever we see, read, or hear anything, our brains must parse the input in order to make some kind of logical sense out of it. This is why parsing is such a crucial technique for a computer programmer—there will often be a need to parse data sets and other forms of input so that applications can work with the information presented to them.

The following are common types of parsed data:

- Data TypeText files

- CSV files

- HTML

- XML

- RSS files

- Command-line arguments

- E-mail/Web page headers

- HTTP headers

- POP3 headers

- SMTP headers

- IMAP headers

To get a better idea of just how parsing works, you first need to consider that in order to parse data you must classify the data you are examining into units. These units are referred to as *tokens*, and their identification is called *lexing*. In Figure 1-1, the units are numbers, and a tab separates each unit; for many lexing tasks, such whitespace identification is adequate. However, for certain sophisticated parsing tasks, this breakdown may not be as straightforward. A recursive approach may also be warranted, since in more nested structures it becomes possible to find units within units. Math equations such as 4*(3+2) provide an ideal example of this. Within the parentheses, 3 and 2 behave as their own distinct units; however, when it comes time to multiply by 4, (3+2) can be considered as a single unit. In fact, it is in dealing with nested structures such as this example that full-scale parsers prove their worth. As you will see later in the "Using Regular Expressions" section, simpler parsing tasks (in other words, those with a known finite structure) often do not require full-scale parsers but can be accomplished with regular expressions and other like techniques.

■**Note** Examples of a well-known lexer and parser are the C-based Lex and Yacc programs that generally come bundled with Unix-based operating systems.

Parse::Lex

Before moving on to more in-depth discussions of parsers, I will introduce the Perl module `Parse::Lex`, which you can use to perform lexing tasks such as lexing the math equation listed previously.

■**Tip** `Parse::Lex` and the other Perl modules used in this book are all available from CPAN (`http://www.cpan.org`). If you are unfamiliar with working with CPAN modules, you can find information about downloading and installing Perl modules on a diversity of operating systems at `http://search.cpan.org/~jhi/perl-5.8.0/pod/perlmodinstall.pod`. If you are using an ActiveState Perl distribution, you can also install Perl modules using the Perl Package Manager (PPM). You can obtain information about its use at `http://aspn.activestate.com/ASPN/docs/ActivePerl/faq/ActivePerl-faq2.html`.

For more detailed information about CPAN and about creating and using Perl modules, you will find that *Writing Perl Modules for CPAN* (Apress, 2002) by Sam Tregar is a great reference.

Philipe Verdret authored this module; the most current version as of this book's publication is version 2.15. `Parse::Lex` is an object-oriented lexing module that allows you to split input into various tokens that you define. Take a look at the basics of how this module works by examining Listing 1-1, which will parse simple math equations, such as 18.2+43/6.8.

Listing 1-1. *Using* `Parse::Lex`

```
#!/usr/bin/perl

use Parse::Lex;
```

```
#defines the tokens
@token=qw(
    BegParen [\(]
    EndParen [\)]
    Operator [-+*/^]
    Number   [-?\d+|-?\d+\.\d*]
    );
$lexer=Parse::Lex->new(@token); #Specifies the lexer
$lexer->from(STDIN); #Specifies the input source

TOKEN:
while(1){ #1 will be returned unless EOI
    $token=$lexer->next;
    if(not $lexer->eoi){
        print $token->name . " " . $token->text . " " . "\n";
    }
    else {last TOKEN;}
}
```

The first step in using this module is to create definitions of what constitutes an acceptable token. Token arguments for this module usually consist of a token name argument, such as the previous BegParen, followed by a regular expression. Within the module itself, these tokens are stored as instances of the Parse::Token class. After you specify your tokens, you next need to specify how your lexer will operate. You can accomplish this by passing a list of arguments to the lexer via the new method. In Listing 1-1, this list of arguments is contained in the @token array. When creating the argument list, it is important to consider the order in which the token definitions are placed, since an input value will be classified as a token of the type that it is first able to match. Thus, when using this module, it is good practice to list the strictest definitions first and then move on to the more general definitions. Otherwise, the general definitions may match values before the stricter comparisons even get a chance to be made.

Once you have specified the criteria that your lexer will operate on, you next define the source of input into the lexer by using the from method. The default for this property is STDIN, but it could also be a filename, a file handle, or a string of text (in quotes). Next you loop through the values in your input until you reach the eoi (end of input) condition and print the token and corresponding type. If, for example, you entered the command-line argument 43.4*15^2, the output should look like this:

```
Number 43.4
Operator *
Number 15
Operator ^
Number 2
```

In Chapter 3, where you will closely examine the workings of full-fledged parsers, I will employ a variant of this routine to aid in building a math equation parser.

Regular expressions are one of the most useful tools for lexing, but they are not the only method. As mentioned earlier, for some cases you can use whitespace identification, and for others you can bring dictionary lists into play. The choice of lexing method depends on the application. For applications where all tokens are of a similar type, like the tab-delimited text file discussed previously, whitespace pattern matching is probably the best bet. For cases where multiple token types may be employed, regular expressions or dictionary lists are better bets. For most cases, regular expressions are the best since they are the most versatile. Dictionary lists are better suited to more specialized types of lexing, where it is important to identify only select tokens.

One such example where a dictionary list is useful is in regard to the recent bioinformatics trend of mining medical literature for chemical interactions. For instance, many scientists are interested in the following:

```
<Chemical A> <operates on> <Chemical B>
```

In other words, they just want to determine how chemical A interacts with chemical B. When considering this, it becomes obvious that the entire textual content of any one scientific paper is not necessary to tokenize and parse. Thus, an informatician coding such a routine might want to use dictionary lists to identify the chemicals as well as to identify terms that describe the interaction. A dictionary list would be a listing of all the possible values for a given element of a sentence. For example, rather than operates on, I could also fill in reacts with, interacts with, or a variety of other terms and have a program check for the occurrence of any of those terms. Later, in the section "Capturing Substrings," I will cover this example in more depth.

Using Regular Expressions

As you saw in the previous Parse::Lex example, regular expressions provide a robust tool for token identification, but their usefulness goes far beyond that. In fact, for many simple parsing tasks, a regular expression alone may be adequate to get the job done. For example, if you want to perform a simple parsing/data extraction task such as parsing out an e-mail address found on a Web page, you can easily accomplish this by using a regular expression. All you need is to create a regular expression that identifies a pattern similar to the following:

```
[alphanumeric characters]@[alphanumeric characters.com]
```

■**Caution** The previous expression is a simplification provided to illustrate the types of pattern matching for which you can use regular expressions. A more real-world e-mail matching expression would need to be more complex to account for other factors such as alternate endings (for example, .net, .gov) as well as the presence of metacharacters in either alphanumeric string. Additionally, a variety of less-common alternative e-mail address formats may also warrant consideration.

The following sections will explain how to create such regular expressions in the format Perl is able to interpret. To make regular expressions and their operation a little less mysterious, however, I will approach this topic by first explaining how Perl's regular expression engine operates. Perl's regular expression engine functions by using a programming paradigm known as a *state machine*, described in depth next.

A State Machine

A simple definition of a state machine is one that will sequentially read in the symbols of an input word. After reading in a symbol, it will decide whether the current state of the machine is one of acceptance or nonacceptance. The machine will then read in the next symbol and make another state decision based upon the previous state and the current symbol. This process will continue until all symbols in the word are considered. Perl's regular expression engine operates as a state machine (sometimes referred to as an *automaton*) for a given string sequence (that is, the word). In order to match the expression, all of the acceptable states (that is, characters defined in the regular expression) in a given path must be determined to be true. Thus, when you write a regular expression, you are really providing the criteria the differing states of the automaton need to match in order to find a matching string sequence. To clarify this, let's consider the pattern /123/ and the string 123 and manually walk through the procedure the regular expression engine would perform. Such a pattern is representative of the simplest type of case for your state machine. That is, the state machine will operate in a completely linear manner. Figure 1-2 shows a graphical representation of this state machine.

■**Note** It is interesting to note that a recursive descent parser evaluates the regular expressions you author. For more information on recursive descent parsers, see Chapter 5.

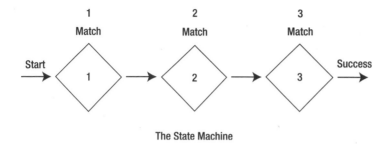

The String in Question = 123

Figure 1-2. *A state machine designed to match the pattern* /123/

In this case, the regular expression engine begins by examining the first character of the string, which is a 1. In this case, the required first state of the automaton is also a 1. Therefore, a match is found, and the engine moves on by comparing the second character, which is a 2, to the second state. Also in this case, a match is found, so the third character is examined and another match is made. When this third match is made, all states in the state machine are satisfied, and the string is deemed a match to the pattern.

In this simple case, the string, as written, provided an exact match to the pattern. Yet, this is hardly typical in the real world, so it is important to also consider how the regular expression will operate when the character in question does not match the criterion of a particular state in the state machine. In this instance, I will use the same pattern (/123/) and hence the same state machine as in the previous example, only this time I will try to find a match within the string 4512123 (see Figure 1-3).

This time the regular expression engine begins by comparing the first character in the string, 4, with the first state criterion. Since the criterion is a 1, no match is found. When this mismatch occurs, the regular expression starts over by trying to compare the string contents beginning with the character in the second position (see Figure 1-4).

As in the first case, no match is found between criterion for the first state and the character in question (5), so the engine moves on to make a comparison beginning with the third character in the string (see Figure 1-5).

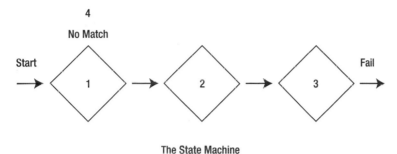

Figure 1-3. *The initial attempt at comparing the string* 4512123 *to the pattern* /123/

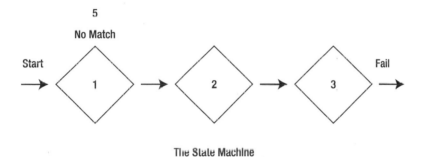

Figure 1-4. *The second attempt at comparing the string* 4512123 *to the pattern* /123/

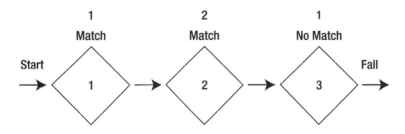

Figure 1-5. *The third attempt at comparing the string* 4512123 *to the pattern* /123/

In this case, since the third character is a 1, the criterion for the first state is satisfied, and thus the engine is able to move on to the second state. The criterion for the second state is also satisfied, so therefore the engine will next move on to the third state. The 1 in the string, however, does not match the criterion for state 3, so the engine then tries to match the fourth character of the string, 2, to the first state (see Figure 1-6).

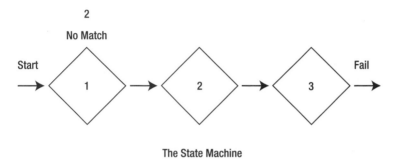

Figure 1-6. *The fourth attempt at comparing the string* 4512123 *to the pattern* /123/

As in previous cases, the first criterion is not satisfied by the 2, and consequently the regular expression engine will begin to examine the string beginning with the fifth character. The fifth character satisfies the criterion for the first state, and therefore the engine proceeds on to the second state. In this case, a match for the criterion is also present, and the engine moves on to the third state. The final character in the string matches the third state criterion, and hence a match to the pattern is made (see Figure 1-7).

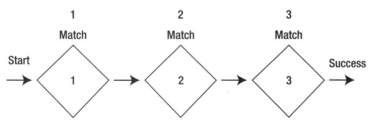

Figure 1-7. *A match is made to the pattern* /123/.

The previous two examples deal with a linear state machine. However, you are not limited to this type of regular expression setup. It is possible to establish alternate paths within the regular expression engine. You can set up these alternate paths by using the alternation ("or") operator (|) and/or parentheses, which define subpatterns. I will cover more about the specific meanings of regular expression syntaxes in the upcoming sections "Pattern Matching," "Quantifiers," and "Predefined Subpatterns." For now, consider the expression /123|1b(c|C)/, which specifies that the matching pattern can be 123, 1bc, or 1bC (see Figure 1-8).

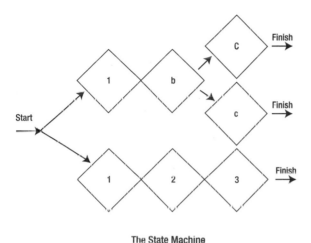

The State Machine

Figure 1-8. *The state machine defined by the pattern* /123|1b(c|C)/

■Note Parentheses not only define subpatterns but can also capture substrings, which I will discuss in the upcoming "Capturing Substrings" section.

As you can see, this state machine can follow multiple paths to reach the goal of a complete match. It can choose to take the top path of 123, or can choose to take one of the bottom paths of 1bc or 1bC. To get an idea of how this works, consider the string 1bc and see how the state machine would determine this to be a match. It would first find that the 1 matches the first state condition, so it would then proceed to match the next character (b) to the second state condition of the top path (2). Since this is not a match, the regular expression engine will backtrack to the location of the true state located before the "or" condition. The engine will backtrack further, in this case to the starting point, only if all the available paths are unable to provide a correct match. From this point, the regular expression engine will proceed down an alternate path, in this case the bottom one. As the engine traverses down this path, the character b is a match for the second state of the bottom path. At this point, you have reached a second "or" condition, so the engine will check for matches along the top path first. In this case, the engine is able to match the character c with the required state c, so no further backtracking is required, and the string is considered a perfect match.

When specifying regular expression patterns, it is also beneficial to be aware of the notations [ ] and [^], since these allow you to specify ranges of characters that will serve as an acceptable match or an unacceptable one. For instance, if you had a pattern containing [ABCDEF] or [A-F], then A, B, C, D, E, and F would all be acceptable matches. However, a or G would not be, since both are not included in the acceptable range.

■**Tip** Perl's regular expression patterns are case-sensitive by default. So, A is different from a unless a modifier is used to declare the expression case-insensitive. See the "Modifiers" section for more details.

If you want to specify characters that would be unacceptable, you can use the [^] syntax. For example, if you want the expression to be true for any character but A, B, C, D, E, and F, you can use one of the following expressions: [^ABCDEF] or [^A-F].

Pattern Matching

Now that you know how the regular expression engine functions, let's look at how you can invoke this engine to perform pattern matches within Perl code. To perform pattern matches, you need to first acquaint yourself with the binding operators, =~ and !~. The string you seek to bind (match) goes on the left, and the operator that it is going to be bound to goes on the right. You can employ three types of operators on the right side of this statement. The first is the pattern match operator, m//, or simply // (the m is implied and can be left out), which will test to see if the string value matches the supplied expression, such as 123 matching /123/, as shown in Listing 1-2. The remaining two are s/// and tr///, which will allow for substitution and transliteration, respectively. For now, I will focus solely on matching and discuss the other two alternatives later. When using =~, a value will be returned from this operation that indicates whether the regular expression operator was able to successfully match the string. The !~ functions in an identical manner, but it checks to see if the string is unable to match the specified operator. Therefore, if a =~ operation returns that a match was successful, the corresponding !~ operation will not return a successful result, and vice versa. Let's examine this a little closer by considering the simple Perl script in Listing 1-2.

Listing 1-2. *Performing Some Basic Pattern Matching*

```perl
#!/usr/bin/perl

$string1="123";
$string2="ABC";
$pattern1="123";

if($string1=~/$pattern1/){
    print "123=123\n";
}

if($string2!~/123/){
    print "ABC does not match /123/\n";
}

if("234"=~/$pattern1|ABC/){
    print "This is 123 or ABC\n";
}
else{print "This is neither 123 nor ABC";}
```

The script begins by declaring three different scalar variables; the first two hold string values that will be matched against various regular expressions, and the third serves as storage for a regular expression pattern. Next you use a series of conditional statements to evaluate the strings against a series of regular expressions. In the first conditional, the value stored in $string1 matches the pattern stored in $pattern1, so the print statement is able to successfully execute. In the next conditional, $string2 does not match the supplied pattern, but the operation was conducted using the !~ operator, which tests for mismatches, and thus this print statement can also execute. The third conditional does not return a match, since the string 234 does not match either alternative in the regular expression. Accordingly, in this case the print statement of the else condition will instead execute. A quick look at the output of this script confirms that the observed behavior is in agreement with what was anticipated:

```
123=123
ABC does not match /123/
This is neither 123 nor ABC
```

Operations similar to these serve as the basis of pattern matching in Perl. However, the basic types of patterns you have learned to create so far have only limited usefulness. To gain more robust pattern matching capabilities, you will now build on these basic concepts by further exploring the richness of the Perl regular expression syntax.

Quantifiers

As you saw in the previous section, you can create a simple regular expression by simply putting the characters or the name of a variable containing the characters you seek to match between a pair of forward slashes. However, suppose you want to match the same sequence of characters multiple times. You could write out something like this to match three instances of Yes in a row:

```
/YesYesYes/
```

But suppose you want to match 100 instances? Typing such an expression would be quite cumbersome. Luckily, the regular expression engine allows you to use quantifiers to accomplish just such a task.

The first quantifier I will discuss takes the form of {number}, where number is the number of times you want the sequence matched. If you really wanted to match Yes 100 times in a row, you could do so with the following regular expression:

```
/(Yes){100}/
```

To match the whole term, putting the Yes in parentheses before the quantifier is important; otherwise, you would have matched Ye followed by 100 instances of s, since quantifiers operate only on the unit that is located directly before them in the pattern expression. All the quantifiers operate in a syntax similar to this (that is, the pattern followed by a quantifier); Table 1-1 summarizes some useful ones.

Table 1-1. *Useful Quantifiers*

Quantifier	Effect
X*	Zero or more Xs.
X+	One or more Xs.
X?	X is optional.
X{5}	Five Xs.
X{5,10}	From five to ten Xs.
X{5,}	Five Xs or more.

When using quantifiers, it is important to remember they will always produce the longest possible match unless otherwise instructed to do so. For example, consider the following string:

```
(123)123(123)
```

If you asked the regular expression engine to examine this string with an expression such as the following, you would find that the entire string was returned as a match, because . will match any character other than \n and because the string does begin and end with (and) as required:

`/\(.*\)/`

■Note Parentheses are *metacharacters* (that is, characters with special meaning to the regular expression engine); therefore, to match either the open or close parenthesis, you must type a backslash before the character. The backslash tells the regular expression engine to treat the character as a normal character (in other words, like *a, b, c*, 1, 2, 3, and so on) and not interpret it as a metacharacter. Other metacharacters are \, |, [, {, ^, $, *, +, ., and ?.

It is important to keep in mind that the default behavior of the regular expression engine is to be greedy, which is often not wanted, since conditions such as the previous example can actually be more common than you may at first think. For example, other than with parentheses, similar issues may arise in documents if you are searching for quotes or even HTML or XML tags, since different elements and nodes often begin and end with the same tags. If you wanted only the contents of the first parentheses to be matched, you need to specify a question mark (?) after your quantifier. For example, if you rewrite the regular expression as follows, you find that (123) is returned as the match:

`/\(.*?\)/`

Adding ? after the quantifier allows you to control greediness and find the smallest possible match rather than the largest one.

Predefined Subpatterns

Quantifiers are not the only things that allow you to save some time and typing. The Perl regular expression engine is also able to recognize a variety of predefined subpatterns that you can use to recognize simple but common patterns. For example, suppose you simply want to match any alphanumeric character. You can write an expression containing the pattern [a-zA-Z0-9], or you can simply use the predefined pattern specified by \w. Table 1-2 lists other such useful subpatterns.

Table 1-2. *Useful Subpatterns*

Specifier	Pattern
\w	Any standard alphanumeric character or an underscore (_)
\W	Any nonalphanumeric character or an underscore (_)
\d	Any digit
\D	Any nondigit
\s	Any of \n, \r, \t, \f, and " "
\S	Any other than \n, \r, \t, \f, and " "
.	Any other than \n

These specifiers are quite common in regular expressions, especially when combined with the quantifiers listed in Table 1-1. For example, you can use \w+ to match any word, use d+ to match any series of digits, or use \s+ to match any type of whitespace. For example, if you want to split the contents of a tab-delimited text file (such as in Figure 1-1) into an array, you can easily perform this task using the split function as well as a regular expression involving \s+. The code for this would be as follows:

```
while (<>){
    push @Array, {split /\s+/ };
}
```

The regular expression argument provided for the split function tells the function where to split the input data and what elements to leave out of the resultant array. In this case, every time whitespace occurs, it signifies that the next nonwhitespace region should be a distinct element in the resultant array.

Posix Character Classes

In the previous section, you saw the classic predefined Perl patterns, but more recent versions of Perl also support some predefined subpattern types through a set of Posix character classes. Table 1-3 summarizes these classes, and I outline their usage after the table.

Table 1-3. *Posix Character Classes*

Posix Class	Pattern
[:alnum:]	Any letter or digit
[:alpha:]	Any letter
[:ascii:]	Any character with a numeric encoding from 0 to 127
[:cntrl:]	Any character with a numeric encoding less than 32
[:digit:]	Any digit from 0 to 9 (\d)
[:graph:]	Any letter, digit, or punctuation character

Posix Class	Pattern
[:lower:]	Any lowercase letter
[:print:]	Any letter, digit, punctuation, or space character
[:punct:]	Any punctuation character
[:space:]	Any space character (\s)
[:upper:]	Any uppercase letter
[:word:]	Underline or any letter or digit
[:xdigit:]	Any hexadecimal digit (that is, 0–9, a–f, or A–F)

Note You can use Posix characters in conjunction with Unicode text. When doing this, however, keep in mind that using a class such as [:alpha:] may return more results than you expect, since under Unicode there are many more letters than under ASCII. This likewise holds true for other classes that match letter and digits.

The usage of Posix character classes is actually similar to the previous examples where a range of characters was defined, such as [A-F], in that the characters must be enclosed in brackets. This is actually sometimes a point of confusion for individuals who are new to Posix character classes, because, as you saw in Table 1-3, all the classes already have brackets. This set of brackets is actually part of the class name, not part of the Perl regex. Thus, you actually need a second set, such as in the following regular expression, which will match any number of digits:

```
/[[:digit:]]*/
```

Modifiers

As the name implies, modifiers allow you to alter the behavior of your pattern match in some form. Table 1-4 summarizes the available pattern modifiers.

Table 1-4. *Pattern Matching Modifiers*

Modifier	Function
/i	Makes insensitive to case
/m	Allows $ and ^ to match near /n (**multiline**)
/x	Allows insertion of comments and whitespace in expression
/o	Evaluates the expression variable only **once**
/s	Allows . to match /n (**single line**)
/g	Allows **global** matching
/gc	After failed **global** search, allows **continued** matching

For example, under normal conditions, regular expressions are case-sensitive. There-fore, ABC is a completely different string from abc. However, with the aid of the pattern modifier /i, you could get the regular expression to behave in a case-insensitive manner. Hence, if you executed the following code, the action contained within the conditional would execute:

```
if("abc"=~/ABC/i){
    #do something
}
```

You can use a variety of other modifiers as well. For example, as you will see in the upcoming "Assertions" section, you can use the /m modifier to alter the behavior of the ^ and $ assertions by allowing them to match at line breaks that are internal to a string, rather than just at the beginning and ending of a string. Furthermore, as you saw earlier, the subpattern defined by . normally allows the matching of any character other than the new line metasymbol, \n. If you want to allow . to match \n as well, you simply need to add the /s modifier. In fact, when trying to match any multiline document, it is advis-able to try the /s modifier first, since its usage will often result in simpler and faster executing code.

Another useful modifier that can become increasingly important when dealing with large loops or any situation where you repeatedly call the same regular expression is the /o modifier. Let's consider the following piece of code:

```
While($string=~/$pattern/){
    #do something
}
```

If you executed a segment of code such as this, every time you were about to loop back through the indeterminate loop the regular expression engine would reevaluate the regular expression pattern. This is not necessarily a bad thing, because, as with any variable, the contents of the $pattern scalar may have changed since the last iteration. However, it is also possible that you have a fixed condition. In other words, the contents of $pattern will not change throughout the course of the script's execution. In this case, you are wasting process-ing time reevaluating the contents of $pattern on every pass. You can avoid this slowdown by adding the /o modifier to the expression:

```
While($string=~/$pattern/o){
    #do something
}
```

In this way, the variable will be evaluated only once; and after its evaluation, it will remain a fixed value to the regular expression engine.

■**Note** When using the /o modifier, make sure you never need to change the contents of the pattern variable. Any changes you make after /o has been employed will not change the pattern used by the regular expression engine.

The /x modifier can also be useful when you are creating long or complex regular expressions. This modifier allows you to insert whitespace and comments into your regular expression without the whitespace or # being interpreted as a part of the expression. The main benefit to this modifier is that it can be used to improve the readability of your code, since you could now write /\w+ | \d+ /x instead of /\w+|\d+ /.

The /g modifier is also highly useful, since it allows for global matching to occur. That is, you can continue your search throughout the whole string and not just stop at the first match. I will illustrate this with a simple example from bioinformatics: DNA is made up of a series of four nucleotides specified by the letters *A, T, C,* and *G*. Scientists are often interested in determining the percentage of G and C nucleotides in a given DNA sequence, since this helps determine the thermostability of the DNA (see the following note).

■**Note** DNA consists of two complementary strands of the nucleotides A, T, C, and G. The A on one strand is always bonded to a T on the opposing strand, and the G on one strand is always bonded to the C on the opposing strand, and vice versa. One difference is that G and C are connected by three bonds, whereas A and T only two. Consequently, DNA with more GC pairs is bound more strongly and is able to withstand higher temperatures, thereby increasing its thermostability.

Thus, I will illustrate the /g modifier by writing a short script that will determine the %GC content in a given sequence of DNA. Listing 1-3 shows the Perl script I will use to accomplish this.

Listing 1-3. *Determining %GC Content*

```
#!usr/bin/perl;

$String="ATGCCGGGAAATTATAGCG";
$Count=0;

while($String=~/G|C/g){
    $Count=$Count+1;
}
$len=length($String);
$GC=$Count/$len;
print "The DNA sequence has $GC %GC Content";
```

As you can see, you store your DNA sequence in the scalar variable $String and then use an indeterminate loop to step through the character content of the string. Every time you encounter a G or a C in your string, you increment your counter variable ($Count) by 1. After you have completed your iterations, you divide the number of Gs and Cs by the total sequence length and print your answer. For the previous DNA sequence, the output should be as follows:

```
The DNA sequence has 0.473684210526316 %GC Content
```

Under normal conditions, when the /g modifier fails to match any more instances of a pattern within a string, the starting position of the next search is reset back to zero. However, if you specified /gc instead of just /g, your next search would not reset back to the beginning of the string, but rather begin from the position of the last match.

Cloistered Pattern Modifiers

In the previous section, you saw how to apply pattern modifiers to an entire regular expression. It is also possible to apply these modifiers to just a portion of a given regular expression; however, the syntax is somewhat different. The first step is to define the subpattern to which you want the modifier to apply. You accomplish this by placing the subpattern within a set of parentheses. Immediately after the open parenthesis, but before the subpattern, you add ?modifiers:. For example, if you want to match either ABC or AbC, rather than using alternation, you write the following:

```
/A(?i:B)C/
```

To create a regular expression that allows . to match /n but only in part of the expression, you can code something like the following, which allows any character to be matched until an A is encountered:

```
/.*?A(?s:.*?)BC/
```

It then allows any character to match, including /n, until a BC is encountered.

■ **Note** Cloistered pattern modifiers are available only in Perl versions 5.60 and later.

Assertions

Assertions are somewhat different from the topics I covered in the preceding sections on regular expressions, because unlike the other topics, assertions do not deal with characters in a string. Because of this, they are more properly referred to as *zero-width assertions*.

Assertions instead allow you to add positional considerations to your string matching capabilities. Table 1-5 summarizes the available assertions.

Table 1-5. *Assertions*

Assertion	Function
\A, ^	Beginning assertions
\Z, \z, $	Ending assertions
\b	Boundary assertion
\G	Previous match assertion

The \A and ^ Assertions

For example, if you want to match only the beginning of a string, you can employ the \A assertion. Similarly, you can also use the ^ assertion, known as the *beginning-of-line* assertion, which will match characters at the beginning of a string. When used in conjunction with the /m modifier, it will also be able to match characters after any new lines embedded within a string. Thus, if you had the regular expressions /\A123/ and /^123/m, both would be able to match the string 123456, but only /^123/m would be able to match the string abd\n123.

The \z, \Z, and $ Assertions

Just as there are assertions for dealing with the beginnings of lines and strings, so too are there assertions for dealing with the character sequences that end strings. The first of these assertions is the \z assertion, which will match the ending contents of a string, including any new lines. \Z works in a similar fashion; however, this assertion will not include a terminal new line character in its match, if one is present at the end of a string. The final assertion is $, which has functionality similar to \Z, except that the /m modifier can enable this assertion to match anywhere in a string that is directly prior to a new line character. For example, /\Z321/, /\z321/, and /$321/ would be able to match the string 654321.

Boundary Assertions

While assertions dealing with the beginning and end of a string/line are certainly useful, assertions that allow you to deal with positions internal to a string/line are just as important. Several types of assertions can accomplish this, and the first type you will examine is the so-called boundary assertion. The \b boundary assertion allows you to perform matches at any word boundary. A word boundary can exist in two possible forms, since you have both a beginning of a word and an end. In more technical terms, the beginning of a word boundary is defined as \W\w, or any nonalphanumeric character followed by any alphanumeric character. An end of a word boundary has the reverse definition. That is, it is defined by \w\W, or a word character followed by a nonword character. When using these assertions, you should keep in mind several considerations, however. The first is that the underscore character is a part of the \w subpattern, even though it is not an alphanumeric character. Furthermore, you need to be careful using this assertion if you are dealing with contractions, abbreviations, or other wordlike structures, such as Web and e-mail addresses, that have embedded nonalphanumeric characters. According to the \w\W or \W\w pattern, any of the following would contain valid boundaries:

```
"can't"
"www.apress.com"
"F.B.I."
"((1+2)*(3-4))"
user@example.com
"(555) 555-5555"
```

The pos Function and \G Assertion

Before I discuss the remaining assertion, I will first discuss the pos function, since this function and the \G assertion are often used to similar effect. You can use the pos function to either return or specify the position in a string where the next matching operation will start (that is, one after the current match). To better understand this, consider the code in Listing 1-4.

Listing 1-4. *Using the* pos *Function*

```
#!usr/bin/perl;
$string="regular expressions are fun";
pos($string)=3;
while($string=~/e/g){
    print "e at position " . (pos($string)-1). "\n";
}
```

If you execute this script, you get the following output:

```
e at position 8
e at position 12
e at position 22
```

Notice how the first e is missing from the output. This is because Listing 1-4 specified the search to begin at position 3, which is after the occurrence of the first e. Hence, when you print the listing of the returned matches, you can see that the e in the first position was not seen by the regular expression engine.

The remaining assertion, the \G assertion, is a little more dynamic than the previous assertions in that it does not specify a fixed type of point where matching attempts are allowed to occur. Rather, the \G assertion, when used in conjunction with the /g modifier, will allow you to specify the position right in front of your previous match. Let's examine how this works by looking at a file containing a list of names followed by phone numbers. Listing 1-5 shows a short script that will search through the list of names until it finds a match. The script will then print the located name and the corresponding phone number.

Listing 1-5. *Using the* \G *Assertion*

```perl
#!/usr/bin/perl

($string=<<'LIST');
John (555)555-5555
Bob (234)567-8901
Mary (734)234-9873
Tom (999)999-9999
LIST

$name-"Mary";
pos($string)=0;
while($string=~/$name/g){
    if($string=~/\G(\s?\(?\d{3}\))?[-\s.]?\d{3}[-.]\d{4})/){
        print "$name $1";
    }
}
```

■**Note** As mentioned earlier, parentheses are metacharacters and must be escaped in order to allow the regular expression to match them.

This script begins with you creating the $string variable and adding the list of names. Next, you define the $name variable as the name Mary. The next line of code is not always necessary but can be if prior matching and other types of string manipulation were previously performed on the string. You can use the pos function to set the starting point of the search to the starting point of the string. Finally, you can use a loop structure to search for the name Mary within your $string variable. Once Mary is located, you apply the \G assertion in the conditional statement, which will recognize and print any phone number that is present immediately after Mary. If you execute this script, you should receive the following output:

```
Mary (734)234-9873
```

Capturing Substrings

After looking at the previous example, you might be wondering how you were able to capture the recognized phone number in order to print it. Looking at the output and the print statement itself should give you the idea that it had something to do with the variable $1, and indeed it did. Earlier in the chapter, I noted that parentheses could serve two purposes within Perl regular expressions. The first is to define subpatterns, and the second is to capture the substring that matches the given subpattern. These captured substrings are stored in the variables $1, $2, $3, and so on. The contents of the first set of parentheses goes into $1, the second into $2, the third into $3, and so on. Thus, in the previous example, by placing the phone number regular expression into parentheses, you are able to capture the phone number and print it by calling the $1 variable.

When using nested parentheses, it is important to remember that the parentheses are given an order of precedence going from left to right, with regard to where the open parenthesis occurs. As a result, the substring is enclosed by the first open parenthesis encountered and its corresponding close parenthesis will be assigned to $1, even if it is not the first fully complete substring to be evaluated. For example, if you instead wrote the phone number regular expression as follows, the first set of parentheses would capture the entire phone number as before:

```
=~/(\s?(\(?\d{3}\)?)?)[-\s.](?\d{3}[-.]\d{4}))/
```

The second set would capture the area code in $2, and the third set would put the remainder of the phone number into $3.

■Note If you do not want to capture any values with a set of parentheses but only specify a subpattern, you can place ?: right after (but before the subpattern (for example, (?:abc)).

Parentheses are not the only way to capture portions of a string after a regular expression matching operation. In addition to specifying the contents of parentheses in variables such as $1, the regular expression engine also assigns a value to the variables $`, $&, and $'. $& is a variable that is assigned the portion of the string that the regular expression was actually able to match. $` is assigned all the contents to the left of the match, and $' is assigned all the contents to the right of the match (see Table 1-6).

Caution When dealing with situations that involve large amounts of pattern matching, it may not be advisable to use $&, $`, and $', since if they are used once they will be repeatedly generated for every match until the Perl program terminates, which can lead to a lengthy increase in the program's execution time.

Table 1-6. *Substring Capturing Variables*

Variable	Use
$1, $2, $3, ...	Stores captured substrings contained in parentheses
$&	Stores the substring that matched the regex
$`	Stores the substring to the left of the matching regex
$'	Stores the substring to the right of the matching regex

Let's take some time now to explore both types of capturing in greater depth by considering the medical informatics example, mentioned earlier, of mining medical literature for chemical interactions. Listing 1-6 shows a short script that will search for predefined interaction terms and then capture the names of the chemicals involved in the interaction.

Listing 1-6. *Capturing Substrings*

```perl
#!usr/bin/perl;

($String=<<'ABOUTA');
    ChemicalA is used to treat cancer.  ChemicalA
    reacts with ChemicalB which is found in cancer
    cells.  ChemicalC inhibits ChemicalA.
ABOUTA

pos($String)=0;
while($String=~/reacts with|inhibits/ig){
    $rxn=$&;
    $left=$`;
    $right=$';
    if($left=~/(\w+)\s+\z/){
        $Chem1=$1;
    }
    if($right=~/(\w+)/){
        $Chem2=$1;
    }
    print "$Chem1 $rxn $Chem2\n";
}
```

The script begins by searching through the text until it reaches one of the predefined interaction terms. Rather than using a dictionary-type list with numerous interaction terms, alternation of the two terms found in the text is used for simplicity. When one of the interaction terms is identified, the variable $rxn is set equal to this term, and $left and $right are set equal to the left and right sides of the match, respectively. Conditional statements and parentheses-based string capturing are then used to capture the word before and the word after the interaction term, since these correspond to the chemical names. It is also important to note the use of the \z assertion in order to match the word before the interaction term, since this word is located at the end of the $left string. If you run this script, you see that the output describes the interactions explained in the initial text:

```
ChemicalA reacts with ChemicalB
ChemicalC inhibits ChemicalA
```

Substitution

Earlier I mentioned that in addition to basic pattern matching, you can use the =~ and !~ operations to perform substitution. The operator for this operation is s///. Substitution is similar to basic pattern matching in that it will initially seek to match a specified pattern. However, once a matching pattern is identified, the substitution will replace the part of the string that matches the pattern with another string. Consider the following:

```
$String="aabcdef";
$String=~s/abc/123/;
print $String;
```

If you execute this code, the string a123def will be printed. In other words, the pattern recognized by /abc/ is replaced with 123.

Troubleshooting Regexes

The previous examples clearly demonstrate that regular expressions are a powerful and flexible programming tool and are thus widely applicable to a wealth of programming tasks. As you can imagine, however, all this power and flexibility can often make constructing complex regular expressions quite difficult, especially when certain positions within the expression are allowed to match multiple characters and/or character combinations. The construction of robust regular expressions is something that takes practice; but while you are gaining that experience, you should keep in mind a few common types of mistakes:

- *Make sure you choose the right wildcard*: For example, if you must have one or more of a given character, make sure to use the quantifier + and not *, since * will match a missing character as well.

- *Watch out for greediness*: Remember to control greediness with ? when appropriate.

- *Make sure to check your case (for example, upper or lowercase)*: For example, typing \W when you mean \w will result in the ability to match different things.

- *Watch out for metacharacters (\,(, |, [, {, ^, $, *, +, ., and ?)*: If a metacharacter is part of your pattern, make sure you turn off its special meaning by prefixing it with \.

- *Check your | conditions carefully*: Make sure all the possible paths are appropriate.

Even with these guidelines, debugging a complex regular expression can still be a challenge, and one of the best, although time-consuming, ways to do this can be to actually draw a visual representation of how the regular expression should work, similar to that found in the state machine figures presented earlier in the chapter (Figure 1-2 through Figure 1-8). If drawing this type of schematic seems too arduous a task, you may want to consider using the GraphViz::Regex module.

GraphViz::Regex

GraphViz is a graphing program developed by AT&T for the purpose of creating visual representations of structured information such as computer code (http://www.research. att.com/sw/tools/graphviz/). Leon Brocard wrote the GraphViz Perl module, which serves as a Perl-based interface to the GraphViz program. GraphViz::Regex can be useful when coding complex regular expressions, since this module is able to create visual representations of regular expressions via GraphViz. The syntax for using this module is quite straightforward and is demonstrated in the following code snippet:

```
Use GraphViz::Regex;

my $regex='((123|ab(c|C))';
my $graph=GraphViz::Regex->new($regex);
print $graph->as_jpeg;
```

When you first employ the GraphViz::Regex module, you place a call to the new constructor, which requires a string of the regular expression that you seek a graphical representation of. The new method is then able to create a GraphViz object that corresponds to this representation and assigns the object to $graph. Lastly, you are able to print the graphical representation you created. This example displays a JPEG file, but numerous other file types are supported, including GIF, PostScript, PNG, and bitmap.

■**Caution** The author of the module reports that there are incompatibilities between this module and Perl versions 5.005_03 and 5.7.1.

■**Tip** Another great tool for debugging regular expressions comes as a component of ActiveState's programming IDE Komodo. Komodo contains the Rx Toolkit, which allows you to enter a regular expression and a string into each of its fields and which tells you if they do or do not match as you type. This can be a rapid way to determine how well a given expression will match a given string.

Using Regexp::Common

As you can imagine, certain patterns are fairly commonplace and will likely be repeatedly utilized. This is the basis behind Regexp::Common, which is a Perl module originally authored by Damian Conway and maintained by Abigail that provides a means of accessing a variety of regular expression patterns. Since writing regular expressions can often be tricky, you may want to check this module and see if a pattern suited to your needs is available. Table 1-7 lists all the expression pattern categories available in version 2.113 of this module.

Table 1-7. Regexp::Common *Patterns*

Pattern Types	Use
Balanced	Matches strings with parenthesized delimiters
Comment	Identifies code comments in 43 languages
Delimited	Matches delimited text
Lingua	Identifies palindromes
List	Works with lists of data
Net	Matches IPv4 and MAC Internet addresses
Number	Works with integers and reals
Profanity	Identifies obscene terms
URI	Identifies diversity of URI types
Whitespace	Matches leading and trailing whitespace
Zip	Matches ZIP codes

Although Table 1-7 provides a general idea of the different types of patterns, it is a good idea to look at the module description available at CPAN (http://www.cpan.org/). The module operates by generating hash values that correspond to different patterns, and these patterns are stored in the hash %RE. When using this module, you can access its predefined subpatterns by referencing the scalar value of a particular hash element. So, if you want to search for Perl comments in a file, you can employ the hash value stored in $RE{comments}{Perl}; or, if you want to search for real numbers, you can use $RE{num}{real}. This two-layer hash of hash structure is fine for specifying most pattern types, but deeper layers are available in many cases. These deeper hash layers represent flags that modify the basic pattern in some form. For example, with numbers—in addition to just specifying real or integer—you can also set delimiters so that 1,234 is interpreted as a valid number pattern rather than just 1234. I will briefly cover some types of patterns, but complete coverage of every possible option could easily fill a small book on its own. I recommend you look up the module on CPAN (http://www.cpan.org) and refer to the descriptions of the pattern types offered by each component module.

Regexp::Common::Balanced

This namespace generates regular expressions that are able to match sequences located between balanced parentheses or brackets. The basic syntax needed to access these regular expressions is as follows:

```
$RE{balanced}{-parens=>'()[]{}'}
```

The first part of this hash value refers to the basic regular expression structure needed to match text between balanced delimiters. The second part is a flag that specifies the types of parentheses you want the regular expression to recognize. In this case, it is set to work with (), [], and {}. One application of such a regular expression is in the preparation of publications that contain citations, such as "(Smith et al., 1999)." An author may want to search a document for in-text citations in order to ensure they did not miss adding any to their list of references. You can easily accomplish this by passing the filename of the document to the segment of code shown in Listing 1-7.

Listing 1-7. *Pulling Out the Contents of* () *from a Document*

```perl
#!/usr/bin/perl -w
use Regexp::Common;

while(<>){
    /$RE{balanced}{-parens=>'()'}{-keep}/
    and print "$1\n";
}
```

■**Note** A more detailed description of the module's usage will follow in the sections "Standard Usage" and "Subroutine-Based Usage," since each of the expression types can be accessed through code in the same manner.

Regexp::Common::Comments

This module generates regular expressions that match comments inserted into computer code written in a variety of programming languages (currently 43). The syntax to call these regular expressions is as follows, where {comments} refers to the base comment matching functionality and {LANGUAGE} provides the descriptor that indicates the particular programming language:

```
$RE{comments}{LANGUAGE}
```

For example, to match Perl and C++ comments, you can use the following:

```
$RE{comments}{Perl}
$RE{comments}{C++}
```

Regexp::Common::Delimited

This base module provides the functionality required to match delimited strings. The syntax is similar to that shown for the Text::Balanced module:

```
$RE{delimited}{-delim=>'"'}
```

In this case, the -delim flag specifies the delimiter that the regular expression will search for and is a required flag, since the module does not have a default delimiter.

■**Note** Table 1-8 summarizes all the Regexp::Common flags.

Regexp::Common::List

The List module can match lists of data such as tab-separated lists, lists of numbers, lists of words, and so on. The type of list matched depends on the flags specified in the expression. Its syntax is as follows:

```
$RE{list}{-pat}{-sep}{-lastsep}
```

The pattern flag specifies the pattern that will correspond to each substring that is contained in the list. The pattern can be in the form of a regular expression such as \w+ or can be another hash value created by the Regexp::Common module. The -sep flag defines a type of separator that may be present between consecutive list elements, such as a tab or a space (the default). The -lastsep flag specifies a separator that may be present between the last two elements in the list. By default, this value is the same as that specified by -sep. As an example, if you wanted to search a document for lists that were specified in the Item A, Item B, ..., and Item N format, you could easily identify such listings using the following expression:

```
$RE{list}{-pat}{-sep=>', '}{-lastsep=>', and '}
```

Regexp::Common::Net

The Net module generates hash values that contain patterns designed to match IPv4 and MAC addresses, and the first hash key specifies which type to match. The next hash key allows you to specify whether the address will be decimal (default), hexadecimal, or octal. You can also use the -sep flag to specify a separator, if required. The following is a sample:

```
$RE{net}{IPv4}{hex}
```

This module comes in handy if you want to monitor the domains that different e-mails you have received originated from. This information is found in most e-mail headers in a format similar to the following:

```
from [64.12.116.134] by web51102.mail.yahoo.com via HTTP;
Mon, 29 Nov 2004 23:33:11 -0800 (PST)
```

You can easily parse this header information to find the IPv4 address 64.12.116.134 by using the following expression:

```
$RE{net}{IPv4}
```

Regexp::Common::Number

The Number module can match a variety of different number types, including integers, reals, hexadecimals, octals, binaries, and even Roman numerals. The base syntax is of the following form, but you should also be aware of a diversity of flags:

```
$RE{num}{real}
```

For example, you can apply the -base flag to change the base of the number to something other than the default of base 10. The -radix flag specifies the pattern that will serve as the decimal point in case you desire something other than the default value (.). If you are dealing with significant figures, you may find the -places flag useful, since it can specify the number of places after the decimal point. As in previous modules, -sep specifies separators; however, in this module, you can also specify the appropriate number of digits that should be present between separators using the -group flag. The default value for this flag is 3, so if you specified a comma (,) as your separator, your expression would be able to recognize values such as 123,456,789. The -expon flag specifies the pattern that will be used to specify that an exponent is present. The default value for this property is [Ee].

Universal Flags

As you saw in the previous sections, many of the base modules have their own flags, which can be used to further refine the pattern your regular expression will match (see Table 1-8). You can use two additional flags, however, with almost all base modules. These flags are the -i flag and the -keep flag. The -i flag makes the regular expression insensitive to alphabetic case so the expression can match both lowercase and capital letters. You can use the -keep flag for pattern capturing. If you specify -keep, the entire match to the pattern is generally stored in $1. In many cases, $2, $3, and other variables are also set, but these are set in a module-specific manner.

Table 1-8. Regexp::Common *Flags*

Flag	Use	Module(s)
-sep	Specifies a separator	Net and List
-lastsep	Specifies the last separator of a list	List
-base	For numbers, makes the base something other than base 10	Number
-radix	Makes a decimal point something other than .	Number
-places	Specifies the number of places after a decimal point	Number
-group	For numbers, specifies the number of digits that should be present between separators	Numbers
-expon	Specifies the exponent pattern	Numbers
-i	Makes the regular expressions case insensitive	All
-keep	Enables substring capturing	All

Standard Usage

You can utilize the patterns located in the module in your source code in a couple of ways. The first of these ways is referred to as the *standard usage method* and has a syntax similar to some of the regular expressions you have already seen in that the expression is placed between the // operator. The only difference is that rather than placing your own regular expression between //, you place one of the modules hash values. Consider the following segment of text:

```
Bob said "Hello".  James
responded "Hi, how are you".
Bob replied "Fine and you".
```

Now let's save this text to a file and execute the Perl code shown in Listing 1-8, making sure to pass the name of the file you just saved as an argument.

Listing 1-8. *Pulling Quotes Out of a Document*

```
#!/usr/bin/perl -w
use Regexp::Common;

while(<>){
    /$RE{delimited}{-delim=>'"'}{-keep}/
    and print "$1\n";
}
```

This short piece of code will read through the contents of the file and identify all the quotes present in the text file. Since you also specified the -keep flag, you are able to capture the quotes and print them. Thus, the output for this script should be similar to the following:

```
"Hello"
"Hi, how are you"
"Fine and you"
```

Subroutine-Based Usage

In addition to the standard usage, you can also access the functionality of this module through a subroutine-based interface, which allows you to perform a matching operation with a syntax similar to a procedural call. If you were to recode the previous example using this alternative syntax, it would look like Listing 1-9.

Listing 1-9. *Pulling Quotes Out via a Subroutine*

```
#!/usr/bin/perl -w
use Regexp::Common 'RE_ALL';

while(<>){
    $_ =~ RE_delimited(-delim=>'"',-keep)
    and print "$1\n";
}
```

You should note several important things here if you choose to use this syntax instead. The first is that when you call the Regexp::Common module, you must append RE_ALL to the end of the line so Perl is able to recognize the alternative syntax. Without this, you will receive a compilation error that says the subroutines are undefined. The second noteworthy thing is that you must explicitly write $_=~ in order to perform the required matching operation. Lastly, you should also note that the flags are read in as arguments separated by commas. Accessing the regular expressions this way can lead to faster execution times since this method does not return objects to be interpolated but, rather, actual regular expressions.

In-Line Matching and Substitution

I will cover these two methods together since they have similar syntax and use an object-oriented interface. In terms of basic pattern matching, they offer no real advantage other than allowing you to create code that may be somewhat more user-friendly to read; their syntax is as follows:

```
if($RE{num}{int}->matches($SomeNumber)){
    print "$SomeNumber is an Integer";
}
```

This interface allows you to easily perform substitutions on a string without changing the original string. For example:

```
$SubstitutedString=$RE{num}{real}->subs($Original=>$Substitution);
```

In this case, $SubstitutedString is a new string that is going to be assigned the value of the $Original string with all substitutions already made, and the $Substitution string specifies the string that is going to be put in place of the characters that were able to match the pattern.

Creating Your Own Expressions

The Regexp::Common module does not limit you to just the patterns that come with it. You also have the ability to create your own regular expressions, at run time, for use within the Regexp::Common module. For example, Regexp::Common does not yet support phone numbers, so let's begin to create a Regexp::Common phone number entry (see Listing 1-10).

Listing 1-10. *Creating Your Own* Regexp::Common *Expression*

```
#!/usr/bin/perl -w
use Regexp::Common qw /pattern/;

pattern name=>[qw(phone)],
    create=>q/(?k:\s?(\(\d{3}\))[-\s.](\d{3}[ .]\d{4}))/,


while(<>){
    /$RE{phone}{-keep}/ and print "$1\n";
}
```

Note You may have noticed that the pattern contains the sequence of characters ?k: in it. Under normal circumstances, capturing through parentheses is not preserved in Regexp::Common, since capturing parentheses are processed out. The ?k: sequence tells the module not to process out these parentheses when the -keep flag is present. This is why you were able to print phone numbers by using $1 in the previous example.

To begin, you must first tell Perl you are going to utilize the pattern subroutine of the Regexp::Common module. Next, you must create a name argument that will specify the name of the pattern and any flags it may take. In this case, the pattern is named phone. If you want to add additional names and/or flags, you can specify them as follows:

```
pattern name=[qw(phone book -flag)]
```

This specifies an entry of $RE{phone}{book}{-flag}.

After you name your pattern, you must next specify a value for the create argument. This argument is the only other required argument and can take either a string that is to be returned as a pattern (as previously) or a reference to a subroutine that will create the pattern. Also, two optional arguments also take subroutine references. These arguments are match and subs, and the provided subroutine will dictate what occurs when the methods match and subs, the matching and substitution methods (respectively), are called. Lastly, one more optional argument, version, can be assigned a Perl version number.

If the version of Perl is older than the supplied argument, the script will not run and a fatal error will be returned.

Summary

This chapter covered how to syntactically construct regular expressions and how you can call upon these expressions within your Perl scripts. Furthermore, I discussed the roles of the different quantifiers, assertions, and predefined subpatterns, as well as how best to debug regular expressions. Lastly, the chapter covered how the Perl module `Regexp::Common` works and how you can utilize it to locate elements of interest.

Now that you have an idea of how you can use regular expressions to match, and hence identify, portions of strings, you are more prepared to tackle the topics of tokens and grammars in greater depth as you delve into the next chapter. Chapter 2 will introduce you to the idea of generative grammars by covering the Chomsky hierarchy of grammars. The upcoming chapter will also demonstrate how you can use Perl code in conjunction with a grammar to generate sentences that comply with the rules specified in the grammar.

CHAPTER 2

■ ■ ■

Grammars

A *parser* is responsible for identifying tokens and making some form of logical sense from them. Before examining how exactly to accomplish this, let's first acknowledge that token identification alone is far from adequate. Consider the following statement:

```
Perl about hook parsing is This
```

While you can easily identify the different tokens found within the statement, it is nonsensical in its current form, thereby illustrating why the rules that govern parsing are considered to be grammars. The statement makes much more sense written in the following form:

```
This book is about Perl parsing
```

When performing parsing tasks, token order is quite important and can often affect the meaning or significance of a given token. For instance, a math equation consists of operands and operators, while a sentence consists of nouns, verbs, adjectives, and so forth. In both cases, the order in which their components are written creates the context. To understand this concept, consider the following two sentences:

```
I saw a bird fly by my window.
```

```
A fly landed on my wall.
```

Within the first sentence, the token fly operates as a verb since it has an action associated with it. However, in the second sentence, the same token operates as a noun. For this reason, most advanced parsing tasks utilize grammars.

In computer science, grammars serve the same purpose as they do for any spoken or written language; they define the orders that tokens can be arranged and thereby help to specify the meaning of the tokens. If the input meets the criteria laid forth by the grammar, then the parser should be able to assign a meaning to the various input tokens. If the grammar criteria are not met, the parser will not be able to make sense of the input, as in the "Perl about book parsing is This" statement. When thinking about parsers in this context, consider how your Perl compiler operates, since much of a compiler's underlying function is the ability to parse computer code for a given programming language. If your code follows proper Perl syntax (grammar), then the program will compile and execute. If syntax errors are present, the Perl compiler loses its ability to properly interpret your code, and you will receive a runtime error message similar to the following:

```
Syntax error at MyPerlScript.pl at line 5, near "xxxx"
Execution of MyPerlScript.pl aborted due to compilation errors.
```

Tip Many books about compiler design can provide highly beneficial resources for furthering your knowledge of parser design and theory. One recommended resource is *Compilers* by Alfred V. Aho, Ravi Sethi, and Jeffrey D. Ullman (Addison-Wesley, 1986).

Now that you have an idea of what a grammar is supposed to accomplish, let's look at how you can implement such functionality; I will now discuss the computer scientist's view of grammars.

Introducing Generative Grammars

In the past, many linguists tried to define grammars that were exact, were finite-sized, and provided a complete description of the language (that is, the allowable sequences of tokens). However, this type of construction led to many problems; in fact, arriving at a complete description that could be proven to hold true against all possible cases in a given language was determined to be a nearly impossible task because of the potentially infinite numbers of combinations of tokens. A good example of this is the text contained within this book, or any book. Every sentence in this book, with the exception of the code listings and the purposely incorrect examples shown previously, adheres to what is considered proper English grammar, yet no two sentences consist of the same combination of words given in the same order. Indeed, it would be difficult to express a finite-sized set of rules that would perfectly match every sentence, especially considering that English, and most other languages, are replete with context-sensitive exceptions. For example, let's take the simple rule of making a verb past tense by adding *ed* at the end so that *walk* becomes *walked*. So far, so good, but what about the verb *run*? In the past tense it is not *runned*; it is *ran*. Therefore, a special rule would need to be established just for this word. Now consider just how many other exceptions there are, how many words there are, and how many different possible ways these words can be combined, and take a moment to ponder how immense a task developing a complete description of a language would be.

Thus, the complete description idea has largely been abandoned, and generative grammars have come into play. Generative grammars do not seek to provide complete descriptions of a language, but rather they specify an exact, fixed-sized recipe for constructing sentences (sequences of tokens) in a given language. In other words, a generative grammar may not be able to be used to create every possible sentence in a given language, but it does guarantee that any sentence generated with it will be in a proper form. This view of grammars has been determined to be more widely applicable and is quite the same view of grammars that computer scientists embrace.

Grammar Recipes

The recipe-based grammar method is based upon the simple principle that a properly formed sequence of objects can be built by starting with a small object and using rules to add objects to it and create a larger structure. This is an underlying principle for all the grammar types discussed in this chapter, since even though the various types of grammars have differing levels of restrictions, they are all generative in nature. To clarify what exactly this entails, let's look at a simple recipe that describes a list of items you might want to pick up at the grocery store (for example, bread, milk, and eggs). Thinking back to grammar-school English classes, you probably recall learning the basic rules for constructing such a list, such as each item other than the second-to-last item and the last item should be preceded by a comma, and there should be an *and* present between the last item on the list and the preceding item, if any. According to these rules, the list should look something like this:

```
Item, Item, Item, ... Item and Item
```

▮Note In the English language, it is also acceptable to have a comma present before the *and* that separates the last item from the second-to-last item, but for purposes of this chapter I will treat the syntax shown in the previous example as the only acceptable syntax.

In this example, I will slightly increase the specificity of the list and generate a recipe that can be used to describe grocery lists containing any of the following items: bread, milk, eggs, and meat. Thus, how do you use the information you know about the list structure to create such a recipe? A logical starting point is to decide that bread, milk, eggs, and meat are all items and thus can replace any of the Item placeholders present in the list. Next you should consider the simplest possible list structure. That is a list that contains only one Item. Therefore, in this simple grammar, any one item can serve as a complete sentence (sequence of tokens). Longer lists can be created by appending , Item to the end of a simpler list. It is also possible for each of these longer lists to serve as a complete sentence, in which the end of the list signifies the end of the sentence. However, to achieve the proper format for the ending element of the list, you must also specify a rule that when , Item is found at the end of a sentence, it must be replaced by and Item.

Now that you have a general understanding of the grammar for a mini "list" language, how do you represent these thoughts in the form of a more formalized grammar? Writing out such a grammar should result in something like this:

```
Item -> bread|milk|eggs|meat
Sentence_s -> Item|List END
List -> Item|Item, List
, Item END-> and Item
```

In this particular notation, tokens that begin with a capital letter are *nonterminals*, and tokens that begin with a lowercase letter are *terminals*. Terminals are items that cannot be further specified. That is, they cannot be made any more specific. In the previous example, bread is a terminal because this grammar considers bread to be a fully specified item; it does not further differentiate between white bread and whole wheat per se. If bread were instead a nonterminal, the grammar would need the following modifications:

```
Item -> bread|milk|eggs|meat
Bread -> white|whole wheat
```

Nonterminals differ in that they can be replaced by even more specific components. For example, the nonterminal Item can be replaced by any of the terminals eggs, bread, milk, or meat. It is also possible to replace nonterminals with other nonterminals, as in the List nonterminal being replaced by the Item nonterminal or the Item, List nonterminals. This ability to replace List with Item, List is especially important since it allows the grammar to be used for generating a list of any length rather than requiring an individual rule for each list of length 2 to length N.

Also in this particular notation, the -> symbol stands for "can be replaced by," and the subscript S defines the *start symbol* for the sequence. The start symbol is important since it represents the point at which sentence generation will begin. Chapter 3 will also show that top-down parsing tasks are initiated at the start symbol, and bottom-up parsers try to work their way back from a complete sentence to the start symbol. Furthermore, all grammars must contain a finite number of terminals, a finite number of nonterminals, and a finite number of production (grammar) rules. Additionally, a start symbol must always be specified in order for a grammar to be fully defined.

■Note Do not get overly caught up in the grammar syntax used in the previous example; it is being used largely for illustrative purposes. Most Perl parsers instead require that grammars be specified in the Backus-Naur format (BNF), which is syntax used to specify a higher-order grammar than that found in the preceding example. I will discuss this format in the upcoming "Backus-Naur Format" section.

Sentence Construction

Now that you have specified a grammar that defines the syntax of an item list language, it is time to put the grammar to the test and determine if it can really be utilized to construct an appropriate list sentence. Therefore, let's begin to sequentially step through the rules laid forth and try to construct a list using only the rules provided by the grammar.

To begin constructing the grocery list sentence, you first call upon the rule with the start symbol, which means you have a new sentential form that consists of the nonterminal Sentence. You can think of a sentential form as a "sentence in progress," since it is a form that contains nonterminals. To construct a fully qualified sentence, you must replace all nonterminals with terminals. Table 2-1 lists the order in which the various rules need to be called and the results they will produce.

Table 2-1. *Application Order of Grammar Rules*

Sentential Form	Rule Used*
List END	Sentence -> List END
Item, List END	List -> Item, List
Item, Item, List END	List -> Item, List
Item, Item, Item, List END	List -> Item, List
Item, Item, Item, Item END	List -> Item
Item, Item, Item and Item	, Item END -> and Item

* The Rule Used column indicates the rule used to create the current sentential form from the previous one.

After establishing that the Sentence nonterminal is going to serve as a start symbol, you can next check to see what rule establishes the valid replacements for Sentence. Looking at the rules established earlier, you see that the nonterminal Sentence can be replaced by the more specific nonterminal List. Thus, by applying this rule, your sentence now consists of List END. You then repeat the process of increasing the specificity of the sentential form by determining what can replace the nonterminal List. In this case, since you want a list of four items, you then apply the rule that List can be replaced by Item, List. You then apply this rule twice more, which yields the following:

Item, Item, Item, List END

Since there is only one list element left to add to the list of four, you then call upon the rule that states List can be replaced by Item in order to eliminate the final List nonterminal, yielding the following:

Item, Item, Item, Item END

You next seek to eliminate the END marker and insert and between the final two items on the list. Thus, you call upon the rule , Item END -> and Item to accomplish this. At this point, you are left with the following:

Item, Item, Item and Item

As a final step, you call upon the rule, which specifies acceptable values for the non-terminal items, and replace those nonterminals with the terminals eggs, milk, bread, and meat. This yields the following sentence:

eggs, milk, bread and meat

To make the preceding process easier to follow, Figure 2-1 demonstrates a production graph (also referred to as a *syntactic graph* by some). The diagram illustrates the syntactic structure used to generate the final sentence.

■**Note** The grammar just discussed is merely one example of how that grammar could be used to generate a valid list sentence. Sentences such as "bread" and sentences such as "bread and eggs" and "eggs, eggs and eggs" would also be valid sentences that could be reproduced according to the grammar provided.

Introducing the Chomsky Method

The type of grammar used to generate the list sentence is referred to as a *phase-structure grammar*. In theory, you can use this type of grammar to lay out the rules for any type of set (sentence) structure. However, as the sentence grows in complexity, so too does the number and types of rules in the grammar. Thus, for complex structures, the design and implementation of a phase-structure grammar can become quite arduous. When performing parsing tasks, the difficulty of working with phase-structure grammars is compounded even further, since no generalized parsing algorithm exists for use with them. More restrictive grammars (most notably Type 2 grammars) lend themselves to being parsed into treelike structures, which can be readily processed using various programming methodologies. As you will see in the upcoming "Type 2 Grammars (Context-Free Grammars)" section, creating a parse tree requires that the rules of the grammar are not subject to context sensitivity/dependency. *Context sensitivity* implies that the meaning of a nonterminal or its proper replacement during sentence generation can be deciphered only by looking at the other nonterminals and terminals surrounding it. A phase-structure grammar's unrestricted nature also allows for the simultaneous replacements of multiple nonterminals and terminals, which also leads to difficulties in their implementations. This lack of restrictions and context dependence creates a lot of "specialized cases" that parser code needs to deal with on an individual basis. Therefore, specialty parsers need to be coded for use with

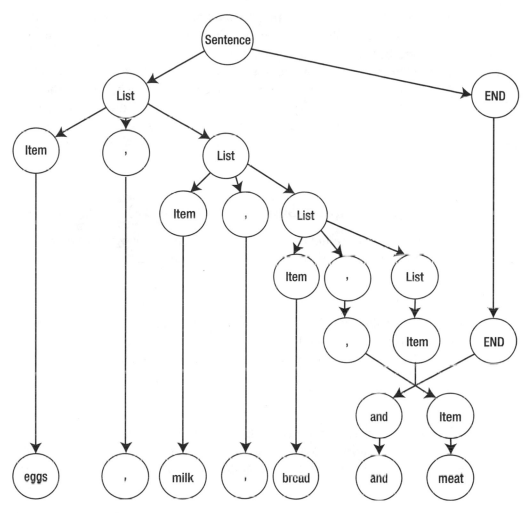

Figure 2-1. *The production graph for the "eggs, milk, bread and meat" sentence*

them, but even this is not always possible and is usually a complex and inefficient process. For this reason, these so-called Type 0 grammars are generally not employed in the real world; instead, a more restricted type of grammar is used for most applications.

■Note The notable exception to where phase-structure grammars or the upcoming context-sensitive grammars are sometimes used is in the field of linguistics. Representing natural language with a more restrictive grammar is sometimes not feasible given the large numbers of exceptions and caveats present in most modern-day spoken and written languages. The difficulty of implementing phase-structure grammars programmatically is a major reason why computer processing of natural language is such a difficult and elusive task.

These shortcomings are addressed in the Chomsky hierarchy of grammars, which seeks to increase the manageability of grammars while still preserving the robustness of the grammar's descriptive abilities. The hierarchy was first proposed by Noam Chomsky in 1942. Under the Chomsky hierarchy, phase-structure grammars are considered Type 0 grammars, since they exist in a fully unrestricted form. The hierarchy has three other types of grammars (Types 1–3), each with increased restrictions over the previous but also with increased manageability. Fortunately, even the more restrictive cases are still quite applicable to many parsing tasks. In fact, some of the most popular Perl parsing modules, such as RecDescent (Chapter 5), utilize Type 2 grammars.

Type 1 Grammars (Context-Sensitive Grammars)

If you look back at the Type 0 grammar you constructed for the list language, you will note that the grammar allowed you to create the following rule:

```
, Item END-> and Item
```

In this rule, you are able to replace three symbols (comma, Item, and END) with just two symbols (and and Item). In a Type 1 grammar, such replacements are unallowable. A grammar is considered context-sensitive if only one symbol gets replaced by one or more other symbols.

■**Note** Type 1 grammars are often referred to as *monotonic grammars*, since a monotonic grammar is defined as a grammar that contains no rules in which the left side consists of more symbols than the right side. This means, by definition, all context-sensitive grammars are also monotonic.

Hence, if you had to rewrite the rules of the list language to adhere to the standards of a Type 1 grammar, you would write the following:

```
Item -> eggs|milk|bread|meat
Sentence_s -> Item|List
List -> EndItem|Item Comma List
Comma EndItem -> and EndItem
and  EndItem -> and Item
Comma -> ,
```

Note how you have to add two nonterminals (Comma and EndItem) and two rules in order to conform to the context-sensitive standard. This prevents the potential complications that could be associated with the simultaneous multiple replacements (see Figure 2-2).

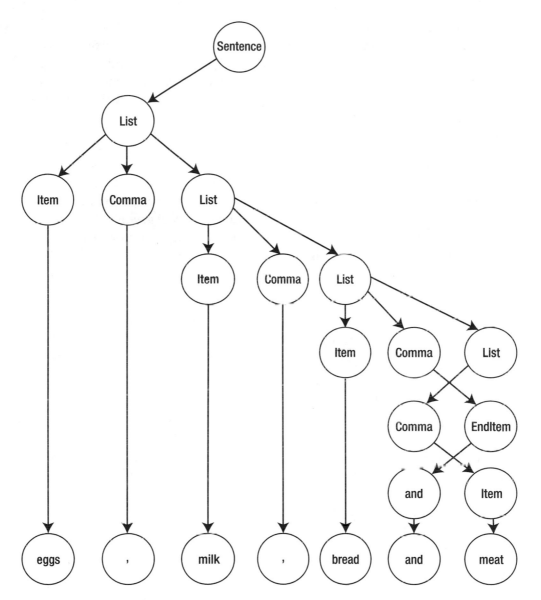

Figure 2-2. *The Type 1 production graph for the "eggs, milk, bread and meat" sentence. The regions where the arrows cross are regions of context sensitivity.*

Constructing Type 1 Grammars

I will explain the construction of Type 1 grammars a little more closely now using the standard computer science example of generating a string that consists of an equal number of *a*'s, *b*'s, and *c*'s. In other words, say you want to define a grammar that will accept the string abc and expand upon it to generate strings such as aabbcc and aaaabbbbcccc.

To begin this grammar, you start with the most straightforward rule, in that Sentence could be replaced by abc. The question arises, however, of how you append things to this string. Since the grammar you are trying to create is a Type 1 grammar, you cannot readily create rules for complex insertions of new characters; therefore, you will create a rule that adds a to the beginning of the string and appends a nonterminal X to the end of the string. This yields a rule of the following form:

```
Sentence -> abc|aSentenceX
```

Since this rule directly takes care of adding a to the beginning of the string, you need to add b and c by creating a rule that states the nonterminal X can be replaced by bc. However, directly appending bc to the end of the string would not give you the result you desire. Thus, you must first create a rule that strategically positions X prior to its replacement with its corresponding terminals. You can do this as follows:

```
cX -> Xc
```

Applying this rule one or more times will eventually result in a sentential of the form bXc. Now if you perform your replacement of X with bc, both the b and c will be appropriately placed. Therefore, the resultant grammar for the string expansion is as follows:

```
Sentence_s -> abc|aSentenceX
cX -> Xc
bXc -> bbcc
```

If you examine the generative nature of this grammar in constructing aabbcc, you will see that the procedure is as follows. First, you apply the following rule:

```
Sentence -> aSentenceX
```

Following this, Sentence can be replaced according to this rule:

```
Sentence -> abc
```

which yields the following:

```
aabcX
```

Now if you apply this rule:

```
cX -> Xc
```

you arrive at this:

```
aabXc
```

Executing the remaining rule, which dictates the replacement of X by bc, you are left with the desired string (see Figure 2-3).

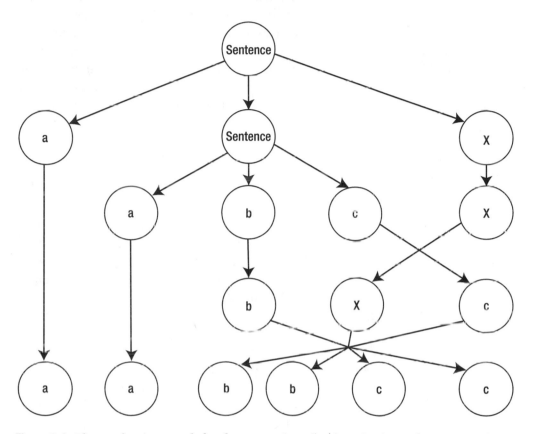

Figure 2-3. *The production graph for the generation of* aabbcc. *Regions where arrows intersect are regions of context sensitivity.*

If you consider each of the previous examples, you will notice that even though only one nonterminal gets replaced in each rule, multiple terminals and nonterminals are still allowed on the left side of each rule. This is what makes these grammars context-sensitive, because a given nonterminal cannot always be replaced with an element on the right side of the rule. Instead, the complete left side of the rule must match so that the substitution occurs only in the event that the context in which the nonterminal is found is proper. Context cannot always be readily determined, however, and with the creation of a larger set of rules, most grammars can be made into context-free grammars (see the next section), which are the preferred type of grammars for parsing tasks. As you will see in the next chapter, the most common classes of parsing algorithms are designed to work with context-free grammars as well.

Type 2 Grammars (Context-Free Grammars)

Grammars of this type are probably most important for dealing with Perl-based parsing routines, since most of the common Perl parsing modules will utilize Type 2 grammars. What distinguishes Type 2 grammars from Type 1 grammars is that Type 2 grammars are considered *context-free* instead of *context-sensitive*. In more technical terms, this means that while context-sensitive grammars are allowed to have one or more nonterminals on their left side, context-free grammars have the additional restriction of being able to have only a single nonterminal on their left side. For example, if you were to rewrite your list language in the form of a Type 2 grammar, it would take the following form:

```
Item -> bread|milk|eggs|meat
Sentence_s -> Item|List and Item
List -> Item, List|Item
```

The significance of obtaining a grammar in a Type 2 format is that since it is context-free, each nonterminal is able to operate independently of its neighbor. In other words, each grammar rule operates as a definition of the element found on the left side. This yields the benefit that the production graph produced will always be in a tree form, and hence Type 2 production graphs are often referred to as *production trees* (see Figure 2-4). The benefit to a tree-type grammar is that the sentences constructed from its rules can be analyzed by both top-down and bottom-up approaches. As you will see in the next chapter, this is ideal for parsing tasks, since recursive descent parsers employ the top-down approach, and shift-reduce parsers utilize the bottom-up approach. Type 2 grammars are probably the most widely used of all the grammar types when it comes to creating parsers, since they allow the data to be parsed into treelike structures. Tree-based analytical methods are quite pervasive throughout computer science. As you will see in upcoming chapters, tree-based parsing is utilized in processing a diversity of data formats, including HTML and the DOM-based parsing of XML documents.

Backus-Naur Format

BNF is named after John Backus and Peter Naur, who were two prominent computer scientists in the area of compiler design in the mid-twentieth century. BNF was originally created as a way of specifying the syntax of the ALGOL programming language but has become one of the standard notations for expressing grammars in computer science. In Perl, grammars are generally structured using BNF. The previous rules written out in BNF would look as follows:

```
<Item>::=       bread|milk|eggs|meat
<Sentence>_s::=  <Item>|<List> and <Item>
<List>::=       <Item>, <List>|<Item>
```

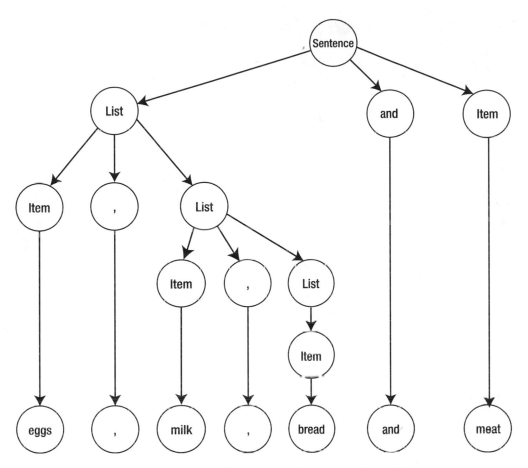

Figure 2-4. *The Type 2 production tree for "eggs, milk, bread and meat"*

Before examining the grammar, let's first examine some of the notations used in BNF:

- Symbols that are encapsulated within a set of <>; BNF notation> are nonterminals; the tokens that are not enclosed in <> are terminals.

- The ::= in BNF notation stands for "may be replaced by," and | is used for alternation of choices in a manner similar to the Perl regular expression syntax.

- The subscript S denotes the start symbol for the sequence, and the start symbol must always be a nonterminal.

AN ALTERNATE SYNTAX FOR TYPE 2 GRAMMARS

Although not widely used by Perl programmers, programmers in other languages sometimes express Type 2 grammars in van Wijngaarden form. This format is as follows:

```
Item: bread symbol; milk symbol; eggs symbol; meat symbol.
Sentence: Item; List and symbol, Item.
List, comma symbol, List; Item.
```

Note the use of ; for alternation and the use of `symbol` after all nonterminals. A comma (,) also has the special meaning of "followed by," and all rules must end in a period.

Constructing Math Equations with Type 2 Grammars

I will begin the explanation of Type 2 grammars by starting with a practical example, that of creating grammar rules that can be used to construct mathematical equations. In particular, I will show you how to create algebraic expressions employing this format:

```
Variable = Expression
```

For example:

```
w = x*(y+z)
```

Now that you have an idea in mind of what you want to accomplish, let's look at how you could go about constructing such an equation via a Type 2 grammar.

```
<Variable>::= w|x|y|z
<Sentence>::= <Variable>=<Expression>
<Expression>::= <Expression>+<Expression>
<Expression>::= <Expression>-<Expression>
<Expression>::= <Expression>*<Expression>
<Expression>::= <Expression>/<Expression>
<Expression>::= (<Expression>)
<Expression>::= <Variable>
```

The previous grammar defines the basic rules essential to constructing fundamental four-function algebraic expressions and will now be put to the test by using it to generate the equation for w presented previously.

Table 2-2 summarizes the order in which the rules are applied to generate the desired algebraic expression, and Figure 2-5 demonstrates the production tree for the process.

Table 2-2. *Application Order of Algebraic Grammar Rules**

Sentential Form	Rule Used
V=E	S::= V=E
V=E*E	E::= E*E
V=E*(E)	E::= (E)
V=E*(E+E)	E::= E+E
V=V*(V+V)	E::= V (applied three times)
w=x*(y+z)	V::= w|x|y|z (applied three times)

* To improve readability, S, V, and E were used to replace <Sentence>, <Variable>, *and* <Expression>, *respectively.*

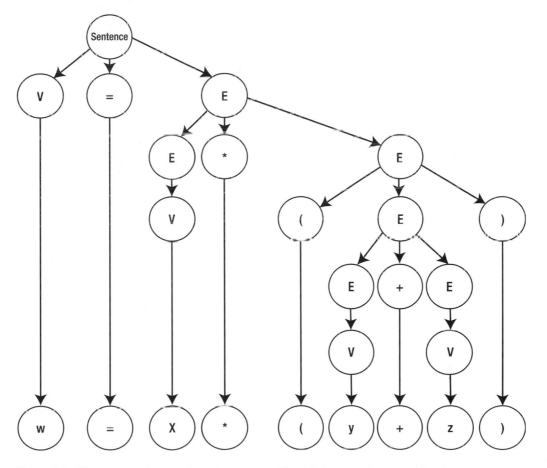

Figure 2-5. *The production tree for the construction of the equation w=x*(y+z)*

Constructing Basic English Sentences

You may recall from middle-school grammar class that a complete sentence in the English language usually has a subject, an object, and a verb, and they are usually present in the order subject, verb, object. To create a slightly more advanced sentence, you may choose to insert an adjective before each noun. So, now the question arises as to how you express this basic sentence structure in the form of a Type 2 grammar. To examine this issue, let's review the following Type 2 grammar:

```
<Sentence>::= <Subject> <Verb> <Object>
<Subject>::= <NounExpression>
<Object>::= <NounExpression>
<NounExpression>::= <Noun>|<Adjective> <NounExpression>
<Noun>::= grammars|parsers
<Adjective>::= Type 2|Backus-Naur|better|Perl
<Verb>::= make
```

Now, if you step through these given rules in the order presented in the production tree shown in Figure 2-6, you arrive with this English sentence:

```
Type 2 Backus-Naur grammars make better Perl parsers
```

However, when constructing English sentences via a grammar, it is important to remember that the limitations imposed by their context-free nature can arise. For example, if you had the following grammar:

```
<Sentence>::= <Subject> <Verb> <Object>
<Subject>::= <NounExpression>
<Object>::= <NounExpression>
<NounExpression>::= <Noun>|<Adjective> <NounExpression>
<Noun>::= cats|bird
<Adjective>::= two|one
<Verb>::= chased
```

you could use it to create the following proper English sentence:

```
two cats chased one bird
```

However, it could also easily generate the incorrect sentence:

```
one cats chased two bird
```

This is an example of how the context-free nature of the Type 2 grammar makes the parser unable to correctly generate sentences where one component affects the

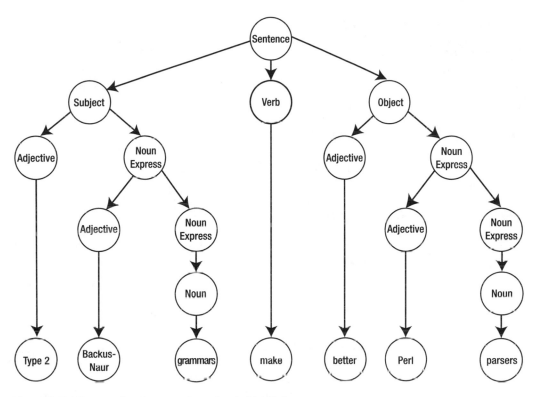

Figure 2-6. *The production tree for a basic English sentence*

appropriateness of another (for example, one should go only before the singular bird).
In this case, you can do several things to remedy the matter, with the first being using a
context-sensitive or phase-structure grammar instead. This, however, tends to become
an arduous process, since both grammars seek to define global relationships through
localized dependencies. Programmers more often choose to create a "context fixing" program instead to fix the output after its context-free grammar generation. In fact, this type
of complication is one of the reasons why certain instances of machine translation pose
a high degree of difficulty. Luckily, most parsing tasks deal with data sets that are much
more finite and regularly structured than human language, and hence routine parsing
tasks generally do not entail these complications.

■Tip Generally speaking, it is best to use the simplest grammar structure you can when solving a problem,
as long as it does not negatively influence the robustness of the parser's ability to process data. By using a
simpler grammar, you will generally get improved execution speed as well as less of a headache in actually
developing the parser.

Extended Context-Free Grammars

Extended context-free grammars are a system of notation designed to improve the read-ability of grammars that require repetition. For example, in the English sentence examples given previously, the grammar is capable of looping through several times to yield multiple adjectives before a noun is placed.

```
<NounExpression>::= <Noun>|<Adjective> <NounExpression>
```

Rather than writing it in this format, an extended context-free grammar would instead allow you to write this:

```
<NounExpression>::= <Noun>|<Adjective>+ <Noun>
```

or an equivalent type statement. The plus (+) sign in this case is a repetition operator and indicates the allowable types of repetition. The + symbol means one or more repetitions, an asterisk (*) means one or more repetitions, and a question mark (?) indicates zero or one repetitions.

Type 3 Grammars (Regular Grammars)

Up until this point, I have dealt with restrictions placed on the left side of a given rule. What distinguishes Type 3 grammars from Type 2 grammars is a right-side restriction. Type 3 grammars are allowed to have only one nonterminal on the right side of any given rule. This restriction means that in order for any form of sentence generation to occur, nonterminals must always be present at the end of a sentential form. For example, if you were to create a Type 3 grammar for your list language, you would write something like the following:

```
Sentence-> [bread|milk|eggs|meat]|List
List-> [bread|milk|eggs|meat], List|[bread|milk|eggs|meat] and
       [bread|milk|eggs|meat]
```

This creates a production chain type of construction, as shown in Figure 2-7.

Despite the restrictions placed on Type 3 grammars, they are actually not without real-world value and can be used for many simple parsing tasks. In fact, anyone who worked their way through Chapter 1 before reading this chapter has actually already employed Type 3 grammars, since such grammars form the basis of regular expressions. When you create a regular expression, you are in essence creating a Type 3 grammar that Perl's regex engine uses to parse strings of text.

■**Note** Keep in mind, though, that authoring generators and parsers for Type 3 grammars is the simplest, so if a Type 3 grammar is sufficient, it is advisable to use it.

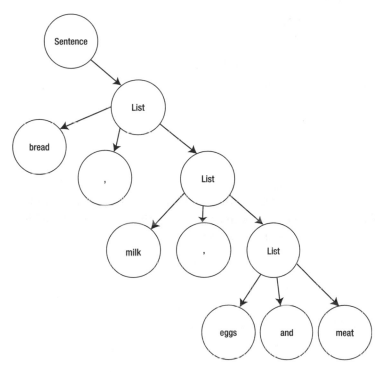

Figure 2-7. *The production chain for the Type 3 construction of your grocery list*

■Tip Another type of restriction is not part of the formal Chomsky hierarchy but still has occasional uses. A finite-choice grammar has the additional restriction that only terminals are allowed on the right side of the rule. You can use this type of grammar to represent a listing of keywords. Finite choice rules are often seen as pieces of larger, less restricted grammars (for example, `<Item>::= milk|eggs|bread|meat`).

Using Perl to Generate Sentences

Although the focus of this book is on parsing existing sentences and data structures, I will digress from this point momentarily to explain how you can utilize grammars, like the ones constructed previously, to generate sentences. Sentence generation is often important when it comes to transforming one document's contents into another format. For example, XML documents are often translated via the rules defined in an XML schema from one format into another so applications can communicate without having to be able to explicitly read the file formats of another application. This not only should give you a better appreciation of the expressive power of grammars but also provides a way in which you can test your grammar for certain common caveats.

Perl-Based Sentence Generation

Now it is time to actually implement one of the context-free (Type 2) grammars in a Perl script and see how well it functions. As a starting point, let's consider your list language grammar one more time and begin by entering the following grammar into a text file:

```
<Sentence>::= <Item>|<List> and <Item>
<List>::= <Item>, <List>|<Item>
<Item>::= bread|milk|eggs|meat
```

It is important to maintain the spacing shown in order to get the following script to execute as is, since you will use regular expressions to parse through the grammar and since for simplicity purposes code was not added in order to eliminate extraneous whitespace. Listing 2-1 shows the script you can utilize to test this grammar.

Listing 2-1. *A List Generator*

```perl
#!/usr/bin/perl

my @rules;
my $SententialForm;
my @rhs;

# read in grammar rules file
while(<>){
    push @rules, [split/::= /];
}

#Sets sentential form equal to <Sentence>
$SententialForm=$rules[0][0];

#While checks for remaining nonterminals
while($SententialForm=~/<\w*>/) {
    $NonTerm=$&;

    #Loops through rules to find nonterminal matches
    foreach $rule (@rules){
        $lhs = $rule->[0];
        $rhs = $rule->[1];
        if($NonTerm=~/$lhs/){
            #If rule matches sets, nonterminal equal to rule rhs
            if($rhs!~/\|/){
                $SententialForm=~s/$NonTerm/$rhs/;
            }
```

```
        #If rule has more than one rhs, picks one at random
        elsif($rhs=~/\|/){
            # @rhs is an array made of the alternate elements of $rhs
            @rhs=split /\|/, $rhs;

            # replace $NonTerm with a random element of @rhs
                $SententialForm=~s/$NonTerm/$rhs[int(rand(@rhs))]/;
        }
    }
  }
}

#When no nonterminals are remaining, prints generated sentence
print $SententialForm;
```

The routine begins by using a while loop to read in the rules of your grammar from a file, which is passed to the script as an argument. The split function is utilized to divide the rules according to their left and right divisions, and the strings corresponding to each of these sides are stored in the array rules.

```
# read in grammar rules file
while(<>){
    push @rules, [split/::= /];
}
```

Next this script assumes that the first rule of the grammar is the start rule and accordingly sets the first sentential form to the nonterminal on the left side of this rule, which in this case is <Sentence>.

```
#Sets sentential form equal to <Sentence>
$SententialForm=$rules[0][0];
```

You next arrive at a loop structure that checks the sentential form for nonterminals, since a complete sentence has been generated once a sentential form containing only terminals has been achieved. If a nonterminal is detected, the variable $NonTerm is set as the leftmost nonterminal value.

```
#While checks for remaining nonterminals
while($SententialForm=~/<\w*>/) {
    $NonTerm=$&;
```

When dealing with context-free grammars, you can perform successive nonterminal replacements in a left-to-right or a right-to-left manner and still end up with equivalent results, but since Perl regular expressions operate in a left-to-right manner, this approach is much easier to code.

Now that you have identified a nonterminal, it is time to cycle through the rules of your grammar in order to locate the rule that specifies what the nonterminal can be changed to. You can accomplish this by comparing the nonterminal to the left-side values stored in the @rules array. Once a match is found, it becomes time to work with the right side of the rule. Conditional statements are used to evaluate whether alternation is present within the right side of the matching rule. If alternation is not present, a substitution is performed to replace the nonterminal with the right side of the rule.

```
#Loops through rules to find nonterminal matches
    foreach $rule (@rules){
    $lhs = $rule->[0];
    $rhs = $rule->[1];
    if($NonTerm=~/$lhs/){
        #If rule matches sets, nonterminal equal to rule rhs
        if($rhs!~/\|/){
            $SententialForm=~s/$NonTerm/$rhs/;
        }
```

■**Note** This routine assumes that the same nonterminal does not exist on the left side of a rule more than once.

If alternation is detected, the right side of the rule is split into its component options and the values stored in the array @rhs. The script then picks a random choice from the @rhs array by successively applying the rand and int functions to the array. In this way, a random integer is used to pick the piece of the right side that will replace the nonterminal in question. To more thoroughly test a grammar, a breadth-first search or depth-first search is often used to produce every possible sentence, but such exhaustive generation is not necessary to demonstrate how the concept works.

```
elsif($rhs=~/\|/){
    # @rhs is an array made of the alternate elements of $rhs
    @rhs=split /\|/, $rhs;

# replace $NonTerm with a random element of @rhs
    $SententialForm=~s/$NonTerm/$rhs[int(rand(@rhs))]/;
}
```

This process will be cycled through until all nonterminals have been replaced by sentences, and at this point the completed sentence will be output. For example, I achieved the following results when I ran this script three times:

```
meat, milk and eggs
milk
meat, eggs, bread, milk, milk, eggs and eggs
```

As you can see, they are all valid lists according to the grammar rules specified.

Tip For those attempting to run this script on Windows, keep in mind that Windows-based text files have a carriage return appended to the end of each line. Unless the carriage returns are removed, they may be substituted into the sentential form along with the right-side text, yielding a correct, but multiline, output.

Avoiding Common Grammar Errors

Among the most common types of grammar errors observed are nonterminals that never break down into anything more meaningful. In other words, you cannot complete your sentence generation, because this type of condition means that one nonterminal can never be converted to a terminal according to the rules defined. This is due to either a missing rule that will add this conversion capability or the presence of a loop condition. Such a loop condition exists in situations like the following:

```
<NonT1> -> <NonT2> -> <NonT3> -> <NonT1>
```

Considering the previous condition, you will notice that a rule exists that allows you to move from <NonT1> to <NonT2>, and likewise a second rule exists that allows you to progress from <NonT2> to <NonT3>. The problem, however, occurs when the rule that specifies <NonT3> is encountered, since this rule specifies that <NonT1> should replace <NonT3>. If this is the only path allowed to you in the grammar, your sentence generator will never be able to exit the loop, thereby making sentence generation impossible.

Another common mistake is the absence of a nonterminal from the right side of any rule in the grammar. For example, consider the following grammar:

```
<Sentence>::=<NonT1>|<NonT2>
<NonT1>::=<NonT4>|Terminal1
<NonT2>::=Terminal1|Terminal2
<NonT3>::=<NonT4>|Terminal3
<NonT4>::=Terminal4|Terminal5
```

Within this grammar, `<NonT3>` is never called from the right side of any rule, which means that `<NonT3>` will never be called by a parser or generator that employs this grammar.

Although such an absence will not affect execution since its absence means it will never appear in any sentential form, this type of error is still indicative of some form of faulty logic. If a rule exists with the nonterminal on the left side, odds are that the nonterminal was expected to occur in the sentential form at some point during sentence generation. This can often be a frustrating error to locate for large grammars because it is likely hard to visually spot and because it may not always hamper sentence generation.

Generation vs. Parsing

As mentioned previously, grammar-based sentence generation can be a useful way for looking for errors within a grammar, but there is also a practical parsing purpose for understanding how this process works. Consider this: When you generate a sentence from a context-free grammar, you basically apply a series of rules in a given order, which in turn generates your production tree and hence your resultant sentence.

Parsing in essence is the reverse of this process (see Figure 2-8). When you perform grammar-based parsing tasks, you start with the resultant sentence; given this sentence and a set of grammar rules, you attempt to reconstruct the production tree. It is through reconstructing the parse tree that you are often able to assign a meaning to the different pieces of your start sentence. This process is called *semantic analysis* and will be covered in the next chapter, where I will discuss the methods employed by both top-down and bottom-up parsers.

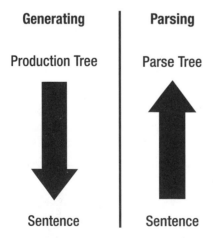

Figure 2-8. *The relationship between parsing and generation*

Summary

This chapter introduced the idea of a generative grammar and the different types of generative grammars that comprise the Chomsky hierarchy. Of all the Chomsky divisions, Type 2 context-free grammars are the most often utilized for real-world parsing applications, since they can be utilized with most existing parsing algorithms and thus do not require the development of custom parsers. This chapter also provided an overview of how you could utilize a generative grammar in a Perl script to create valid sentences.

In Chapter 3, you will examine the two common classes of parsing algorithms, bottom-up and top-down, and see how you can utilize them in conjunction with a set of grammar rules to parse math equations. Chapter 3 will also touch upon how parsers are utilized in the real world to evaluate content in which the format is not rigidly structured.

CHAPTER 3

■■■

Parsing Basics

The previous chapter explored grammars and explained how you can utilize them to generate a sentence string from a series of simple rules. As you saw, grammars provide a powerful generative tool, and when properly formulated, even the more "restrictive" context-free grammars can create intricate sentence structures. Toward the end of the chapter, I alluded to the idea that understanding grammar-based sentence generation is also important, since in effect sentence generation is the opposite of parsing. While sentence generation seeks to build up a sentence by continually turning abstract nonterminals into more definitive terminals, parsing seeks to determine the set of rules used to generate the sentence. In other words, the goal of parsing is to reconstruct the production tree used to create the sentence and the order in which the rules are applied. In this way, a parser can tell you if a sentence is proper, since the parse tree should be constructible only for a sentence that properly follows the rules laid forth in the grammar.

When thinking of parsing applications, however, it is important to not just think of language-based possibilities such as translation, even though the terms *sentence* and *grammar* tend to favor this line of reasoning. Parsing has many other applications as well, including interpreting the different tags and nodes of HTML and XML documents and a variety of other document types that possess a similarly loose structure. A *loosely structured* document is one in which the different elements that comprise it are not always found in the same order, number, and/or position every time, such as the text of this book. The book is organized into chapters, with differing levels of sections dividing each chapter, but each chapter has differing numbers of subsections and is divided a little differently; however, each chapter is still a valid chapter.

As you will come to understand in this chapter, context-free grammar-based parsers fall into two main categories: those that take a bottom-up approach, and those that take a top-down approach. *Bottom-up parsers* operate by starting with terminals and trying to work backward to the most abstract nonterminal, which is generally the start nonterminal. One of the most common examples where a bottom-up parser is used is for compiler design, since although they are typically harder to program than top-down parsers, they tend to run much more efficiently because fewer parsing possibilities exist when terminals are identified first. *Top-down parsers* take the opposite approach. They start with the most abstract nonterminal and try varying applications of the grammar rules in an effort to re-create the correct series of terminals. Top-down parsers are generally used for smaller parsing tasks, since they are simpler to program.

In the ensuing discussion of both approaches, it is important to keep in mind that all parsing tasks have the potential for some degree of ambiguity with the parse tree that results. Parsers will verify that a sentence is grammatically correct (in other words, could be constructed from the grammar), but in many instances differing rule application orders could result in the same end product. In other words, the reconstructed parse tree may not consist of the exact set or rule ordering used to create the sentence but, rather, is just a set of rules that could have generated that sentence. While this does place some limitations on what can be accomplished with parsers, as you will see in this chapter and the remainder of the book, parsers are still highly versatile tools, and they can help in a variety of tasks that computer programmers face.

Exploring Common Parser Characteristics

Before discussing the individual types of parsers, I will cover some commonplace characteristics shared by all types of parsers. If you think about parsing in general terms, parsers must accomplish two major types of tasks in order to properly do their job, regardless of whether they are top-down or bottom-up parsers. The first is they need a method to perform substitutions between terminals and nonterminals. In other words, in order to re-create a production tree (top-down parser) or develop a reverse production tree (bottom-up parser), the parser needs to be able to appropriately interchange terminals and nonterminals in order to traverse to the next level of the production tree. This substitution component is most often addressed using a *nondeterministic automaton* (NDA). The substitution mechanism is an automaton because it automatically performs a given action based on the instructions laid forth in the computer code, and it is considered nondeterministic because this action is not predetermined but, rather, dependent on the information provided to it by the control mechanism. For a top-down parser, the NDA consists of the grammar rules; for a bottom-up parser, the NDA is simply the reverse grammar rules.

While essential, the ability to perform substitutions is far from adequate by itself. This is where the control mechanism enters. The control mechanism basically controls what substitutions will be made by dictating what information is provided to the NDA. For example, when I cover bottom-up parsing theory, I will explain that tokens from the input string are removed and shifted onto a stack. The control mechanism is responsible for deciding whether another token should be shifted onto the stack or if the contents of the stack should be passed to the NDA for reduction to a nonterminal that more closely approaches the start symbol. In other words, the control mechanism dictates when it is appropriate for the parser to replace elements that match one side of a grammar rule with the other side of the rule.

■**Note** Which side is replaced (for example, the left side with the right, and vice versa) depends on whether the parser is a top-down or bottom-up parser.

Control mechanisms vary greatly in terms of architecture and complexity, and they can operate in a variety of ways. These ways, however, vary in their ease of creation, their speeds of operation, and their ability to deal with certain types of grammars. For example, some operate in grammar-independent manners, and others frequently use the grammar rules. The techniques also range from brute-force techniques such as breadth-first searches to table-driven techniques such as those employed by LL and LR parsers, and a range of techniques in-between.

An *LL parser* is the name given to a table-driven form of top-down parser because the algorithm it employs is also known as left-to–right left derivative parsing, which is a technique that is more commonly referred to as *recursive descent*. (See Chapter 5 for more details.) *LR parsers* are a bottom-up form of parser that use a left–to–right right derivative parsing, such as that performed by Yacc and Yapp. (See Chapter 4.)

Table-driven techniques include grammar-derived tables that are almost always considered too cumbersome to hand-program and thus are generally created using parser generators. I will cover parser generators in more detail when I discuss the module Yapp in Chapter 4. In this chapter, I will simply focus on the basic theory that underlies top-down and bottom-up parsers.

Introducing Bottom-Up Parsers

The coverage of parsers begins with an examination of the functionality behind bottom-up parsers. As I mentioned in the introduction to this chapter, bottom-up parsers operate by starting with a complete sentence and attempting to use this sentence to create a reverse production tree. One of the basic underlying methodologies behind these types of parsers is that of *shift* and *reduce*. Hence, bottom-up parsers are also sometimes referred to as *shift-reduce parsers*.

The shift element comes in because shift and reduce parsers take advantage of a stack-based approach, where an element of the input string is first shifted onto the stack in a left-to-right manner. At this point the parser has the ability to shift a contiguous element onto the stack, or if the element matches the right side of a grammar rule, the parser could also choose to reduce the element to a less-defined one (for example, a terminal to a nonterminal). The easiest way to gain an understanding of how this works is to consider an example, so let's recall the grammar you used to define your four-function algebraic equations:

```
<Variable>::= w|x|y|z
<Sentence>::= <Variable>=<Expression>
<Expression>::= <Expression>+<Expression>
```

```
<Expression>::= <Expression>-<Expression>
<Expression>::= <Expression>*<Expression>
<Expression>::= <Expression>/<Expression>
<Expression>::= (<Expression>)
<Expression>::= <Variable>
```

Now let's consider the equation you generated using this grammar in Chapter 2:

```
w=x*(y+z)
```

Now that you have your starting sentence and your grammar defined, let's take a look at a series of possible shift and reduce steps that a bottom-up parser may undergo to construct a possible parse tree. Table 3-1 summarizes these steps.

Table 3-1. *Shift and Reduce Steps Used to Construct a Parse Tree**

Stack	Sentence	Operation Performed
	w=x*(y+z)	
w	=x*(y+z)	Shift
<V>	=x*(y+z)	Reduce
<V>=	x*(y+z)	Shift
<V>=x	*(y+z)	Shift
<V>=<V>	*(y+z)	Reduce
<V>=<E>	*(y+z)	Reduce
<V>=<E>*	(y+z)	Shift
<V>=<E>*(	y+z)	Shift
<V>=<E>*(y	+z)	Shift
<V>=<E>*(<V>	+z)	Reduce
<V>=<E>*(<E>	+z)	Reduce
<V>=<E>*(<E>+	z)	Shift
<V>=<E>*(<E>+z	)	Shift
<V>=<E>*(<E>+<V>	)	Reduce
<V>=<E>*(<E>+<E>	)	Reduce
<V>=<E>*(<E>	)	Reduce
<V>=<E>*(<E>)		Shift
<V>=<E>*<E>		Reduce
<V>=<E>		Reduce
<S>		Reduce

*The symbols <V>, <E>, *and* <S> *were substituted for* <Variable>, <Expression>, *and* <Sentence>, *respectively, in order to allow the table to fit in the page's space constraints. The Operation Performed column indicates the operation that was performed on the previous row's stack and sentence values in order to generate the current row's stack and sentence values.*

Examining Table 3-1, you can see that the first step in your parsing process is to shift the first element onto the stack, which in this case is the terminal w. This element is reducible, so it is therefore next reduced to the nonterminal <Variable>. Looking back at the grammar, you can see that <Variable> is further reducible to <Expression>, but if this reduction was made, problems would develop further down the line, since the final reduction must be in the following form:

```
<Variable>=<Expression> -> <Sentence>
```

Thus, if you were writing a parser designed to work with this grammar, you may want to specify in the control element that <Variable> can be further reduced only if it appears after an equal (=) sign. In this way, the format <Variable>=<Expression> will always be preserved.

After this initial reduction, you execute two more shift operations, until you shift x onto the stack. You are now allowed to reduce x twice, first to <Variable> and then to <Expression>, since x occurs after an equal sign. At this point, your stack contains the following expression:

```
<Variable>=<Expression>
```

Therefore, when programming a control element for your parser, you must take measures to ensure that this stack expression is not prematurely converted into the sentence nonterminal, since this nonterminal should be achieved only at the end of the bottom-up parse tree. If you allowed premature conversion to remain, an erroneously formatted equation (for example, w=x+) could still lead to a successful parse because your parser would be able to achieve the sentence nonterminal. The occurrence of such false successes would greatly hamper the utility of the parser and make the results not trustable.

A series of three shift operations are then performed in order to shift the next terminal, y, onto the stack. Once again, a series of two reductions can be carried out in order to convert y to the nonterminal <Expression>. This process of shifting and reducing is then repeated until the final terminal, z, has been reduced to <Expression> as well.

Once z has been reduced to <Expression>, you are once again left with a series of nonterminals that matches the right side of the grammar rule, as follows:

```
<Expression>::= <Expression>+<Expression>
```

Thus, you can further simplify <Expression>+<Expression> to <Expression>. Next you shift the remainder of the original sentence,), onto the stack, yielding (<Expression>), an element that is reducible to <Expression>. Now you are left with a right side of the algebraic equation that reads <Expression>*<Expression>, which in turn can be reduced to <Expression>. This leaves you a stack containing <Variable>=<Expression>, which corresponds to the right side of the grammar rule, which specifies <Sentence>. Hence, a final reduction means you have successfully constructed a parse tree for the equation.

This process of shifting and reducing is the underlying mechanism of the majority of bottom-up parsers. The main differences in the parsers arise in the control mechanism of the parsers. Depending on the grammar rules specified, control mechanisms have to decide whether it is appropriate to shift or to reduce. Even in the previous example, you would need your control mechanism to decide that it is possible to reduce <Variable> only after an equal sign. Of course, more complex grammars will require even more sophisticated sets of controls. In fact, this is why many bottom-up parsers are generated using parser generators, as you will later see in Chapter 4. Parser generators like these will determine when and where it is best to shift or reduce and will store these determinations in one or more tables. The control mechanism of the parser generated will then rely upon these tables to shift or reduce in the appropriate places. Thus, in practice bottom-up parsers are generally not hand-coded, since the logic can require a high degree of complexity and the code base for such a parser can grow to be very large. Bottom-up parsers are normally constructed using parser generators such as the well-known Unix program Yacc or the Perl port of Yacc, Yapp. (See Chapter 4 for more details.) Bottom-up parsers have one distinct advantage, however, in that a well-coded bottom-up parser tends to be much faster than a parser that uses a top-down approach.

Coding a Bottom-Up Parser in Perl

The previous example supplied a reasonable conceptual illustration of how bottom-up parsers operate, but examining Perl code that accomplishes this type of parsing is invaluable. So, let's consider how you could go about programming the previous routing in Perl. First, as you witnessed in the sentence generation code given in the previous chapter, it is often valuable to use regular expressions to locate elements of grammar rules in your stack. However, since this is a parser that is dealing with algebraic equations, you must keep in mind that some of the characters that compose these grammar rules are specialized symbols that have a specialized meaning in the Perl regular expression syntax. Thus, prior to utilizing the grammar rules in your parser, let's make the following changes to the grammar:

```
<Variable>::= W|X|Y|Z
<Sentence>::= <Variable>=<Expression>
<Expression>::= <Expression>\+<Expression>
<Expression>::= <Expression>-<Expression>
<Expression>::= <Expression>\*<Expression>
<Expression>::= <Expression>\/<Expression>
<Expression>::= \(<Expression>\)
<Expression>::= <Variable>
```

Looking closely at the grammar, you will see that you need to make two changes. The first is that the special meanings of all the regular expression metasymbols are made negligible by placing backslashes before each of these characters in the grammar. In this way, when the rule is used as a regular expression, the backslash will ensure that the regular expression engine ignores the special meanings of the characters and just treats them as a regular character. The second change is a little subtler. If you use the grammar rules as regular expressions, you raise the possibility that the x in the right side of the variable rule (<Variable>::= w|x|y|z) can match the x in the nonterminal <Expression>. Thus, in order to eliminate erroneous substitutions, you allow the grammar to deal with only uppercase variables.

Now that you have changed the grammar into a format that will be easier to work with, you can begin to consider Perl code that will allow you to perform the aforementioned bottom-up parsing. Listing 3-1 shows code that performs such parsing.

Listing 3-1. *A Simple Bottom-Up Parser*

```perl
#!/usr/bin/perl -w
use strict;
my @rules;
my $Expression;
my $Sentence="W=X*(Y+Z)";
my $Stack;
my $i;
my $k=0;
my @rhs;

# read in grammar rules to @rules array
while(<>){
    push @rules, [split/::= /];
}

#shift first token onto stack
$Stack=substr($Sentence,$k,1);
print $Stack . "\n";

#loop which processes the entire input string until
# it has been reduced to the start token.
while($Stack!~/<Sentence>/) {
    for($i=0;$i<=$#rules;$i++){
        if($i!=7 && $Stack=~/$rules[$i][1]/){
```

```
#Ensures that V=E not reduced until entire string is processed
        if($i!=1){
            $Stack=~s/$rules[$i][1]/$rules[$i][0]/;
            print $Stack . "\n";
        }
        elsif($i==1 && $Stack!~/\+|-|\*|\/|\(/){
            $Stack=~s/$rules[$i][1]/$rules[$i][0]/;
        }
    }

#only allows V to be reduced if it occurs on rhs of =
    elsif($i==7){
        if($Stack=~/=/){
            @rhs=split /=/, $Stack;
            if($rhs[1]=~/($rules[7][1])/){
                $rhs[1]=~s/$rules[$i][1]/$rules[$i][0]/;
                print $rhs[0] ."=". $rhs[1] . "\n";
            }
            $Stack=$rhs[0] ."=". $rhs[1];
        }
    }
}

$shifts next token onto $Stack
    $k=$k+1;
    $Stack=$Stack . substr($Sentence,$k,1);
    if($k<=8){print $Stack . "\n";}
}
print $Stack . "\n";
```

This code begins by first reading in the file that specifies the grammar rules and uses the split function to divide each rule into its left and right sides, where both sides of each rule are stored in the two-dimensional array @rules:

```
while(<>){
    push @rules, [split/::= /];
}
```

Next, you begin the actual parsing code by shifting the first element of the sentence onto the stack, which in this case is W:

```
$Stack=substr($Sentence,$k,1);
```

■**Note** Several print statements appear throughout the program code. These print statements do not serve any functional parsing purpose but are merely present so you can verify upon execution that your program performs the expected shift and reduce steps.

Once the first value has been shifted onto the stack, you are able to enter a nondeterministic loop, which will allow your parser to perform continued shift and reduce operations until you end up with the start nonterminal <Sentence>. Within the nondeterministic while loop you'll see the following for loop that will work to iterate through the different rules that compose the grammar and allow for matches to be made between elements in the sentence and elements of the grammar:

```
while($Stack!~/<Sentence>/) {
    for($i=0;$i<=$#rules;$i++){
```

When a match is found, a substitution is made that replaces the piece of the stack that matches the right side of a grammar rule with the corresponding left side of the rule. If no matches are found, the variable $k is incremented and another element shifted onto the $Stack.

Within the for loop you will notice a series of conditional statements; for this simple parser the series serves as a control mechanism. The first control mechanism checks to see if the current grammar is the rule stored in the rules array element with the index of 7. This particular rule states <Expression>::= <Variable>.

The previously demonstrated (Table 3-1) shift-reduce process required to successfully parse this algebraic equation specified that the nonterminal <Variable> should be further reduced to the nonterminal <Expression> only if <Variable> is located to the right of an equal sign. Thus, when this particular rule arises, the parsers will execute a regular expression that will first check for the presence of an equal sign. If an equal sign is present, the right side of the equal sign is split off separately from the remainder of the stack and a substitution is attempted on the right side. This ensures that a <Variable> found on the left side of an equal sign will never be reduced to <Expression>.

```
    elsif($i==7){
        if($Stack=~/=/){
            @rhs=split /=/, $Stack;
            if($rhs[1]=~/($rules[7][1])/){
                $rhs[1]=~s/$rules[$i][1]/$rules[$i][0]/;
                print $rhs[0] ."=". $rhs[1] . "\n";
            }
            $Stack=$rhs[0] ."=". $rhs[1];
        }
    }
}
```

The second control conditional tests to see if the rule with the rules index of 1 is currently in play. This rule (<Sentence>::= <Variable>=<Expression>) also needs to be controlled for because it is likely that shifts and reductions will cause the <Variable>=<Expression> sequence of nonterminals to appear prior to all sentence and stack terminals and nonterminals being processed. Thus, you need to ensure that the <Sentence> substitution is not made prematurely, which would cause the parser to terminate before a full parse tree was generated. In this case, the control conditional checks for the presence of mathematical operators and parentheses before performing this substitution. If a mathematical operator or parentheses are present in the stack, it is indicative that further shifts and reductions need to be made. If these operators are absent, then the parser can proceed with the <Sentence> reduction.

```
if($i!=1){
    $Stack=~s/$rules[$i][1]/$rules[$i][0]/;
    print $Stack . "\n";
}
elsif($i==1 && $Stack!~/\+|-|\*|\/|\(/){
    $Stack=~s/$rules[$i][1]/$rules[$i][0]/;
}
}
```

Now that you have a basic understanding of how the code works, let's execute the code found in Listing 3-1 and use the print statements to view the shifts and reductions performed by the parser. The output should look something like the following:

```
W
<Variable>
<Variable>=
<Variable>=X
<Variable>=<Variable>
<Variable>=<Expression>
<Variable>=<Expression>*
<Variable>=<Expression>*(
<Variable>=<Expression>*(Y
<Variable>=<Expression>*(<Variable>
<Variable>=<Expression>*(<Expression>
<Variable>=<Expression>*(<Expression>+
<Variable>=<Expression>*(<Expression>+Z
<Variable>=<Expression>*(<Expression>+<Variable>
<Variable>=<Expression>*(<Expression>+<Expression>
<Variable>=<Expression>*(<Expression>+<Expression>)
```

```
<Variable>=<Expression>*(<Expression>)
<Variable>=<Expression>*<Expression>
<Variable>=<Expression>
<Sentence>
```

Compare the output from the Perl parsing routine to the manual walk-through you performed earlier in this chapter (Table 3-1), and you will see that shift and reduce operations performed are highly similar. Now that you understand just how bottom-up parsers work, it's time to move on and begin exploring a different approach to parsing, that of top-down parsers.

Introducing Top-Down Parsers

In the bottom-up parser approach, you started with the complete sentence of terminals and worked your way back to the starting nonterminal. As you consider the top-down approach, you will reverse this and begin with the start symbol to work your way up to a complete sentence that matches the one you seek to parse. Thus, if your parser can correctly arrive at this sentence using the rules specified in the grammar, you can conclude that your sentence is formed in a grammatically correct manner. Therefore, top-down parsing is similar to the principles of sentence generation, only you need to make some changes to your control mechanism to ensure you can arrive at your specific sentence of interest rather than just any grammatically correct sentence. Before you get into any coding of an actual top-down type parser, let's first review what a possible top-down parse tree for such a sentence could look like by examining the possible parse steps shown in Table 3-2.

Table 3-2. *Possible Top-Down Parsing Steps*

Sentential Form	Grammar Rule
V=E	S::= V=E
V=E*E	E::= E*E
V=E*(E)	E::= (E)
V=E*(E+E)	E::= E+E
V=V*(V+V)	E::= V (applied 3X)
W=X*(Y+Z)	V::= W|X|Y|Z (applied 3X)

As you can see from Table 3-2, if you apply your grammar rules in the appropriate order, it is quite possible to generate the mathematical sentence of interest. You start with the right side of the start rule and are gradually able to expand the right side of the equation until all the proper algebraic operations are represented in the equation. Once all the key algebraic operands are in place, you can begin to substitute your `<Expression>` non-terminal for the `<Variable>` nonterminal. Finally, you are able to replace the `<Variable>` nonterminal with the appropriate terminal values of W, X, Y, and Z. This generative-type approach is the basic approach used by all top-down parsers, with the major difference between top-down parser types being present in the control mechanism. As with bottom-up parsers, these control mechanisms can range from highly complex table-driven approaches (LL parsers) to simple but time-consuming brute-force approaches. Among Perl programmers, probably the most popular top-down parsing approach is to use a technique called *recursive descent*. I will reserve any discussion of this approach, however, for Chapter 5, when I introduce the recursive descent module `Parse::RecDescent`. The key is for you to determine what best meets your parsing needs. For a simple example such as the math equation w=x*(y+z), a brute-force approach is probably not such a bad choice, since the computational time required to solve this problem is negligible even if you consider all possibilities. Thus, the programming time saved by taking a simple approach may be in your best interest. For more complex parsing tasks (in other words, tasks that involve many more possible combinations of terminals and nonterminals or tasks with very large input strings), the computational time may no longer be negligible, which will warrant a more complex control mechanism, even if it adds to amount of development time required. The key is for you to find the correct balance between the amount of development time required vs. the required turnaround time for parser results.

Coding a Top-Down Parser in Perl

As mentioned in the previous section, for a simple application like this, which is going to be used to parse only simple algebraic equations, a brute-force choice is probably not that horrible a choice. For most modern computers and the processor speeds they support, computing all possible variations of an equation of that length would still be nearly instantaneous, so I will show an approach that is somewhat brute force. Rather than attempting a fully brute-force approach such as breadth-first search, I will instead show how to allow your control mechanism to perform in a more depth-first search manner by allowing the control mechanism to look ahead to the sentence and determine whether your parse tree is headed in the right direction. In this way, the parser will explore only the avenue that is likely to yield the correct answer and will not waste time exploring paths that will result in sentences that do not match the sentence of interest. Listing 3-2 shows how to construct the parser.

Listing 3-2. *A Simple Top-Down Parser*

```perl
#!/usr/bin/perl -w
use strict;

my @rules;
my $Expression;
my $Sentence="W=X*(Y+Z)";
my $NonTerm;
my $i;

#Read in grammar rules
while(<>){
    push @rules, [split/::= /];
}

#Set $Expression to start rule rhs
$Expression=$rules[1][1];
print $Expression;

#Allows for the replacement of <Expression>
while($Expression=~/<Expression>/){

    #Directs replacement by pulling appropriate operators out of $Sentence
    if($Sentence=~/\+|-|\*|\\|\(/g){
        $NonTerm=$&;
        if($NonTerm ne '-'){
            $NonTerm="\\" . $NonTerm;
        }
        for($i=0;$i<=$#rules;$i++){
            if($rules[$i][1]=~/$NonTerm/){
                $Expression=~s/<Expression>/$rules[$i][1]/;
                print $Expression;
            }
        }
    }

    #Controls replacement of E with V
    if($Expression=~/<Expression>/ and $NonTerm ne '\('){
        $Expression=~s/<Expression>/<Variable>/;
        print $Expression;
    }
}
```

```
#Resets $Sentence position to beginning
pos($Sentence)=0;

#Directs replacement of V by pulling appropriate nonterminals out of $Sentence
while($Expression=~/<Variable>/){
    if($Sentence=~/W|X|Y|Z/g){
        $NonTerm=$&;
        $Expression=~s/<Variable>/$NonTerm/;
        print $Expression;
    }
}
```

■**Note** This code is not a full depth-first search implementation, since it does not allow the ability to back-track if the selected path does not turn out to be the correct path, but this robust a mechanism is not needed to parse such simple equations. Oftentimes depth-first search is used in a predict and match scenario, where the parser makes a substitution and then checks to see if the substitution is correct before deciding whether to backtrack or proceed.

This code starts in basically the same manner as the bottom-up parser in that the code first uses a nondeterministic loop to read in the grammar rules that your parser is going to work with. For this particular parser, use the following grammar:

```
<Variable>::= W|X|Y|Z
<Sentence>::= <Variable>=<Expression>
<Expression>::= <Expression>+<Expression>
<Expression>::= <Expression>-<Expression>
<Expression>::= <Expression>*<Expression>
<Expression>::= <Expression>/<Expression>
<Expression>::= (<Expression>)
<Expression>::= <Variable>
```

In this case, stick with using the capital letters for your variable terminals; you do not need to prefix any metacharacters with a backslash, since you handle this issue directly in the program code. Next, since your top-down parsing design requires that you begin at the start symbol, you set your $Expression variable to the right side of the <Sentence> rule and print this value to the output so that later you can evaluate how well your parser works.

You next enter a while loop that will continue to run as long as the <Expression> nonterminal is present within your developing $Expression. As I mentioned earlier, you will allow your control mechanism to direct the progress of your parser, so you will use a regular expression to determine what algebraic operands are contained within the sentence in a left-to-right manner. If an operand is detected, it is stored in the variable $NonTerm, and if the operand is a metacharacter (any operand other than -), then it is prefixed with a backslash so it can later be used in a regular expression. At this point all the grammar rules are sequentially examined until the rule that contains the operand of interest is found. The right side of this rule is then substituted for the <Expression> non-terminal, and the new value of $Expression is output.

```
while($Expression=~/<Expression>/){
    if($Sentence=~/\+|-|\*|\\|\(/g){
        $NonTerm=$&;
        if($NonTerm ne '-'){
            $NonTerm="\\" . $NonTerm;
        }
        for($i=0;$i<=$#rules;$i++){
            if($rules[$i][1]=~/$NonTerm/){
                $Expression=~s/<Expression>/$rules[$i][1]/;
                print $Expression;
            }
        }
    }
}
```

After the iteration through the grammar rules has completed, you arrive at another conditional that your control mechanism uses to check for the presence of parentheses. If parentheses are not currently stored in the $NonTerm variable, this conditional will allow the <Expression> nonterminal to be replaced with the <Variable> nonterminal. If parentheses are the current operand of interest, this substitution is prevented in order to eliminate the possibility that any algebraic operations within the parentheses are replaced with <Variable> before they could be fully evaluated.

```
if($Expression=~/<Expression>/ and $NonTerm ne '\('){
    $Expression=~s/<Expression>/<Variable>/;
    print $Expression;
}
```

At the point when all <Expression> nonterminals have been converted into <Variable> nonterminals, you will leave the while loop and reset the current $Sentence position. You can then enter a second while loop, which will allow you to use the same look-ahead logic you employed previously so you can correctly replace the <Variable> nonterminals with their proper terminals and print the results to output. Once this loop has finished executing, the value of $Expression should match the value of the sentence, indicating that the sentence was correctly parsed. If you execute Listing 3-2 by passing the previous grammar to it, you should get the following results:

```
<Variable>=<Expression>
<Variable>=<Expression>*<Expression>
<Variable>=<Variable>*<Expression>
<Variable>=<Variable>*(<Expression>)
<Variable>=<Variable>*(<Expression>+<Expression>)
<Variable>=<Variable>*(<Variable>+<Expression>)
<Variable>=<Variable>*(<Variable>+<Variable>)
W=<Variable>*(<Variable>+<Variable>)
W=X*(<Variable>+<Variable>)
W=X*(Y+<Variable>)
W=X*(Y+Z)
```

Now that you have the results of your program execution, you can compare these results to the parse tree laid out in Table 3-2 and determine that your parser operated in the expected manner.

Using Parser Applications

Now that you understand how the different classes of parsers operate, it is time to consider some practical applications of parsers. In fact, most of the remainder of the book will highlight how you can use different Perl parsing modules to solve real-world parsing tasks, but for now let's take a moment to consider what the real strength behind a parser is. You can do this by considering some commonly used applications that support parsing. For example, let's consider the average Web browser, such as Mozilla, Firefox, Opera, or Internet Explorer. While an application such as this seems somewhat routine and unexciting by today's standards, it is really quite remarkable what a Web browser actually does. When you think of a Web browser displaying a Web page, you probably think of an image similar to Figure 3-1.

However, let's take a moment to ponder the underlying mechanism behind the page displayed in the browser window. What you see in a Web browser is not what is transferred over the network to your computer but rather a rendition created by the browser based upon HTML markup that is transmitted to the Web client. For example, the HTML markup that the browser actually sees resembles something similar to the HTML code found in Figure 3-2.

So, the question that remains is, how does the Web browser use the HTML document as a basis for creating the Web page display? The answer is by using an HTML parser that is able to make sense of the structure and content of the various markup tags and use this as a basis for creating a set of rendering instructions. Chapter 6 is devoted to parsing HTML, so I will not go much into specifics here, but the take-home point is that the portion of the program that renders the Web page does not know in advance what to render. The

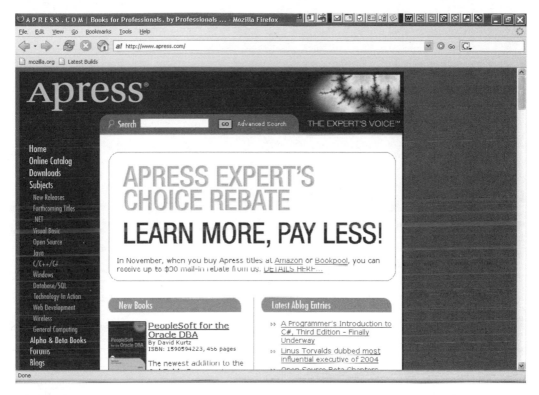

Figure 3-1. *A Web browser displaying the Apress Web site*

content of the graphical display is pulled out of the HTML markup by an HTML parser. What is so highly significant about this is that you can use different markups to create a diversity of displays that your Web browser will be able to render as long as they adhere to the proper HTML syntax (grammar). You can easily assess the truth behind this statement by examining just a few of the billions of pages found on the World Wide Web.

In other words, the presence of a parsing engine within the browser allows the browser to interpret content dynamically, which is an extraordinary feat. While many data sources can produce tabular output with static columns or the like, which can be readily broken down into components by counting whitespace, far more data is probably available in formats that are much less rigid, such as word processing documents, XML documents, HTML, source code, and so on. It is in situations like these that the true virtues of a parser become apparent. A parser can take this data, check to see that it complies with a grammar, break it down into its component pieces, and potentially transform the data into something else that may be of greater use for your current application. In the next section, you can explore this concept a little bit by coding a simple parser that can take any simple four-function math problem and dynamically evaluate it in order to return the result of the expression.

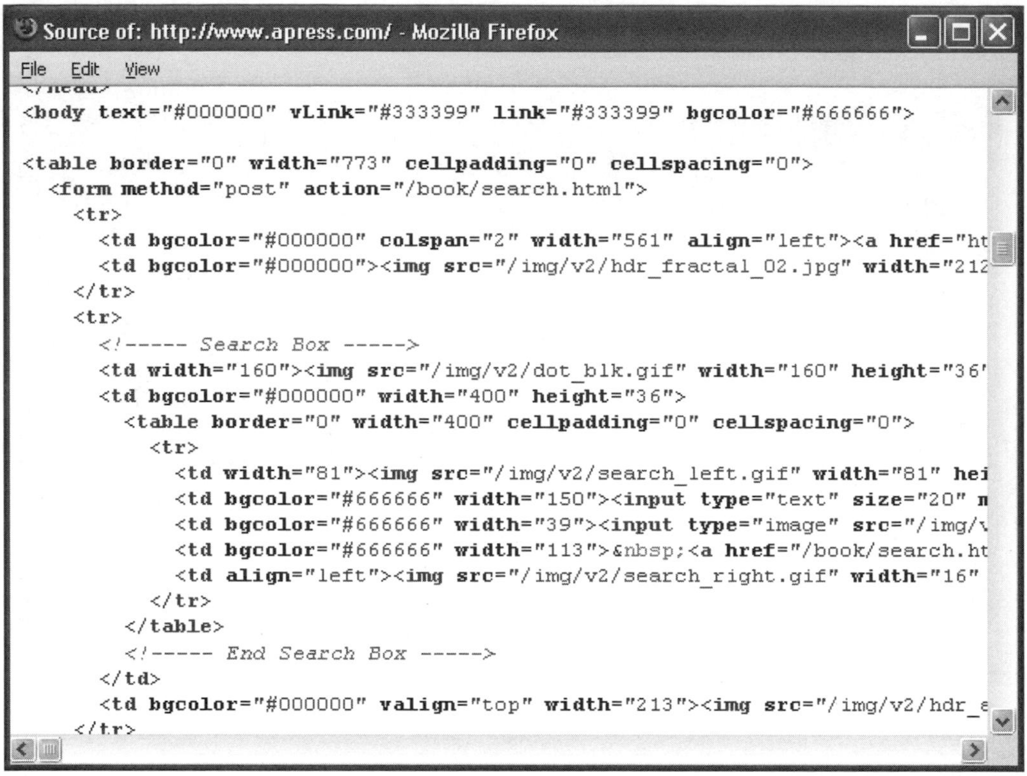

Figure 3-2. *A portion of the HTML markup behind the Apress Web page*

Programming a Math Parser

To show you how to code this parser, I will use a bottoms-up approach to solve the problem, but you do not need to develop a full-fledged grammar to evaluate the expression. Since this is a mathematical expression, a known methodology already exists for evaluating the symbols present within the expression in the correct sequence, namely, the order of operations. Your parser will be able to evaluate math statements that contain the four basic algebraic operands (+, -, *, /) in addition to parentheses. Thus, for these purposes, the order of operations will be as follows:

- *Parentheses*: ( )

- *Multiplication and division*: *, /

- *Addition and subtraction*: +, -

This order of operations specifies that parts of the equation listed in parentheses will be evaluated first. After these components are evaluated, multiplication and division operands will next be evaluated in a left-to-right manner, followed by addition and subtraction operations in a left-to-right manner.

Now that you understand how to approach this problem, let's take a look at some Perl code that can accomplish this (see Listing 3-3).

Listing 3-3. *Four-Function Math Parser*

```perl
#!/usr/bin/perl -w
use strict;
my $Expression="1+3*(((4*7)-29))/3+(90/5)";
my $ParenExpression;
my $ParenContents;

sub evaluate{
    my $Expr=join("",@_);
    my $A;
    my $B;
    my $C;
    my $X;

#Order of while loops preserves order of operations
    while($Expr=~/((-?\d+|-?\d+\.\d+)\*(-?\d+|-?\d+\.\d+))/){

#Math broken down into extra steps to make simplify logic
        $A=$2;
        $B=$3;
        $C=$A*$B;
        $Expr=~s/((-?\d+|-?\d+\.\d+)\*(-?\d+|-?\d+\.\d+))/$C/;
    }
    while($Expr=~/((-?\d+|-?\d+\.\d+)\/(-?\d+|-?\d+\.\d+))/){
        $A=$2;
        $B=$3;
        $X=$1;
        $C=$A/$B;
        # Does not check for division by zero
        $Expr=~s/((-?\d+|-?\d+\.\d+)\/(-?\d+|-?\d+\.\d+))/$C/;
    }
```

```
    while($Expr=~/((-?\d+|-?\d+\.\d+)\+(-?\d+|-?\d+\.\d+))/){
        $A=$2;
        $B=$3;
        $C=$A+$B;
        $Expr=~s/((-?\d+|-?\d+\.\d+)\+(-?\d+|-?\d+\.\d+))/$C/;
    }
    while($Expr=~/((-?\d+|-?\d+\.\d+)-(-?\d+|-?\d+\.\d+))/){
        $A=$2;
        $B=$3;
        $X=$1;
        $C=$A-$B;
        $Expr=~s/((-?\d+|-?\d+\.\d+)-(-?\d+|-?\d+\.\d+))/$C/;
    }
    return $Expr;
}


#Evaluates contents of parenthesis first
while($Expression=~/(\((.*?)\))/){
    $ParenContents=$2;
    $ParenContents=evaluate($ParenContents);
    $Expression=~s/(\((.*?)\))/$ParenContents/;
}


#Evaluates elements not in parenthesis
$Expression=evaluate($Expression);
print $Expression;
```

Within this script, you can enter any proper algebraic expression and set it as the variable $Expression. The key here is the word *proper*, since you are not employing a grammar, which means you did not establish a means of checking your expression's syntax prior to evaluating it. The routine will then take this expression and first check for the presence of a parentheses-enclosed expression in a nongreedy manner and will send the contents of the parentheses to the evaluate subroutine. The parentheses match must be nongreedy to ensure that only the contents of a single set of parentheses are sent to the evaluate subroutine in the event that multiple and/or nested sets of parentheses exist within $Expression.

The evaluate subroutine then evaluates the expression segment it is sent by first taking care of all the multiplication operations within a left-to-right manner; it does this by taking advantage of a regular expression that uses substring capturing to identify the numbers on the left and right of the operator. These numbers are then multiplied and substituted back into the expression. The process is then repeated for division, addition, and subtraction operations, respectively, and the result is returned to the main program body. This process of calling the evaluate routine and passing it the contents of a set of parentheses is then repeated until all the parentheses have been eliminated from the expression. Once this has occurred, the entire contents of $Expression are then passed to the evaluate subroutine and the result outputted to the user.

If you were to run this routine with the value currently specified in $Expression, the parser would yield a result of 18, which is the correct answer to the problem. If you so choose, you could readily change the $Expression variable and evaluate a different mathematical expression. The parser is able to deal with the data that it is presented on the fly, which is an ability that is being considered more and more crucial to how the increasingly interconnected and computerized world properly functions.

Perhaps one of the best examples of the increasing reliance on data that can be readily reformatted to suit differing needs is the rapid adoption of XML as a standard for the exchange of information. XML lends itself well to parsing and using schemas (which share much in common with grammars), and this is a large part of XML's ability to be adaptable to a wide variety of applications and a wide variety of end-user processing tasks. (See Chapter 7 for more information.) As you can see, the uses for parsing and the need for programmers that are competent in parsing techniques will continue to grow.

Summary

This chapter introduced the two major classes of parsers, bottom-up parsers and top-down parsers, and the methodologies that each type of parser employs. Bottom-up parsers use a shift and reduce approach to evaluate the content of a sentence and gradually reduce to the sentence to the start nonterminal. Top-down parsers utilize the opposite approach and begin with the start nonterminal and then apply the grammar rules in an attempt to reconstruct the sentence of interest. Each of these approaches has its own advantages and disadvantages, with the advantage of bottom-up parsers being rapid execution time and the disadvantage being that they can become quite cumbersome to program. Top-down parsers, on the other hand, tend to be much simpler to program but can also be very slow on the execution since they often require backtracking to generate the appropriate sentence. You also examined a simple math parser that enabled the dynamic evaluation of four-function math equations, and I hinted at the true power and utility that more advanced parsing approaches covered in upcoming chapters will provide. Therefore, turn the page and continue to see how you can practically apply parsing approaches to real-world problems.

CHAPTER 4

■ ■ ■

Using Parse::Yapp

Chapter 3 introduced you to bottom-up parsers and the series of shift-reduce operations they perform to reduce a sentence to the start symbol specified in the grammar. The previous chapter also mentioned how hand-coding such bottom-up parsers is not practical and that programmers generally use parser generators to solve such problems.

In this chapter, you will examine one such parser generator, the Perl module Parse::Yapp by François Desarmenien. Yapp (which stands for Yet Another Perl Parser) is a Perl port of the common Unix parsing utility Yacc (which stands for Yet Another Compiler Compiler). Both parser generators operate by reading rules from a grammar file and using the rules to generate tables that specify when it is appropriate for either a shift or a reduce operation to be performed. These tables form the basis of the parser that is generated.

Unlike a module such as Parse::RecDescent (see Chapter 5), neither Yapp nor Yacc provides integrated lexing ability, so it becomes necessary for users of the parser to supply a lexing routine that will sequentially shift the input tokens onto the parser's stack for evaluation. This chapter will cover how to format Yapp grammar files and how you can use these grammar files to generate a parser. The chapter will also walk you through how to code a lexing routine that you can use in conjunction with the generated parser to process input strings.

■**Tip** Yapp and Yacc share many similarities; in fact, a well-formed Yacc grammar will in many cases be completely compatible with Yapp (although the reverse may not be true). Thus, it may be advantageous to keep in mind that reading Yacc documentation can be a valuable source of information about designing grammars for Yapp parser generation. You can find a good source for Yacc information at http:// dinosaur.compilertools.net/.

Creating the Grammar File

Prior to using the Yapp parser generator, you must first create a grammar file to serve as the basis for parser generation. The typical Yapp grammar file consists of three sections, including an optional header section, a rule section, and an optional footer section, which are laid out in the file in the following format:

```
Optional Header Section
%%
Rule Section
%%
Footer Section
```

The Header Section

The header section of the grammar file is not required but can serve a variety of purposes, including specifying one or more code blocks that will execute when the parsing module is first called. These code blocks are often used for declaring global variables that will be used to store information during the parsing process.

Also, you can use the header section to list precedence declarations, which are often a useful way of reducing shift-reduce conflicts that may arise if a parser could interpret a given token set in multiple ways. For example, consider the following typical math formula:

```
X+Y+Z
```

While the rules of algebra tell you to evaluate this formula in a left-to-right manner (that is, X+Y first), a formula such as this may lead to a conflict for the parser, since the parser will not know whether to evaluate X+Y first or Y+Z. Thus, if you had a + token in your grammar, it would be advisable to use the header to specify it as having left precedence (see Table 4-1), which you can accomplish as follows:

```
%left '+'
```

In contrast, consider the equal (=) sign in a math equation such as the following:

```
W=X+Y+Z
```

Here you would not want to use left precedence. It would not be appropriate to have the parser operate on W=X first. Rather, what is on the right of the equal sign should be evaluated prior to the equal sign being evaluated. Thus, an = sign has right precedence, which you can specify as follows:

```
%right '='
```

The grammar syntax also allows for the precedence declaration of %nonassoc, which specifies that there is no associativity between the operators and that nested operators should be considered syntax errors.

Table 4-1. *Precedence Declarations*

Declaration	Meaning
%left	Nested operator is evaluated in a left-to-right manner.
%right	Nested operator is evaluated in a right-to-left manner.
%nonassoc	No associativity. Nested operators are syntax errors.

Your final consideration when specifying precedence declarations is the order the declarations are written in the header. Declarations that appear later in the file will have a higher precedence than those that appear earlier and will thus be parsed first. Therefore, if you had a math equation that involved both addition and multiplication, it would be proper to have the following declaration in the header file:

```
%left '+'
%left '*'
```

If written in the previous order, it would set multiplication operations as having a higher precedence than addition operations and enable your parser to conform to the typical algebraic order of operations.

In addition to specifying precedence declarations, the header section can also specify the start rule of a grammar. For example, if you had a rule named rule1 that functioned as a start rule, you could declare it the start in the header using the following line of code:

```
%start rule1
```

If a start rule is not specified, as in the earlier case, Yapp will automatically assume that the first rule of the grammar is the start rule. Therefore, if your starting rule is first, this declaration can be ignored, but if the start rule appears later in the grammar rule listing, this declaration will be required for proper parser generation and function.

Lastly, the header section of the grammar file allows for token declarations; however, declaring tokens is not required, since any symbol that does not appear on the left side of any rule is automatically treated as a token. The ability of Yapp to handle token declarations is a feature designed to instill compatibility with Yacc grammars, since Yacc requires explicit token declarations.

The Rule Section

From this point onward, the coverage of the Yapp grammar file will correspond to code that will be used to create a parser for the grocery list language that was developed in Chapter 2.

The rule declarations in a Yapp grammar file are actually quite similar to the ones shown in the following Backus-Naur format, with several slight differences:

```
<Sentence>s::=   <Item>|<List> and <Item>
<List>::=        <Item>, <List>|<Item>
<Item>::=        bread|milk|eggs|meat
```

The first difference is that nonterminals are not encased in <> but are rather just written without brackets of any kind. Second, terminals, such as bread, are enclosed in single quotes in a Yapp grammar. Lastly, the right side of rules and the left side are not separated by ::= but rather just a single :. Thus, if you had to rewrite the previous grammar in proper Yapp syntax, you would write it as shown in Listing 4-1.

Listing 4-1. *The Yapp Grammar Rules for the List Language*

```
%%
Sentence:   List | List 'and' Item ;
List:       Item ',' List | Item ;
Item:       'bread'|'milk'|'eggs'|'meat';
%%
```

■ **Note** Remember to enclose the rule section of the grammar between sets of %% even if a header and/or a footer section is not present in the grammar file.

Now that you have laid out a set of Yapp grammar rules, enter the rules into a text editor and save the progress under the filename MyGrammar.yp. The .yp extension is the file extension recommended by the Parse::Yapp module author to signify a Yapp grammar file. For this particular parser, header information is not needed since there are no operations present that could result in shift-reduce conflicts and no need for any code blocks to be specified. Before you use the grammar to generate a parser, however, you will have to consider the footer section of the grammar.

The Footer Section

The footer section is also an optional section like the header, but it can be a useful place to enter code that is required for the parser to function, such as the lexing routine. This is not essential, and you can instead add lexing code to the Perl script that will use the generated parser. However, placing lexing code in the footer section will ensure that the lexing routine becomes a component of the generated parsing module and will simplify the authoring of Perl scripts that will use the module.

In this particular case, you need to develop a lexing routine that will identify the various items that comprise the list (in other words, the bread, milk, eggs, and meat tokens) as well as the commas and the and that work to separate those list items. Listing 4-2 shows a lexing routine for this example.

Listing 4-2. *The Lexing Subroutine*

```perl
sub Lexer{
    my($parser)=shift;

    #Checks to see if data to be parsed is present
    $parser->YYData->{INPUT} or return('',undef);

    $parser->YYData->{INPUT}=~s/^[ \t]//;

    #Returns tokens to parser
    for($parser->YYData >{INPUT}){
        s/^(bread)// and return ('bread', $1);
        s/^(milk)// and return ('milk', $1);
        s/^(eggs)// and return ('eggs', $1);
        s/^(meat)// and return ('meat', $1);
        s/^(,)// and return (',',$1);
        s/^(and)// and return ('and',$1);
    }
}
```

The lexing routine first seeks to ensure that a data string intended to undergo parsing has been passed to the parser module or has already been entirely consumed by the lexing operation. This data string is stored in a hash under the {INPUT} key. If the {INPUT} element is empty, the lexing routine will return undefined. If a data string is present, the lexer will first remove all leading whitespace from the string by using a regular expression–based substitution. The lexer then uses a for loop to process the entire data string and remove encountered tokens in a left-to-right fashion. The token removed from the string is then returned to the parser.

The token is returned as a list of two variables, with the first being the name of the token and the second being the actual value of the token. In this example, these two variables will be identical in all cases. However, if you were writing a math parser (see the later example in the "Evaluating Dynamic Content" section), the token name could be number and the value variable the actual numeric value (for example, 5.3). Together these two values allow the parser to both parse the input string and process the data that is being parsed (for example, adding up two numbers).

■**Caution** It is never a good idea to have a token named `error` when using a Yapp parser, since this token name is used by the parser's own error-reporting system. Using such a token can lead to parsing problems, such as premature termination, because of an inability to correctly handle the `error` token.

In addition to a lexing subroutine, `Parse::Yapp`–generated parsers also have the ability to generate error messages if the parser is for some reason unable to successfully generate a complete parse tree. As was the case with the lexing routine, it is a good idea to add an error-reporting routine to the grammar file's footer, so error reporting is built into the generated module and does not have to be handled externally in the Perl script that will use the module. Listing 4-3 shows a typical error-reporting subroutine for a Yapp-generated parser.

Listing 4-3. *The Error-Reporting Routine*

```
sub Error {
    exists $_[0]->YYData->{ERRMSG}
    and do {
        print $_[0]->YYData->{ERRMSG};
            return;
    };
    print "Syntax error\n";
}
```

When a parser error is encountered, such as an invalid token, the parser will make a call to this routine. In this particular case, the subroutine will check to see if a specific error message has been generated with regard to the data input into the parser or with regard to the function of the parser rules. If this is the case, the specific error message is printed to STDOUT. If an error is encountered that does not have a specific error message associated with it, the user of the parser will simply be provided with the generic error message Syntax error.

Unlike the lexing routine, an error-reporting routine is actually optional. If you choose not to provide an error-reporting routine, users of the module will simply be provided with the generic error message Parser error whenever an error is encountered. When writing an error-reporting routine, it is also possible to force the parser to proceed despite the error by invoking the following method in the error-reporting routine:

```
$_[0]->YYErrok;
```

This method tells the parser that it is OK to resume processing the remainder of the input text. When using this method, it is a good idea to make sure the module user is aware that an error does exist despite the parser's ability to consume the entire input string. Therefore, be sure to include the appropriate warning messages in your error-reporting routine's output.

Lastly, it is always a good idea to take the time to insert one additional method into the footer section of the grammar file, in the form of a parse method for the generated parser object. As with the lexing and error-reporting routines, this can also be laid out in the Perl script calling the parser object. However, placing the code in the grammar file directly (and hence in the parser module after grammar file compilation) reduces the amount of code required to implement the module later and therefore reduces sources of errors further down the line when the parser module is implemented in Perl scripts. The parse method should look something like Listing 4-4.

Listing 4-4. *The* parse *Method*

```
sub parse{
  my ($self, $input) = @_;
  $self->YYData->{INPUT} = $input;
  my $result = $self->YYParse(yylex => \&Lexer, yyerror => \&Error,
yydebug=>0x1F);
  return $result;
}
```

The parse method will accept an input string upon invocation and pass the input string to the {INPUT} key of the YYData hash of the parser, which stores the string that the parser will attempt to parse. Next, the parse method invokes the Yapp-generated parser's YYParse method, which is responsible for actually performing the parsing and which passes the location of the lexing and error-reporting subroutines to the method. In this case, the optional yydebug parameter is also set. When present, this parameter can be set to one of several hexadecimal bit values that dictate the kind of debugging information that the parser will output (see Table 4-2).

Table 4-2. *Debugging Bit Values*

Bit Value	Information Output
0x1F	Complete debugging information
0x01	Tokens read
0x02	State information
0x04	Shift, reduce, and token acceptance actions
0x08	Dump of parse stack
0x10	Error recovery information

Tip The great advantage to using bit values is that they can be added to create debugging outputs that have more than one type of information output. For example, if both tokens read information and state information were desired, the yydebug parameter could be set to 0x03. Or, if state information and a parse stack dump were desired, the parameter could be set to 0x0A. With the bit values specified in Table 4-2, the combination of any set of bit values (excluding 0x1F) should yield a unique hexadecimal value that can be assigned to the yydebug parameter. If every debugging option other than 0x1F is combined, the resultant bit value will equal 0x1F. If you do not understand the addition of hexadecimal bit values, you can perform such addition in any calculator capable of processing hexadecimals.

BIT MASK OPERATION

To understand more fully how bit masks operate, it is first important to consider the binary basis for the previous bit masks. Let's begin by looking at a binary number that is equivalent to a bit mask stating that all yydebug outputs are not to be used. This binary representation is as follows:

00000

Basically, each position within this binary number is considered to be representative of one type of yydebug output, and if a 0 is found at that position, that particular debugging information feature is turned off; but if a 1 is present, the feature is turned on. Thus, to turn on the tokens read output, use the following the binary number representation:

00001

If you instead want to turn on the tokens read output and error recovery output, use the following binary representation:

10001

If you want all types of debugging output, use the following binary representation:

11111

The values that you set the yydebug parameter to in this example are the hexadecimal equivalents to these various binary representations, which is a conversion that can be readily performed in many calculators. For those not used to working with hexadecimals, it may be easier to decide what debugging outputs you desire and create the corresponding binary representation that turns on the chosen output types. You can then easily convert this binary into the proper hexadecimal for use with the Yapp-generated module.

On production-level parsers, specifying a yydebug value may not be a good idea, since it can generate lengthy output, but specifying full debugging output is a useful way to track down the cause of parse errors and see the actual shift and reduce operations the parser performs to yield its final answer. For example, the following is the complete debugging output from the list language example for a parse of the input string eggs, milk and bread:

```
In state 0:
Stack:[0]
Need token. Got >eggs<
Shift and go to state 4.
```

```
In state 4:
Stack:[0,4]
Don't need token.
Reduce using rule 7 (Item,1): Back to state 0, then go to state 3.
```

```
In state 3:
Stack:[0,3]
Need token. Got >,<
Shift and go to state 9.
```

```
In state 9:
Stack:[0,3,9]
Need token. Got >milk<
Shift and go to state 2.
```

```
In state 2:
Stack:[0,3,9,2]
Don't need token.
Reduce using rule 6 (Item,1): Back to state 9, then go to state 3.
```

```
In state 3:
Stack:[0,3,9,3]
Need token. Got >and<
Reduce using rule 4 (List,1): Back to state 9, then go to state 12.
```

```
In state 12:
Stack:[0,3,9,12]
Don't need token.
Reduce using rule 3 (List,3): Back to state 0, then go to state 1.
```

```
In state 1:
Stack:[0,1]
Shift and go to state 8.
```

```
In state 8:
Stack:[0,1,8]
Need token. Got >bread<
Shift and go to state 5.
```

```
In state 5:
Stack:[0,1,8,5]
Don't need token.
Reduce using rule 5 (Item,1): Back to state 8, then go to state 11.
```

```
In state 11:
Stack:[0,1,8,11]
Don't need token.
Reduce using rule 2 (Sentence,3): Back to state 0, then go to state 7.
```

```
In state 7:
Stack:[0,7]
Need token. Got ><
Shift and go to state 10.
```

```
In state 10:
Stack:[0,7,10]
Don't need token.
Accept.
```

Using yapp

Now that you have created a completed grammar module, it is time to think about using that grammar module to actually generate a parser. You can accomplish this by using yapp, which serves as a front end to the Parse::Yapp module and allows for the easy compilation of Parse::Yapp grammars into object-oriented parser modules.

yapp actually functions as a command-line utility and thus can be executed at the shell level in Unix/Linux systems and from the command prompt under the Windows operating systems. yapp is installed in the Perl system path (/usr/bin or usr/local/bin for Linux and C:\Perl\bin for Windows) when the Parse::Yapp module is installed, so there is no need to go looking on CPAN for an additional yapp application.

At the most basic level, you use yapp by simply typing the following command:

```
yapp MyGrammar.yp
```

This command takes the grammar information specified in MyGrammar.yp and creates a parsing module named MyGrammar.pm, which can then be used in any Perl script. If you run this command on the grammar file that you generated for your list language, the code for the resultant module should look like Listing 4-5.

Listing 4-5. *The Generated Parser Module*

```perl
####################################################################
#
#    This file was generated using Parse::Yapp version 1.05.
#
#        Don't edit this file, use source file instead.
#
#            ANY CHANGE MADE HERE WILL BE LOST !
#
####################################################################
package MyGrammar;
use vars qw ( @ISA );
use strict;

@ISA= qw ( Parse::Yapp::Driver );
use Parse::Yapp::Driver;



sub new {
        my($class)=shift;
        ref($class)
    and $class=ref($class);

    my($self)=$class->SUPER::new( yyversion => '1.05',
                                  yystates =>
```

```
[
        {#State 0
                ACTIONS => {
                        "milk" => 2,
                        "bread" => 5,
                        "eggs" => 4,
                        "meat" => 6
                },
                GOTOS => {
                        'List' => 1,
                        'Item' => 3,
                        'Sentence' => 7
                }
        },
        {#State 1
                ACTIONS => {
                        "and" => 8
                },
                DEFAULT => -1
        },
        {#State 2
                DEFAULT => -6
        },
        {#State 3
                ACTIONS => {
                        "," => 9
                },
                DEFAULT => -4
        },
        {#State 4
                DEFAULT => -7
        },
        {#State 5
                DEFAULT => -5
        },
        {#State 6
                DEFAULT => -8
        },
        {#State 7
                ACTIONS => {
                        '' => 10
                }
        },
```

```
        {#State 8
                ACTIONS => {
                        "milk" => 2,
                        "bread" => 5,
                        "eggs" => 4,
                        "meat" => 6
                },
                GOTOS => {
                        'Item' => 11
                }
        },
        {#State 9
                ACTIONS => {
                        "milk" => 2,
                        "bread" => 5,
                        "eggs" => 4,
                        "meat" => 6
                },
                GOTOS => {
                        'List' => 12,
                        'Item' => 3
                }
        },
        {#State 10
                DEFAULT => 0
        },
        {#State 11
                DEFAULT => -2
        },
        {#State 12
                DEFAULT => -3
        }
],
                                yyrules  =>
[
        [#Rule 0
                '$start', 2, undef
        ],
        [#Rule 1
                'Sentence', 1, undef
        ],
```

```
            [#Rule 2
                    'Sentence', 3, undef
            ],
            [#Rule 3
                    'List', 3, undef
            ],
            [#Rule 4
                    'List', 1, undef
            ],
            [#Rule 5
                    'Item', 1, undef
            ],
            [#Rule 6
                    'Item', 1, undef
            ],
            [#Rule 7
                    'Item', 1, undef
            ],
            [#Rule 8
                    'Item', 1, undef
            ]
    ],
                                        @_);
        bless($self,$class);
}

#line 7 "MyGrammar.yp"


sub Lexer{
    my($parser)=shift;

    $parser->YYData->{INPUT} or return('',undef);
    $parser->YYData->{INPUT}=~s/^[ \t]//;
    for($parser->YYData->{INPUT}){
        s/^(bread)// and return ('bread', $1);
        s/^(milk)// and return ('milk', $1);
        s/^(eggs)// and return ('eggs', $1);
        s/^(meat)// and return ('meat', $1);
        s/^(,)// and return (',',$1);
        s/^(and)// and return ('and',$1);
    }
}
```

```
sub Error {
    exists $_[0]->YYData->{ERRMSG}
    and do {
        print $_[0]->YYData->{ERRMSG};
        delete $_[0]->YYData->{ERRMSG};
        return;
    };
     print "Syntax error\n";
}

sub parse{
  my ($self, $input) = @_;
  $self->YYData->{INPUT} = $input;
  my $result = $self->YYParse(yylex => \&lexer, yyerror => \&Error,
yydebug=>0x1F);
  return $result;
}
1;
```

The yapp front end also allows you to use several flags, which add some functionality. Table 4-3 summarizes these flags, and I will describe several of the more useful flags in upcoming sections.

Table 4-3. yapp *Flags*

Flag	Purpose
-v	Creates the .output file that shows the rules and states used by the parser. It also shows any conflicts the parser may face.
-s	Creates a stand-alone parser module that can function without Parse::Yapp being installed on the deployment machine.
-n	Disables source file (grammar file) line numbering. Source file line numbering is actually useful for debugging purposes and probably not a good idea to disable.
-m	Specifies the name of the module if you want to have a different name than the one specified in the root of the grammar file.
-b	Adds a shebang to the top of the generated parser module.
-V	Displays the current version of Parse::Yapp.
-h	Displays the help screen.

The -v Flag

You should use the -v flag when creating parser modules from your grammar files for several reasons. First, it provides warnings of any parser conflicts that may be encountered, which may provide clues about why certain errors occur. Second, it lists the various rules and states that the parser utilizes, along with the numerical index assigned to each rule and state. This is highly useful when taking advantage of the integrated debugging parameter, since debugging output will refer to the rules and states implemented by these numbers.

■**Tip** You can also garner the numeric indices of rules and states from the module source code, but reading the output file is often easier than trying to sort through code.

To examine how -v works and what its output looks like, run the following command on your grammar file:

```
yapp -v MyGrammar.yp
```

After running this command, look in the directory that contains the grammar file; you will see a file called MyGrammar.output. This is the file generated by the -v flag, whose content should resemble Listing 4-6.

Listing 4-6. MyGrammar.output

```
Rules:
____

0:      $start -> Sentence $end
1:      Sentence -> List
2:      Sentence -> List 'and' Item
3:      List -> Item ',' List
4:      List -> Item
5:      Item -> 'bread'
6:      Item -> 'milk'
7:      Item -> 'eggs'
8:      Item -> 'meat'

States:
____-

State 0:

        $start -> . Sentence $end    (Rule 0)

        'bread'shift, and go to state 5
        'eggs' shift, and go to state 4
        'meat' shift, and go to state 6
        'milk' shift, and go to state 2
```

```
List    go to state 1
Item    go to state 3
Sentence        go to state 7
```

State 1:

```
Sentence -> List .   (Rule 1)
Sentence -> List . 'and' Item      (Rule 2)

'and'  shift, and go to state 8

$default      reduce using rule 1 (Sentence)
```

State 2:

```
Item -> 'milk' .     (Rule 6)

$default      reduce using rule 6 (Item)
```

State 3:

```
List -> Item . ',' List     (Rule 3)
List -> Item .     (Rule 4)

','    shift, and go to state 9

$default      reduce using rule 4 (List)
```

State 4:

```
Item -> 'eggs' .     (Rule 7)

$default      reduce using rule 7 (Item)
```

State 5:

```
Item -> 'bread' .     (Rule 5)

$default      reduce using rule 5 (Item)
```

State 6:

    Item -> 'meat' .   (Rule 8)

    $default   reduce using rule 8 (Item)

State 7:

    $start -> Sentence . $end   (Rule 0)

    $end   shift, and go to state 10

State 8:

    Sentence -> List 'and' . Item   (Rule 2)

    'bread'shift, and go to state 5
    'eggs' shift, and go to state 4
    'meat' shift, and go to state 6
    'milk' shift, and go to state 2

    Item   go to state 11

State 9:

    List -> Item ',' . List   (Rule 3)

    'bread'shift, and go to state 5
    'eggs' shift, and go to state 4
    'meat' shift, and go to state 6
    'milk' shift, and go to state 2

    List   go to state 12
    Item   go to state 3

State 10:

    $start -> Sentence $end .   (Rule 0)

    $default   accept

State 11:

    Sentence -> List 'and' Item .   (Rule 2)

    $default   reduce using rule 2 (Sentence)

State 12:

    List -> Item ',' List .   (Rule 3)

    $default   reduce using rule 3 (List)

Summary:
———

Number of rules   : 9
Number of terminals   : 7
Number of non-terminals : 4
Number of states   : 13

In the previous case, there are no conflicts reported, but if conflicts were present, they would be listed at the top of the output file as follows:

Conflicts:
———

Conflict in state 11 between rule 13 and token '-' resolved as reduce.
Conflict in state 11 between rule 13 and token '^' resolved as shift.

The -m Flag

This flag is useful if you want to change the name of your parser module to something other than MyGrammar.pm, which is the name given to it by default. It is much more logical to have your resulting parser module named MyParser.pm. To accomplish this, you can use the -m flag as follows:

yapp -m MyParser MyGrammar.yp

The -s Flag

Normally, to execute a Parse::Yapp–generated parser module, the Parse::Yapp module needs to be installed because the generated module needs to invoke functionality contained within the Parse::Yapp::Driver module. The -s flag (that is, the stand-alone flag) allows this dependency to be eliminated by embedding the Driver functionality directly into the generated module. When you use this flag, you can run the resultant module on any system capable of running Perl regardless of whether `Parse::Yapp` is installed.

Using the Generated Parser Module

Now that you have generated a parser module, it is time to try implementing that module in an actual Perl script. You can accomplish this with the Perl code shown in Listing 4-7.

Listing 4-7. *Using a* `Parse::Yapp`–*Generated Parser Module*

```
#!/usr/bin/perl

#Note MyParser.pm should be in the same directory as the script
use MyParser;

my $input="eggs, milk and bread";

$parser=new MyParser();
my $result=$parser->parse($input);

print $parser->YYNberr();
```

Implementing the parser module is actually quite simple, since you embedded the lexing, error-reporting, and `parse` method functionality in the footer section of your grammar file (and hence your parser module). You simply need to create a reference to your module and then create an instance of the parser object. An input string to be parsed is then passed to the parser object's `parse` method.

To see if your parse was successful, print the `YYNberr` value, which will return the number of times that the error-reporting subroutine has been called. In the case of a successful parse, this number should be zero. If the parse fails, a number other than zero will be output. For example, if you add a comma after `milk` in the input string, you end up with the following output:

```
Syntax error
1
```

The `Syntax error` part of the output stems from your error-reporting routine and the `1` is the result of printing `YYNberr` to output.

Evaluating Dynamic Content

In the preceding example, a Parse::Yapp parser checked the syntax of an input sequence for errors, which is a task that often has its uses. However, you can further extend the utility of a parser by not only checking the syntax of input strings but also by using the parser to dynamically evaluate the content of an input string and return a result based on the contents of the input. For example, you could create a parser that evaluated simple algebraic operations, such as adding or dividing two numbers, and returned the result of the algebraic operation. You could do this by using production rules.

After each grammar rule is specified, both Yapp and Yacc allow the grammar author to specify a production rule, which will allow the parser to perform a certain action every time it encounters a terminal or nonterminal that matches the right side of the rule. As an example, let's create a grammar file called MyMathGrammar.yp; consider the grammar header and rule sections shown in Listing 4-8.

Listing 4-8. *Simple Math Parser Grammar* (MyMathGrammar.yp)

```
%left    '+' '-'
%left    '*' '/'

%%
sentence:       expression;
expression:     addition|subtraction|multiplication|division;
addition:       number '+' number {$_[1]+$_[3]};
subtraction:    number '-' number {$_[1]-$_[3]};
multiplication:      number '*' number {$_[1]*$_[3]};
division:       number '/' number {if($_[3]==0)
                    {print "Division by Zero";}else{$_[1]/$_[3];}};
%%
```

■**Note** The header precedence declarations are not needed for this particular example, since for purposes of simplicity the grammar is not equipped to deal with nested operators. However, the precedence declarations are shown, since for most mathematical applications these precedences are standard.

The grammar rules state that a valid mathematical expression can consist of one of the four standard algebraic operations (that is, addition, subtraction, multiplication, and division). The grammar then specifies a rule for each of these operations that lays out what the proper syntax for each of the operations should look like (for example, number '+' number). However, if you look next to each of the grammar rules associated with each of the algebraic operation's syntax, you will notice the presence of a second rule enclosed in curly braces ({}). It is this second rule that is the production rule.

The production rule is able to execute a segment of code and in doing so can reference an array that stores the tokens involved in the current match for use within the code segment. The tokens are stored in the array with indices beginning with 1. For example, if you considered the addition rule, the $_[1] position would hold the first number in the expression, the $_[2] position would store the + symbol, and the $_[3] position would store the second number. Thus, you can add the two numbers by executing $_[1]+$_[3]. The parser will then return the result of this operation.

Before you can test this code, however, you first need to develop a lexer and should also develop an error-reporting routine as well as a parse method. As in the previous example, you will add the code that comprises these routines to the footer of the grammar file (after the rules found in Listing 4-7). Listing 4-9 shows the code for these routines.

Listing 4-9. *Simple Math Grammar Footer* (MyMathGrammar.yp, *Continued*)

```
sub Lexer{
    my($parser)=shift;

    $parser->YYData->{INPUT} or return('',undef);
    $parser->YYData->{INPUT}=~s/^[ \t]//;
    for($parser->YYData->{INPUT}){
        s/^(\+)// and return ('+', $1);
        s/^(-)// and return ('-', $1);
        s/^(\*)// and return ('*', $1);
        s/^(\/)// and return ('/', $1);
        s/^(\d+)// and return ('number',$1);
    }

}


sub Error {
    exists $_[0]->YYData->{ERRMSG}
    and do {
        print $_[0]->YYData->{ERRMSG};
        delete $_[0]->YYData->{ERRMSG};
        return;
    };
    print "Syntax error\n";
}
```

```perl
sub parse{
  my ($self, $input) = @_;
  $self->YYData->{INPUT} = $input;
  my $result = $self->YYParse(yylex => \&Lexer, yyerror => \&Error);
  return $result;
}
```

The code for both the error-reporting routine and the parse method are left entirely unchanged from the previous example, since these routines provide functionality that is fairly generic to most parsing tasks. However, you need to modify the lexing routine to recognize a different set of tokens. Rather than using regular expressions to match tokens such as , and bread, the lexer now needs to recognize tokens such as + and needs the ability to recognize integer numbers. It is imperative to remember that +, *, and / are all metacharacters. Thus, in order to get the lexing routine to tokenize them properly, you must precede them with a backward slash (\) so that the regex engine treats them as normal characters and not metacharacters.

Now that the grammar file is complete, it is time to once again use the yapp front end to generate a parser module by using the following command:

```
yapp -m MyMathParser MyMathGrammar.yp
```

For consistency with the upcoming example code, you should generate a module named MyMathParser.pm, since this is the module name employed in the example. Listing 4-10 shows the code script that uses the MyMathParser module.

Listing 4-10. *Using the Simple Math Parser*

```perl
#!usr/bin/perl
use MyMathParser;
my @input=("6 + 5","7 - 15","8 * 5","9 / 19");

$parser=new MyMathParser();

foreach $expression(@input){
    my $result=$parser->parse($expression);
    print $result . "\n";
}
```

This Perl script creates a small list of input strings stored in @input and then creates a new instance of the parser. A for loop then iterates through the different elements of @input, each of which is a string that is fed to the parser. The result returned by the parser is assigned to the $result variable and then printed to output. In this case, the result obtained for each input string is the result of the algebraic operation. Thus, the output of the script shown in Listing 4-9 should appear as follows:

```
11
-8
40
0.473684210526316
```

Summary

This chapter examined the parser generator Yapp, which generates object-oriented, bottom-up parser modules. The chapter laid out the syntax and organization of the grammar file as well as how you can use the yapp utility to generate a Perl parsing module from a grammar file. The chapter also delved into writing lexing routines for use with the parser module and touched upon methods of error handling and debugging Yapp parsers. Lastly, the chapter illustrated how you can use Parse::Yapp parsers for both syntax checking and for the dynamic evaluation of input strings.

In the next chapter, I will cover a second parser generator: Parse::RecDescent. Unlike Parse::Yapp, Parse::RecDescent takes a top-down approach to parsing tasks.

■ ■ ■

## CHAPTER 5

Performing Recursive-Descent Parsing with Parse::RecDescent

This chapter will cover what is probably the most robust and flexible of all the Perl parsing modules available on CPAN, Parse::RecDescent. The Parse::RecDescent module enables top-down parsing by generating recursive-descent parsers. The current version of the module, authored by Damian Conway, is 1.94.

In this chapter, you will also see how to write grammars for Rec::Descent so that it can generate appropriate parsers. If you are familiar with other open-source parsers such as Bison, Yacc, and Yapp, you will be at home here. In addition, you will learn how to precompile your parsers to improve the speed of your parsing tasks, should that be a problem.

Tip Although this chapter should provide robust enough coverage to allow you to utilize most features of Parse::RecDescent, two other recommended resources are the Parse::RecDescent FAQs, which are available on CPAN and in Damian Conway's article "The man(1) of Descent" in Issue 12 of *The Perl Journal* (1998).

Examining the Module's Basic Functionality

The basic functionality of the Parse::RecDescent module is to accept a grammar specification and, based on this grammar specification, generate a recursive-descent parser. I will cover this grammar specification in depth in the next section, but at the basic level it is similar to the Backus-Naur variant used by other parsers such as Bison, Yacc, and Yapp. A reference to the generated parser is then passed back to the Perl program, which can then conduct parsing tasks. To get a clearer understanding of how to invoke this type of functionality, consider the Perl script in Listing 5-1.

Listing 5-1. *Basic Usage of* Parse::RecDescent

```perl
#!/usr/bin/perl -w

use Parse::RecDescent;

my $grammar=q{
    startrule:      Item eofile|List 'and' Item eofile
    List:           Item',' List|Item
    Item:           'bread'|'milk'|'eggs'|'meat'
    eofile:         /^\Z/
};

my $parser=new Parse::RecDescent($grammar)
    or die "parser generation failure";

my @lists=( "bread, milk and eggs",
            "meat and eggs",
            "bread and milk and eggs",
            "meat, milk, eggs",
            "bread and bread",
            "milk, eggs, and",
            "meat, eggs, milk,"
            );


foreach my $list(@lists){
    print $list . '= ' .
    (defined($parser->startrule($list))?"CORRECT":"INCORRECT") . "\n";
}
```

Here, you first specify the grammar by assigning a string to the $grammar variable. If you look back to Chapter 2, you will see that the grammar from that chapter for specifying the structure of a list is what you are using in this case, with one small addition. This grammar includes an additional token called eofile. This grammatical change is necessary because Parse::RecDescent differs from bottom-up parsers in that it does not seek to find the longest possible match to a problem; instead, it indicates a successful parse at the earliest point that correctly satisfies the grammar. For this reason, you use the eofile nonterminal to ensure that the whole input text is parsed. Otherwise, a string such as meat, eggs, and milk would be a successful match for the grammar, even though there is an extra comma after milk.

Now that you have specified the grammar, you can pass it to the parsing object via the new command, at which point the RecDescent module will try to generate a parser based on the grammar rules. The or die command terminates the execution of the program if the parser generation fails. After the parser is generated, a blessed reference to the parser is returned that can be used to carry out any required parsing tasks.

■Note Blessed references are used as part of Perl's object-oriented programming capabilities.

Once you have constructed the parser, you can put it to work by parsing some actual lists to see if they are in the proper format. You can do this by creating an array of lists, @lists, and iterating through each member of the list. Each member will be passed to the parser object, which will check its syntax. If the syntax parses successfully, the script will print "CORRECT"; if it fails to parse successfully, "INCORRECT" will print. After executing the script, you should see the following results:

```
bread, milk and eggs= CORRECT
meat and eggs= CORRECT
bread and milk and eggs= INCORRECT
meat, milk, eggs= INCORRECT
bread and bread= CORRECT
milk, eggs, and= INCORRECT
meat, eggs, milk,= INCORRECT
```

■Tip It is possible to have more than one concurrent parser in an application. Creating other parsers is possible by following the same syntax as in Listing 5-1, with the only difference being that the other parsing objects created should be assigned to an alternate variable name (for example, $otherparser, $parser2, and so on).

Constructing Rules

The basic structure of a rule in a RecDescent grammar is as follows:

```
RuleName: productions
```

Here, productions can be any set of nonterminals or terminals. As you saw in the previous example, nonterminals (also referred to as *subrules* in the RecDescent documentation) correspond to the names of other rules within the grammar, and they are written without quotes. Terminals, on the other hand, are specified as a string of text and are surrounded by a set of single quotes (for example, 'milk'). It is also possible to specify a token by using a regular expression, as you saw for the eofile rule. Furthermore, as in the standard Backus-Naur specification, you specify alternative productions by placing a pipe (|) between them.

One added flexibility that RecDescent allows, when specifying your grammar rules, is that you can append your rules at a later time. Thus, if you consider the item rule from the previous example and later decide you want to add fruits and vegetables to the list of possible terminals, you would lay out the grammar as follows:

```
my $grammar=q{
    startrule:      Item eofile|List 'and' Item eofile
    List:           Item',' List|Item
    Item:           'bread'|'milk'|'eggs'|'meat'
    eofile:         /^\Z/
    Item:           'fruit'|'vegetables'
};
```

This would be equivalent to having the following single Item rule in the grammar:

```
Item:      'bread'|'milk'|'eggs'|'meat'|'fruit'|'vegetables'
```

When constructing your grammar rules, however, it is important to remember that Parse::RecDescent will consider a rule as properly matching at the earliest possible point and will not seek out the terminal that provides the longest possible match. This can make the order in which you write your productions important. For example, consider the following rule:

```
Myrule:  'run'|'running'
```

If this rule is used to parse a sentence that contains the word *running*, there may be some problems, because the parse would match the *run* portion of *running* and try to move on to the next rule, leaving an inappropriate *nning* for the parser to try to handle. You should instead write this rule as follows:

```
Myrule:  'running'|'run'
```

Subrules

The simplest way to define a subrule is as a nonterminal, since a subrule indicates that the current rule should try calling the named production rule in order to obtain a match. For example:

```
List:      Item',' List|Item
```

Within the rule List, there is the subrule Item, which means the parser should also call the Item rule in order to determine whether the current token of interest is going to be a successful match. In this context, List also acts as a subrule of itself, demonstrating the ability for the parser to operate in a recursive manner. When specifying a recursive subrule, it is important to keep in mind that RecDescent will not allow a recursive subrule to be declared as the leftmost production. This is designed as a safety factor, since the parser will always try to match productions in the order they are listed, and listing a recursive call as the first production could lead to an infinite loop.

LEFT VS. RIGHT RECURSION

A grammar rule uses left recursion when the leftmost symbol of the right side of the grammar rule is a recursive symbol. Right recursion occurs when the rightmost symbol of the right side of the grammar rule is a recursive symbol. For recursive-descent parsers, left recursion should always be eliminated to prevent the parser from getting hung up in an infinite loop. However, when using a left-recursion-based parser such as Yapp, Yacc, or Bison, left recursion is preferable.

Although a subrule is basically a nonterminal production, the RecDescent module allows some additional capabilities when dealing with subrules. These additional capabilities come mainly in the form of quantifiers that control how many times a given rule is allowed and/or expected to match before the production is considered complete. Table 5-1 summarizes these quantifiers, and Listing 5-2 demonstrates their usage.

Table 5-1. *Subrule Quantifiers*

Quantifier	Purpose
Mysubrule(?)	Match is optional
Mysubrule(s)	Match one or more times
Mysubrule(s?)	Match zero or more times
Mysubrule(X)	Match X times
Mysubrule(X..Y)	Match between X and Y times (inclusive)
Mysubrule(..Y)	Match between one and Y times (inclusive)
Mysubrule(X..)	Match at least X times

Listing 5-2. *Using Subrule Repetition*

```
use Parse::RecDescent;

my $grammar=q{
    startrule:      String(2..5) eofile
    String:         'a'
    eofile:         /^\Z/
};

my $parser=new Parse::RecDescent($grammar)
    or die "parser generation failure";

my @lists=( "a",
            "aa",
            "aaa",
            "aaaa",
            "aaaaa",
            "aaaaaa",
            "aaaaaaa"
            );


foreach my $list(@lists){
    print $list . '= ' .
    (defined($parser->startrule($list))?"CORRECT":"INCORRECT") . "\n";
}
```

This script will attempt to match a string of *a*'s of various lengths. However, according to the grammar specification, a successful match should occur only if the String subrule is matched between two and five times. This listing again employs the eofile subrule to ensure that the parser considers the whole string that it is passed. If you execute this listing, you should obtain the following results:

```
a= INCORRECT
aa= CORRECT
aaa= CORRECT
aaaa= CORRECT
aaaaa= CORRECT
aaaaaa= INCORRECT
aaaaaaa= INCORRECT
```

As demonstrated by this output, the parser failed to match any of the strings in which the number of occurrences of a was fewer than two or exceeded five.

When employing quantifiers like the previous ones, it is also possible to employ a separator between repeated occurrences of each subrule match. For example, if you want your *a*'s separated by commas, you use a startrule rule like the following:

```
startrule:      String(2..5 /,/) eofile
```

If you instead desire another separator, you simply replace the comma with whatever string of characters meets your needs.

Introducing Actions

The previous sections demonstrate how you can use Parse::RecDescent for the simple verification of syntax, but a parser becomes much more useful if it allows you to actually do something with the content you are parsing. This is where *actions* come in. Actions are basically blocks of Perl code that the parser can execute at a specified point within a production.

Before you learn how to use such actions, however, I should note that the RecDescent parser namespace has a series of predefined runtime variables available that can be of great benefit in programming actions. I will first cover these variables and then illustrate how to use these actions in examples. Table 5-2 summarizes these parsing variables; I will discuss the most useful variables in the upcoming sections.

Table 5-2. *Predefined Parser Variables*

Variable	Use
@item, %item	Stores values associated with each subrule, token, or action in the current production
@arg, %arg	Stores arguments passed from one rule to another
$return	Allows a value to be returned if a production succeeds
$commit	Stores the parser's current state of commitment
$skip	Stores the terminal prefix used by parser (the default is whitespace)
$text	Stores the remaining unparsed text
$thisline	Stores the current line number the parser is acting on
$prevline	Stores the line number of the last item parsed
$thiscolumn	Stores the current column number the parser is acting on
$prevcolumn	Stores the column number of the last item parsed
$thisoffset	Stores the offset of the current character from the beginning of the text being parsed

Continued

Table 5-2. *Continued*

Variable	Use
$prevoffset	Stores the offset of the last character parsed from the beginning of the text being parsed
$thisparser	Stores a reference to the Parse::RecDescent parser object
$thisrule	Stores a reference to the Parse::RecDescent::Rule object for the current rule
$thisprod	Stores a reference to the Parse::RecDescent::Production object for the current production
$score	Stores the best production score when the score directive is employed

@item and %item

The item array and hash variable store values that are associated with each item (subrule, token, or action) in the current production, which can be useful for capturing a specific value to print to output or utilize programmatically in some other way. @item works by storing values in the form of an array with the name of the rule as the zero element. Each item in the production is stored in an additional element of the array in positional increments of 1, based on the order in which they appear. For instance, consider the task of parsing a file that contains customer IDs, last names, first names, addresses, cities, and states, in that order. Say you want to use the RecDescent parser to parse the information in the file and output text that could be used as mailing labels. You can accomplish this using the @item array and an associated action as follows:

```
myrule: ID last first Address city state
{print "$item[3] $item[2] \n $item[4] \n $item[5] $item[6] \n"}
#Note: Assumes subrules exist for matching ID, last, etc.
```

If you execute the previous code, you will find the names and addresses in the data file written out as follows:

```
First name Last Name
Address
City State
```

This is the typical format for U.S.-based addresses.

Tip The @item array also allows negative indexing, starting from the most current production matched. Thus, you can also refer to the city by using $item[-2], for example. If you require an item at the end of a long list of productions, this may be an easier option.

The %item hash works in a similar way to the array, in that it stores matched productions; however, in some ways it may be easier to use since it allows you to recall the match by referring to the production by name. This feature is especially useful if the productions are not always going to be matched to the same index value, such as if an optional production is present, since you do not need to keep track of the order in which the productions are matched. Thus, if you rewrite the previous segment of code with the hash format, it will look like the following:

```
myrule: ID last first Address city state
{print "$item{first} $item{last} \n $item{Address} \n
$item{City} $item{State} \n"}
#Note: Assumes subrules exist for matching ID, last, etc.
```

@arg and %arg

These variables provide array-based and hash-based access to any arguments based on the current rule from any other rule. These variables are generally useful only for viewing arguments, however, since any changes made to either variable will not be passed on to other rules. Listing 5-3 shows a parser that uses the @arg variable to perform a formatting conversion of a list of names (that is, from "last, first" to "first last").

Listing 5-3. *Using* @arg

```
#!/usr/bin/perl -w

use Parse::RecDescent;

my $grammar=q{
    startrule:      LastName ',' FirstName argrule[$item[1],$item[3]]
    LastName:       /\w+/
    FirstName:      /\w+/
    argrule:        { print "Name= $arg[1] $arg[0]\n";}
    };

my $parser=new Parse::RecDescent($grammar)
    or die "parser generation failure";

my @lists=("Frenz, Chris",
           "Smith, Robert",
           "Doe, John");
```

```
foreach my $list(@lists){
   $parser->startrule($list);
}
```

This script specifies a grammar that reads in names in the "last name, first name" format and then calls the rule named argrule. The script then uses the @item array to pass the LastName and FirstName rule matches to argrule. argrule can then access these arguments via the @arg array and use its action to perform the format conversion. The output for this script is as follows:

```
Name= Chris Frenz
Name= Robert Smith
Name= John Doe
```

$return

In the previous examples, the @item array and %item hash allowed match values to be used for inline processing. However, many inline processing tasks will want to do more than just print a few matches to output and will probably involve some matches being used in some form of calculation or as parameters for some kind of routine. More likely than not, these calculations and/or routines will yield a value that is in some way impor-tant; therefore, this value will need to be returned for use in further processing. This is where the $return variable comes in, because it can be assigned a value during an action and upon successful completion of a production will return that value to the production. As an example, Listing 5-4 shows a Perl script; it contains a simple grammar that allows for the addition, subtraction, multiplication, or division of two numbers.

Listing 5-4. *Using the* $return *Variable*

```
#!/usr/bin/perl -w

use Parse::RecDescent;

my $grammar=q{
   startrule:        expression eofile {$return=$item[1]}
   expression:       addition|subtraction|multiplication|division
   addition:         number '+' number {$return=$item[1]+$item[3]}
   subtraction:      number '-' number {$return=$item[1]-$item[3]}
   multiplication:   number '*' number {$return=$item[1]*$item[3]}
   division:         number '/' number {if($item[3]!=0){
```

```
                                          $return=$item[1]/$item[3]}
                                          else{print "division by zero";
                                          $return=""}}

    number:              /\d+/
    eofile:              /^\Z/
};

my $parser=new Parse::RecDescent($grammar)
    or die "parser generation failure" ;

my @lists=("1+7",
           "3+5",
           "12-6",
           "22/12",
           "15|8",
           "2*6",
           "3-2"
           );

foreach my $list(@lists){
    print $list . '- ' .
    $parser->startrule($list) . "\n";
}
```

If you look closely at any of the grammar rules associated with an algebraic operation, you will see that elements of the item array are used to provide the numbers matched by the number subrule. These elements have indices of 1 and 3, respectively, since the element with an index of 2 will contain the algebraic operand. The number-containing elements then undergo the appropriate algebraic operation and are assigned to the $return variable, where they will be returned to the production that initiated the action, which in this case is expression. Within the startrule, you also have a return action that is used to return the value of expression (the answer to the algebraic problem) to the Perl script. Thus, running the script should yield the following output:

```
1+7= 8
3+5- 8
12-6= 6
22/12= 1.83333333333333
15+8= 23
2*6= 12
3-2= 1
```

$text

This variable stores any text that has not yet been parsed; it can be of significance because if a production is successful, any changes made to this variable during that production's action will be passed on to future productions. Thus, you can use this variable to dynamically alter the text being parsed. For example:

```
MyRule:     MyProduction {$text='MyNewText'}
```

Likewise, you can use an action involving the text variable to append something to the current parsing text by performing an action such as the following:

```
{$text='MyNewText' . $text}
```

■**Caution** Modifying the contents of $text will throw off the values returned by $thisline and $prevline (see the next section). Thus, if you plan to use either of these variables with a modified $text variable, you should reset their counters by using this line of code: Parse::RecDescent::Line➥ Counter::resync($thisline). Modifying the contents of $text may also throw off the values returned by $thiscolumn and $prevcolumn.

$thisline and $prevline

$thisline and $prevline are tied hash values used to store line numbers associated with the parsed text. $thisline values start from 1 and store the line number of the current item being parsed. $prevline stores the line number associated with the previous item that was parsed. If you desire to have your parser use a line number value other than its current value, you can accomplish this via assignment to the $thisline variable, such as the following action, which would set the line number equal to 5:

```
{$thisline=5}
```

It is also possible to establish an alternate starting line number value at the point at which the parser is first called by a second integer argument, as follows:

```
$parser->startrule($mytext, 5);
```

This sets the starting line number to a value of 5.

■**Tip** The utility of tied hashes is that they promote code efficiency by preventing shared values from being recomputed.

$thiscolumn and $prevcolumn

Like the previous variables, these two variables are also tied hashes. However, in this case, $thiscolumn stores the column number of the current item being parsed, starting from a column position of 1. The $prevcolumn variable stores the column number associated with the previous item that was parsed. Unlike the $thisline variable, however, assignment to these variables is not advisable, since it will result in the following parser error:

```
Can't set column number via $thiscolumn
```

Tip The value stored by $thiscolumn includes any whitespace that appears before the token, as long as it is considered valid to skip over the whitespace when reading in the token.

$thisoffset and $prevoffset

$thisoffset and $prevoffset are tied hashes that store the current parsing position and the last character successfully parsed, respectively. These variables begin at 0, and their count is not affected if the $text variable is modified. However, these variables cannot be modified, and attempting to change their value will result in an error.

Note You can flip to the "Introducing Startup Actions" section to see an example that uses the $thisoffset variable.

$thisparser

This variable stores a reference to the current parsing object; hence, assignment to this variable allows subrules from alternate parsers to be utilized in the current parsing task. For example, consider the following grammar rule:

```
MyRule:     subrule1|subrule2
            |{$thisparser = $::MyOtherParser} <reject>
            |subrule3|subrule4
```

This rule will look to the current parser's rule set for matches to subrule1 and subrule2, but then $thisparser reference is set to instead refer to the parser object MyOtherParser. Thus, the parser will seek out subrule3 and subrule4 from the MyOtherParser object.

■**Caution** Although this can facilitate the sharing of rule sets between parsers, it is important to make sure that the rule-naming conventions between the parser match up. For example, in order for the previous example to work, you need to have a `subrule3` and `subrule4` defined by the other parser object. In general, you should avoid using this feature, unless there is no other means of solving the problem at hand.

$thisrule and $thisprod

These variables store references to the `Parse::RecDescent::Rule` and `Parse::RecDescent::Production` objects that are associated with the current match.

$score

When the `<score>` directive is employed, this variable is used to store a score that ranks how well a given production matches. The `<score>` directive will then allow the determined score to be compared to the scores of past productions and the best match chosen. This deviates from the typical "take the first match" behavior of the parser. I will provide more information on this topic in the upcoming "Introducing Directives" section.

Introducing Startup Actions

Startup actions are actions that are executed before the rules of the grammar are compiled into a parser object. They are listed in brackets, just like other actions, but appear in the grammar definition before any rules that comprise the grammar. Startup actions are executed only once and as such are usually used to declare variables that will be used to process the data consumed by the parser.

For example, consider a common example from bioinformatics. DNA sequences are basically just a long string of the characters *A*, *T*, *C*, and *G*. However, as you can imagine, certain combinations/orders of these characters are extremely important. One such sequence of characters is called a *restriction site*, and that sequence of characters encodes a region where a type of enzyme, known as a *restriction enzyme*, can cut the DNA. Scientists are often interested in determining where these restriction sites occur. In this case, the restriction site of interest is GAATTC; when encountered, the enzyme will cut the DNA after the *G*. It is your job to take a sequence of DNA and determine the position at which the enzyme will cut the DNA. You will accomplish this using the `RecDescent` module and the Perl code in Listing 5-5.

Listing 5-5. *Declaring a Variable As a Startup Action*

```
use Parse::RecDescent;

my $grammar=q{
   {my $position='???';}
   startrule:      DNA(s) eofile {$return=$position;}
   DNA:            CutSite|/[ATCG]/
   CutSite:      /GAATTC/ {$position=$thisoffset-5;}
   eofile:           /^\Z/
};

my $parser=new Parse::RecDescent($grammar)
    or die "parser generation failure";

my @lists=("ATTGAATTCTTAAG",
           "GTCGGGAGAATTCGGCCT",
           "CGAATTCA",
           );

foreach my $list(@lists){
   print $list . ' Cutsite after position ' .
   $parser->startrule($list) . "\n";
}
```

Looking at the grammar specification, you can see that prior to defining any rules of the grammar, you need to specify a startup action that defines the variable $position. The grammar rules then specify what should constitute a proper DNA sequence and a proper CutSite sequence.

In the DNA rule specification, it is worth noting that the CutSite sequence is defined prior to the definition that specifies [ATCG] is acceptable, because the RecDescent parser will take the first match. [ATCG] will always match the characters that make up the CutSite sequence, and this would prevent the parser from ever properly matching the CutSite rule. When the CutSite rule is defined, an action is also specified that calculates the position of the cut and stores it in the $position variable so that the value can be returned to the program code.

Within the calculation, the $thisoffset variable is called to get the last position of the CutSite sequence and then 5 is subtracted so that the returned cut position is the position following the *G*, as specified previously. Upon executing this script, you should receive the following output:

```
ATTGAATTCTTAAG Cutsite after position 4
GTCGGGAGAATTCGGCCT Cutsite after position 8
CGAATTCA Cutsite after position 2
```

Tip When working with startup actions, it is important to keep in mind that any variables declared in them are scoped to occur within the namespace of the parser (`Parse::RecDescent::namespace000001` by default).

Introducing Autoactions

Autoactions are a special type of action that establishes a default action that will be executed at the successful completion of any production, unless another action for that production is explicitly defined. Unlike startup actions, however, they are not defined in the grammar but, rather, need to be defined in the body of the Perl code that is used to generate the parser.

You can use autoactions to give an idea of how the parser is functioning by creating an action designed to print the name of the rule that corresponds to each production matched. You can do this with code like in Listing 5-6.

Listing 5-6. *Using Autoactions*

```perl
#!/usr/bin/perl -w

use Parse::RecDescent;
$::RD_AUTOACTION=q{print $item[0] . "\n"};

my $grammar=q{
    startrule:      Item eofile|List 'and' Item eofile
    List:           Item',' List|Item
    Item:           'bread'|'milk'|'eggs'|'meat'
    eofile:         /^\Z/
};

my $parser=new Parse::RecDescent($grammar)
    or die "parser generation failure";
```

```
my @lists=( "bread, milk and eggs");

foreach my $list(@lists){
    ($parser->startrule($list));
}
```

Executing this code should yield the following output:

```
Item
Item
Item
Item
List
List
Item
eofile
startrule
```

This list yields some information about the parser's behavior when you combine knowledge of the grammar specification with the known functionality of RecDescent. For example, the parser begins with the start rule, which has two options. Given that RecDescent assigns priorities by order of occurrence, the first option is explored first. By invoking the Item rule, a successful match to bread can be made, and thus the name of the rule is printed.

However, when the parser attempts to match the eofile pattern, the match fails, and the parser moves on to the second startrule option. The parser is then directed to the List rule and then the Item rule again, where it is once again able to successfully match bread, resulting in the name Item being printed to output again. This process then continues until the parser is able to successfully match the entire input string (as indicated by it printing the name startrule).

Introducing Autotrees

Looking at the previous example, it becomes evident that it is indeed possible to use autoactions to yield a crude parse tree, but it is not a straightforward process, since the previous code also printed results from failed paths that the parser attempted as well as the successful path. For a simple parser like this, tracing the logic is not that daunting a task, but imagine doing it for a parser with many rules. The task would not be a pleasant undertaking.

You can improve things by creating an increasingly complex autoaction; however, as it turns out, that is not necessary. The RecDescent module contains a built-in parse tree generator that you can call simply by specifying the autotree directive in your application code. Therefore, if you wanted to create a more sophisticated parse tree for the previous parser, you would modify the code as shown in Listing 5-7.

Listing 5-7. *Using Autotrees*

```
use Parse::RecDescent;
use Data::Dumper;

my $grammar=q{
    <autotree>
    startrule:      Item eofile|List 'and' Item eofile
    List:           Item',' List|Item
    Item:           'bread'|'milk'|'eggs'|'meat'
    eofile:         /^\Z/
};

my $parser=new Parse::RecDescent($grammar)
    or die "parser generation failure";

my @lists=( "bread, milk and eggs");

foreach my $list(@lists){
    my $result=($parser->startrule($list));
    print Dumper($result);
}
```

Upon executing this code, the information generated by the autotree directive is stored in the variable $result, and the Data::Dumper module (available on CPAN) is used to print all the data stored within the autotree-generated hash. This should yield the following output:

```
$VAR1 = bless( {
                'List' => bless( {
                                'List' => bless( {
                                                '__RULE__' => 'List',
                                                'Item' => bless( {
```

```
'__VALUE__' => 'milk'
                                                                    }, 'Item' )
                                                    }, 'List' ),
                              '__RULE__' => 'List',
                              'Item' => bless( {
                                                    '__VALUE__' => 'bread'
                                                }, 'Item' ),
                              '__STRING1__' => ','
                          }, 'List' ),
                '__RULE__' => 'startrule',
                'Item' => bless( {
                                      '__VALUE__' => 'eggs'
                                  }, 'Item' ),
                'eofile' => bless( {
                                        '__VALUE__' => ''
                                    }, 'eofile' ),
                '__STRING1__' => 'and'
          }, 'startrule' );
```

Caution The `autotree` directive works by adding the appropriate autoactions to each production at the time of parser generation. If an action is explicitly specified for a given production, this will override the autoaction and may prevent the generation of a complete parse tree.

Introducing Autostubbing

This is a useful feature when you want to start testing elements of a grammar prior to completing the grammar. For a grammar to be considered complete, every rule and subrule within the grammar must be fully defined. *Autostubbing* allows you to bypass this necessity by placing a *stub* in the place of missing subrules. These stubs are automatically generated when autostubbing is turned on, but they have the following form:

```
subrule: 'subrule'
```

In this example, `subrule` could be any name. This means you can match an undefined rule or subrule by simply typing the name of that rule/subrule within your input string. You can turn off autostubbing by defining `$::AUTOSTUB` in the program code, as follows:

```
$::AUTOSTUB=1;
```

■**Tip** While parsers and grammars are in the developmental stage, it may also be beneficial to set `$::RD_HINT=1;` and `$::RD_TRACE=1;`, as these may provide some useful information as to how the parser may be improved and how the parser is working, respectively. For more in-depth hint and trace information, you can also set these variables to a value of 2 or 3 (the most information).

Introducing Directives

As you saw with the `autotree` directive, *directives* are a set of predefined actions that modify the behavior of the parser. Directives thus allow you to adapt and fine-tune your parser's capabilities. They can be great timesavers because they generally require you merely to add the name of the directive at the proper place in the parser's grammar, rather than forcing you to explicitly define a series of actions that would allow you to obtain similar results. Table 5-3 summarizes the directives available in `RecDescent`; I will cover the most commonly used directives in more depth in the upcoming sections.

Table 5-3. `Parse::RecDescent` *Directives*

Directive	Action
`<commit>`	Causes the rule to skip subsequent productions if the current "committed" one fails
`<uncommit>`	Ends the effects of `<commit>` and allows the parser to attempt matching productions again
`<reject>`	Causes the current production to fail
`<skip>`	Allows the terminal prefix to be modified
`<resync>`	Causes text to be consumed up to and including `/n` or some other specified pattern
`<error>`	Allows for the automatic generation of error messages
`<matchrule>`	Allows for the creation of context-sensitive subrules
`<defer>`	Specifies an action that will occur only if the production is used as part of the successful parsing solution
`<perl_quotelike>`	Parses quote-like operators in Perl (for example, `'`, `{`, `/`, and so on)
`<perl_variable>`	Matches Perl variable specifications
`<perl_codeblock>`	Matches `{}`-delimited blocks of Perl code
`<autoscore>`	Allows the best match to be chosen using custom criteria—applies to all productions in the rule
`<score>`	Allows the best match to be chosen using custom criteria—applies to a single production

<commit> and <uncommit>

As you can imagine, the larger and more complex grammars become, the longer the time each parsing task is likely to take, since there are simply more options to explore. When used properly, however, these directives can help reduce parsing time by preventing the parser from pursuing dead ends. For example, consider the following grammar rules:

```
rule1:    mysubrule1 mysubrule2
          |mysubrule3 mysubrule2
```

If the first production of rule1 successfully matches mysubrule1 but the overall production still fails (for example, fails to match mysubrule2), it is not worth attempting to match the second production since this will also fail (in order to succeed, it would also need to match mysubrule2). Therefore, there is no reason to waste time trying to match something that is going to fail, so you can modify the grammar as follows:

```
rule1:    mysubrule1 <commit> mysubrule2
          |mysubrule3 mysubrule2
```

This ensures that if the first production failed any subsequent productions would not be tried.

You can use the <uncommit> directive to negate the effects of a previous <commit> directive. Consider the following grammar:

```
rule1:    mysubrule1 <commit> mysubrule2
          |mysubrule3 mysubrule2
          |mysubrule4 mysubrule2
          |<uncommit> mysubrule5
```

In this example, the parser will skip over the second and third productions if the first one fails but, because of the <uncommit> directive, will try to match the final production, which is appropriate, since it does not depend on the successful matching of mysubrule2 like the other productions.

Note While not directly related to parsing, it is interesting to note the proven effectiveness of eliminating incorrect paths. For large-scale combinatorial problems, a technique known as *dead-end elimination* is often used to eliminate such dead ends early on and in doing so dramatically reduces the number of possible paths that the program must consider. This technique is frequently employed for tasks such as protein engineering, which often involves extremely lengthy calculations, even in a high-performance computing environment.

<reject>

This directive can be somewhat useful when a parser is being tested for its behavior in response to a production failing to match, since this directive will cause a given production to fail. You can guarantee the failing of a production by using the following syntax:

```
Myrule: myproduction <reject>
```

It can also be conditional using the following syntax:

```
Myrule: myproduction <reject: mycondition>
```

As an example, let's reconsider the simple equation solver from Listing 5-4. The example originally dealt with division by zero by using an if statement in the production and outputting an error message to the user if division by zero was encountered, which is probably the most user-friendly way of handling this issue. If, however, you want to prevent division in case a zero denominator is encountered, you can use the reject statement, as shown in Listing 5-8.

Listing 5-8. *Using the* <reject> *Directive*

```perl
#!/usr/bin/perl -w

use Parse::RecDescent;
$::RD_HINT=1;

my $grammar=q{
    startrule:        expression eofile {$return=$item[1]}
    expression:       addition|subtraction|division|multiplication
    addition:         number '+' number {$return=$item[1]+$item[3]}
    subtraction:      number '-' number {$return=$item[1]-$item[3]}
    multiplication:   number '*' number {$return=$item[1]*$item[3]}
    division:         number '/' number <reject: $item[3]==0>
                        {$return=$item[1]/$item[3]}
    number:           /\d+/
    eofile:           /^\Z/
};


my $parser=new Parse::RecDescent($grammar)
    or die "parser generation failure";
```

```
my @lists=("12/0",
           "22/10"
           );
foreach my $list(@lists){
    print $list . '= ' .
    $parser->startrule($list) . "\n";
}
```

The output generated from this script should resemble the following:

```
12/0=
22/10= 2.2
```

For the expression that involves division by zero, the production was not executed, and no "division by zero" error message was generated; however, for the division by 10, the production executed appropriately.

■**Caution** If you specify a condition that requires < or >, enclose the condition in a do{ } block, since the parser cannot distinguish between the < and > in the directive name and those in the conditional.

<skip>

The default behavior of the parser is to assume that some whitespace may exist between terminals, but the <skip> directive allows you to change this assumption in cases where this does not hold true. For example, if you have a production that uses terminals separated by dashes, you can use the <skip> directive as follows to deal with the dashes present between terminals:

```
Myrule:      <skip: "-"> mysubrule
```

When using <skip>, it is important to consider that it applies only to the current production. If the terminal prefix must be modified for a subsequent production, it must be declared again using <skip>.

A common question asked about the <skip> directive is how to skip over blanks lines within the text being parsed. You can address blank lines by using the following <skip> directive:

```
<skip: '^\s+$'>
```

■Caution If you are using a version of RecDescent older than version 1.51, then you will notice that a different mechanism was used to specify terminal separators.

<resync>

This directive is useful for passing over text that the parser cannot match properly. By default, the parser consumes text up until it encounters a newline, which it will also consume. For example, assume multiline input along with the following grammar:

```
Myrule:     myproduction1
            |myproduction2
            |<resync>
```

In the case that both myproduction subrules fail, the parser will skip directly ahead to the next line of text and begin parsing that instead. If it is desirable to skip ahead to something other than a newline, you can also specify a custom pattern in this format:

```
<resync: pattern>
```

In this example, pattern can be any regular expression, since pattern is equivalent to /pattern/ followed by the action {$return=0}.

<error>

You can use this directive to output error messages to users in response to a failure to match a given rule. The syntax of the directive is as follows:

```
Myrule: mysubrule1|<error: My error message>
```

If a custom error message is not specified, the directive will output what was expected and what it found instead. The default error messages, however, are often not very clear in terms of what is responsible for the error. An example of the default error message is as follows:

```
ERROR (line 1): Invalid expression: Was expecting addition, or
                        subtraction, or division, or multiplication
```

<defer>

The <defer> directive can almost be thought of as a delayed action, in the sense that after the successful match of a production, deferred directives are queued and are executed only in the event that the production they are associated with is actually part of the final matching solution (that is, the parser's complete match of the input string). The <defer> directive is placed after a production and has the following syntax:

```
<defer: myaction>
```

In this example, myaction can be any valid piece of Perl code, such as a print statement, the addition of two variables, and so on.

<perl ....>

You can use these directives as productions to match their respective types of Perl text: Perl quote-like operators, Perl variables, and Perl code blocks. The patterns defined by these directives use the Text::Balanced module. Therefore, for more information about the types of patterns that these directives involve, you may want to skip ahead to Chapter 8, where I cover the Text::Balanced module.

Listing 5-9 demonstrates how to use these directives.

Listing 5-9. *The* <perl_quotelike> *Directive*

```
use Parse::RecDescent;

my $grammar=q{
    startrule:      String eofile
    String:         <perl_quotelike>
    eofile:         /^\Z/
};

my $parser=new Parse::RecDescent($grammar)
    or die "parser generation failure";

my @lists=("/abc/",
            "'a string'",
            "abcd"
            );

foreach my $list(@lists){
    print $list . '= ' .
    (defined($parser->startrule($list))?"CORRECT":"INCORRECT") . "\n";
}
```

This routine should correctly match any string of characters that meets the definition of a Perl quote-like string as defined by the Text::Balanced routine, and the code is tested against three possible input strings, of which the first two can be considered valid Perl "quotes." Running this routine should thus yield output like the following:

```
/abc/= CORRECT
'a string'= CORRECT
abcd= INCORRECT
```

<score> and <autoscore>

These two declarations have similar functionality in that they allow the parser to deviate from its default behavior of selecting the first match and instead allow it to select the best match. The major difference between the two is their scope. The <score> directive applies to a single production, while the <autoscore> directive will affect every production within a given rule. In addition to specifying one of the previous directives, you must also specify a scoring subroutine as well. You must specify the scoring subroutine within the namespace of the parser object; hence, a good place to specify it is in the startup actions section of the grammar. The following is a sample grammar that utilizes the autoscore directive:

```
my $grammar=q{
{sub myscore{
    my $string=@_;
    my $score=length($string);
    return $score;
}}
    startrule:      String eofile
    String:         'a'  <autoscore: myscore>
                        |'ab'
                        |'abc'
    eofile:         /^\Z/
};
```

Of course, it is possible for you to have a more complex scoring function as your needs dictate, but in this example the longest match is simply considered the best match. The String production in this example is not in an optimal order if you were relying on the default behavior of the parser, since the a would always prohibit the matching of ab or abc, but with the <autoscore> directive all possible productions are tried and the optimal match determined by which has the highest score.

Precompiling the Parser

One of the major disadvantages of any recursive-descent parser is speed, since the top-down approach is very much a trial-and-error approach in many ways. When using the RecDescent module, the speed can sometimes become an even bigger concern because, before the parser can even begin its parsing process, the grammar must first be compiled into a parser object. For a large grammar, this process of parser generation can actually have a noticeable impact on the program's execution time, so this is currently one of the major drawbacks to the RecDescent module.

RecDescent does allow you, however, to precompile parsers in order to eliminate the time it takes to generate the parser from the application's execution time. If you have a large grammar that does not need to be frequently modified, this is an option worth considering.

The RecDescent module allows you to accomplish this using the Precompile method, which works as follows:

```
use Parse::RecDescent;
Parse::RecDescent->Precompile($grammar, "PreCompParser");
```

This creates a module with the name PreCompParser.pm, which you could then use in your application.

Alternatively, if you do not want to write a short parser-generation script, the module also allows you to create a parser at the command line using the following syntax:

```
perl -Mparse::RecDescent - grammar PreCompParser
```

Here, grammar is the name of a file containing the grammar, and PreCompParser is the name of the Perl module that will be generated upon execution.

To use the pregenerated parser, simply implement the following code:

```
use Parse::RecDescent;
use PreComParser.pm;

my $parser=PreCompParser->new();
```

Summary

In this chapter, you examined the Parse::RecDescent module and how it generates top-down, recursive-descent parsers. This module is probably the most powerful and flexible of the Perl parsing modules, and it has the added bonus that it is easier to implement than a Yapp-based solution. RecDescent also has the advantage of coming equipped with many ready-to-implement directives and actions that greatly aid critical parsing tasks such as tree generation.

The next chapter will move away from generic parsing modules such as Yapp and RecDescent and will begin the coverage of specialized parsing modules designed to deal with data in a specific format. Thus, you will look at parsing HTML, which will provide insights into how to access data from the plethora of pages available on the World Wide Web. To aid programmatic processing of HTML, you will also learn about the LWP module, which will allow your application to directly access information from the Web.

■■■

## CHAPTER 6

Accessing Web Data with HTML::TreeBuilder

Over the course of the past decade, the World Wide Web has undoubtedly become one of the greatest means of information dissemination in existence. From consumer products to scholarly treatises on any subject imaginable, the Web truly possesses a plethora of information. For this reason, the automated extraction of data from the Web represents a highly useful tool for rapidly aggregating large amounts of information.

To perform this type of task, you will need to understand how basic Hypertext Markup Language (HTML) documents are structured, since documents written in HTML form most of the foundation of the Web. Thus, this chapter will begin with an overview of the basics of HTML syntax. Once the coverage of HTML syntax is complete, you will examine the LWP::Simple and LWP modules; these modules enable Perl scripts to access Web content and thus can acquire HTML pages for a parser or for an information extraction routine to use. Finally, you will examine the HTML::TreeBuilder module and learn how you can utilize it to parse HTML documents and access information within a specific section of the document.

Caution Although it is true that the Web has an unrivaled amount of information available on it, much of the Web is never reviewed for accuracy. Thus, when obtaining information from the Web, either programmatically or manually, it is important to consider the source of the information or at least whether multiple independent resources yield similar information.

Introducing HTML Basics

HTML is a standard format for publishing content on the Web and is based on Standard Generalized Markup Language (SGML). The current HTML standard is HTML 4.01, and the standard specifications are laid down by the World Wide Web Consortium (W3C). According to these specifications, HTML documents are designed to follow a standard format, although it is important to note that not all HTML documents comply with these standards. In fact, some browsers, such as the different Internet Explorer variants, will render a number of nonstandard tags and extensions. This is the reason that certain Web pages render well only in IE. Well-formed HTML should render equally well in any W3C-compliant browser. Lack of standards compliance is one of the difficulties faced when trying to manually parse HTML, with the other major difficulty being the nested nature of HTML.

Note Readers interested in learning more about the HTML 4.01 standard can go to the W3C Web site (http://www.w3.org) for more information. If you are interested in SGML, you can obtain more information from http://www.isgmlug.org/sgmlhelp/g-index.htm.

In the following sections, I will discuss some of the standard practices for authoring simple HTML documents. When reading these sections, keep the following in mind: Although specialized WYSIWYG editors for HTML exist, a standard text editor is sufficient for creating HTML documents as long as you are willing to specify the proper tags yourself. In fact, probably the best way to truly learn HTML is to use a text editor for authoring, since it is the only way to see how different tags will affect rendering within a browser.

So, to follow along with the examples in the following sections, fire up your favorite text editor (for example, NEdit, emacs, vi, Notepad, and so on) and use it to enter the samples as you go along. Just remember to change the file extension to .html before trying to display the document in your browser, or you are likely to see the text you typed rather than the rendering of the HTML document.

Specifying Titles

Every HTML document needs a title that will be displayed as the caption across the top of the browser window and, in the case of tabbed browsers, as the name of the tab. Titles in HTML are designated by enclosing the title text between a specialized set of tags. An opening <title> tag signifies the start of the title text, and the closing </title> tag specifies the end of the title text. Thus, to create a title for the sample document, add the following markup to your HTML file:

```
<title>Pro Perl Parsing Sample</title>
```

If you load this sample file into your Web browser, you will see the browser's caption shown in Figure 6-1.

Figure 6-1. *Browser caption displaying the sample title*

Specifying Headings

You use headings just as you would use them in any text document. They define the different sections of the document by dividing it into a series of sections and/or subsections. Six levels of headings are available within the HTML specification, with level one being the largest and most prominent heading type and subsequent heading levels decreasing in size and prominence. Thus, you may want to have a level-one heading providing the heading for the overall document, a level-two heading defining the major sections of the document, and a level-three heading defining different subsections within any given section.

Tip The HTML specification does not state that you need to use HTML heading levels sequentially. Therefore, you could just as easily use heading levels one, three, and five instead of one, two, and three. In fact, this may even make the visual distinction between sections more prominent and may serve as a better choice.

As with titles, headings are also specified with opening (<hN>) and closing (</hN>) tags, where N is the level of the heading. So, to specify the heading level, you simply need to replace the N in these tags with the number of the desired heading level (1 through 6). Add headings to the sample document by adding the following markup to your file:

```
<h1>The Main Page Heading</h1>
<h3>A Section Heading</h3>
<h5>A Subsection Heading<h5>
```

Rendering this file in a Web browser should display results like those shown in Figure 6-2.

Note The previous markup was rendered with Mozilla's Firefox Web browser. Your results may differ slightly in terms of font and size, since how elements render is somewhat browser-specific, but the relative sizes of headings should be proportional to their level.

The Main Page Heading

A Section Heading

A Subsection Heading

Figure 6-2. *Some sample HTML headings*

Specifying Paragraphs

Paragraphs contain the bulk of the textual information within a Web page, since paragraph elements are essentially equivalent to what you would consider a paragraph in a book or any text document. The beginning of a paragraph is represented by the start <p> tag, and the end of a paragraph is represented by the end </p> tag. To add some textual information to the sample document, you can edit the document's markup as follows:

```
<h1>The Main Page Heading</h1>
<h3>A Section Heading</h3>
<p>This is the first paragraph of this section.  An HTML
document is likely composed of many such paragraphs.</p>
<p>This is a second paragraph.  More text could go here.</p>
<h5>A Subsection Heading<h5>
```

If this markup is rendered, it should look like Figure 6-3.

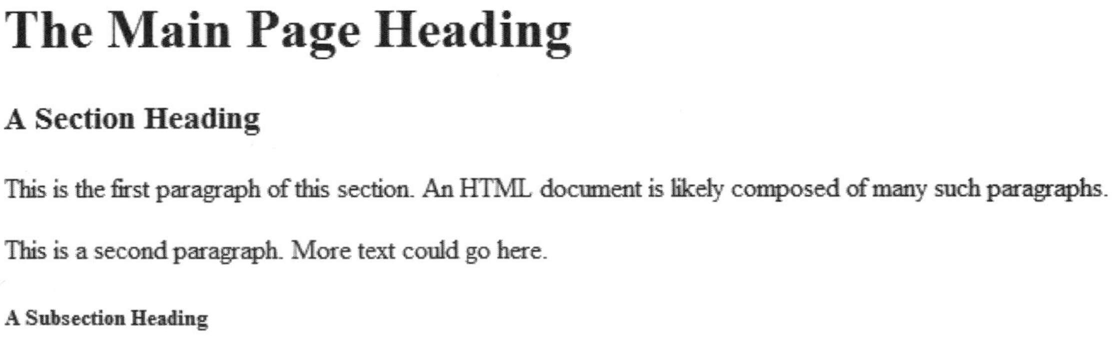

The Main Page Heading

A Section Heading

This is the first paragraph of this section. An HTML document is likely composed of many such paragraphs.

This is a second paragraph. More text could go here.

A Subsection Heading

Figure 6-3. *The sample document with the addition of two paragraphs*

Specifying Lists

HTML markup allows three types of lists to be specified, and each of these lists will be displayed in the browser window in a different style. The lists are an ordered list, an unordered list, and a definition list. The following sections briefly cover each of these types.

Ordered Lists

An *ordered list* is a numbered listing of elements, where the first item is prefixed with a 1, the second with 2, and so on. An ordered list starts with the opening tag <ol> and ends with the closing tag </ol>. You specify each element on the list with the tags <li> and </li>. The following is an example of an ordered list:

```
<ol>
   <li>Element 1</li>
   <li>Element 2</li>
   <li>Element 3</li>
</ol>
```

When a browser renders this markup, the output will look like Figure 6-4.

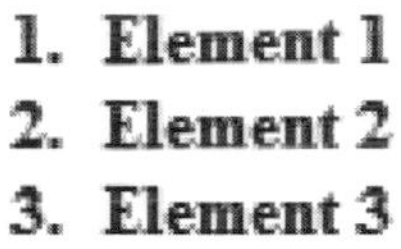

1. **Element 1**
2. **Element 2**
3. **Element 3**

Figure 6-4. *An ordered list*

Unordered Lists

Unordered lists are bulleted lists. Thus, rather than being prefixed with a number, each element will instead appear with a bullet of some sort. The markup for unordered lists is almost the same as for ordered lists, except that the opening and closing tags are <ul> and </ul>, respectively. If you changed the list tags in the previous example to their unordered list counterparts, you will see the list displayed in Figure 6-5.

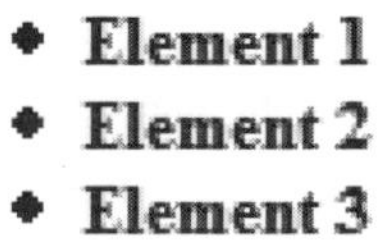

- **Element 1**
- **Element 2**
- **Element 3**

Figure 6-5. *An unordered list*

Definition Lists

Definition lists display an element within a list and then provide some information, such as a definition, about that element. As with the other list types, the start and finish of definition lists are specified with a start tag (<dl>) and an end tag (</dl>). The list elements, however, are defined in two parts. One part lists the element of the list, and the second part provides the definition of that element. The element itself is enclosed in a set of <dt></dt> tags, while the definition is enclosed in <dd></dd> tags. The following is some sample markup for a definition list:

```
<dl>
  <dt>Element 1</dt>
  <dd>Definition of element 1</dd>
  <dt>Element 2</dt>
  <dd>Definition of element 2</dd>
  <dt>Element 3</dt>
  <dd>Definition of element 3</dd>
</dl>
```

Figure 6-6 shows a rendered version of this markup.

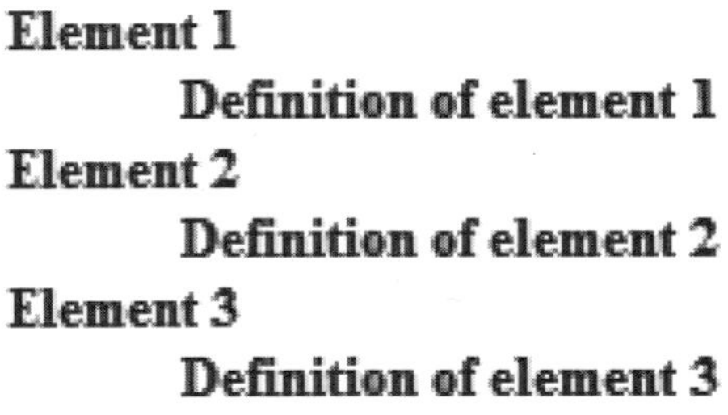

Element 1
> **Definition of element 1**

Element 2
> **Definition of element 2**

Element 3
> **Definition of element 3**

Figure 6-6. *A definition list*

Embedding Links

One of the most useful features of the Web is that a Web page can contain not only its own information but also links to other pages that may contain useful information. Within HTML documents, links are contained between <a> and </a> tags. You can link to http://www.apress.com from an HTML document by entering the following markup:

```
<a href="http://www.apress.com/">Apress Web site</a>
```

When this markup is rendered, the underlined text "Apress Web site" will be displayed, as shown in Figure 6-7, but the browser will proceed to the URL http://www.apress.com when the link is accessed.

Apress Web site

Figure 6-7. *A link to the Apress Web site*

■**Note** The previous sections cover the most basic HTML structures, but most modern Web pages will contain many more markup elements than those discussed. These additional markup items control the formatting of the content as well as embed other items such as pictures and animations. The basics covered here are adequate for understanding how HTML parsing works, but anyone who wants to perform sophisticated types of HTML authoring or parsing should consult a more comprehensive resource on HTML, such as the W3C HTML page at http://www.w3.org/MarkUp/.

Understanding the Nested Nature of HTML

When working with HTML documents, it is important to remember that it is also possible to nest tags. For example, an HTML document can easily contain a list of links:

```
<dl>
  <dt><a href="http://www.apress.com/">Apress Web site</a></dt>
  <dd>Apress sells high-quality computer books</dd>
  <dt><a href="http://www.apress.com/about.index.html/">About Apress</a></dt>
  <dd>You can learn about Apress at this link</dd>
  <dt>
    <a href="http://www.apress.com/author/authorDisplay.html?aID=37">
      Chris Frenz's Apress Books
    </a>
  </dt>
  <dd>See all the books written by Chris Frenz here</dd>
</dl>
```

When a Web browser renders this markup, it yields a definition style list that contains a set of embedded links and descriptions of the content that can be found at each link (see Figure 6-8).

<u>Apress Web site</u>
> **Apress sells high-quality computer books**

<u>About Apress</u>
> **You can learn about Apress at this link**

<u>Chris Frenz's Apress Books</u>
> **See all the books written by Chris Frenz here**

Figure 6-8. *A definition list containing hyperlinks*

It is this nested nature that often makes HTML pages difficult to parse. The HTML specifications are not as stringent as they could be; thus, for many elements, opening tags are required but closing tags are not. The closing tag is often considered implicit; in other words, the opening of another tag of the same type is probably indicative that the previous instance of the tag should have been closed. Implicit tag closing is frequently observed with <p> tags. However, it is a good idea to consider the possibility of implicit tag closing for all tag types.

You can accomplish some basic parsing tasks using regular expressions or a simple grammar and a module such as RecDescent, but a likelihood exists that such code will not work for every Web page, since you may encounter cases of badly formed HTML that contains unbalanced tags. An example of using a regular expression to parse HTML documents would be using a loop structure to try to extract all the Web addresses used in a document's various link structures. The following is the code to accomplish this:

```
while ($CurrentLine=<>){
    if($CurrentLine=~/href="(.*?)"/){
        print $1 . "\n";
    }
}
```

The previous code searches for href=", which prefixes every linked URL and then uses substring capturing to return the URL located between the quotes. Executing the previous code on the markup from the previous example yields the following list of URLs:

```
http://www.apress.com/
http://www.apress.com/about.index.html/
http://www.apress.com/author/authorDisplay.html?aID=37
```

Accessing other tagged elements, such as headings, could be problematic with this approach, since if closing tags were not used, it would be hard to specify where the heading actually ends. Also, even link extraction is not always this straightforward in more complex HTML documents, and you should avoid this method for all but the simplest parsing tasks.

It is in these instances that a specialized HTML parser, such as HTML::TreeBuilder, comes in handy, since these types of parsers have been fine-tuned to deal with implicit tag closings. If, for some reason, using an HTML parsing module is not an option, you may want to try a utility such as HTML Tidy to try to fix the HTML syntax before your custom parser acts on it. HTML Tidy is an open-source utility available at http://tidy.sourceforge.net. Assuming you have it installed on your system already, you could place the following line of code before any parsing is executed on your file of interest:

```
system("tidy", "-m", "MyHTMLFile.html");
```

The system command causes your script to open a child process and wait for the child process to complete before moving on. In this case, the tidy utility executes as that child process with -m and MyHTMLFile.html passed as arguments. The -m flag tells tidy to modify the file so that it is closer to well-formed HTML syntax, while MyHTMLFile.html is the name of the file on which tidy will be operating.

Generally, however, regular expression–based extraction is recommended only for parsing content from the same Web site repeatedly. One example is a program that checks a local weather site daily (see Listing 6-1 in the next section). In this way, you can view the source of the page and cater your regular expression to the style used for that particular Web page. Since the format of the Web page is unlikely to change frequently, the script should not encounter problems often.

Accessing Web Content with LWP

Before learning how to parse HTML with the HTML::Treebuilder module, it is a good idea to lay out a methodology to retrieve HTML documents from the Web so that the parsing module has something to act upon. The LWP module provides methods for accessing HTML content over HTTP connections.

HTTP is a communication protocol and is designed to operate in a client-server environment. The first step in conducting an HTTP transfer is for the client (in this case, the LWP module) to contact the server and request the HTML document of interest with an HTTP GET method (this happens behind the scenes and is handled by the client, so you do not have to worry about it). The server will then respond to the client by either returning the HTML document or sending back notification that the request failed.

■**Note** HTTP also allows you to send data to a server using the POST method. I will cover this method in due course.

Using LWP::Simple

The most straightforward way of accessing Web data is to use the `LWP::Simple` module. However, as you will see, this module is also the most limited in terms of functionality. The `get` function of the `LWP::Simple` module allows you to retrieve an HTML document by simply specifying the URL of the document as the function's argument. Thus, if you wanted to fetch the HTML document found at `http://www.apress.com`, you would simply use the following lines of code in your application:

```
use LWP::Simple;
$mydocument=get("http://www.apress.com");
```

If, for some reason, the Apress Web site was unavailable, the `get` function would return `undef`.

If you instead wanted to download the document as a file to be saved for later manipulation, you could instead employ the `getstore` function. The `getstore` function takes both a URL and a filename as an argument and has the advantage that it returns some status information. The syntax of `getstore` is as follows:

```
$reqstatus=getstore("http://www.apress.com", "myfile.html");
die unless is_success($reqstatus);
```

This code segment will request the document found at `http://www.apress.com`; if the document is successfully returned, it will be stored as `myfile.html`, and the `$reqstatus` variable will be set to the status code of the transaction. The `die` statement will then employ the `is_success` method to determine if the transaction was successful and will terminate the script if the request failed. This will prevent the script from trying to process a nonexistent HTML file.

Using LWP

The `LWP::Simple` module is straightforward to use for retrieving documents but is limited in that it can perform HTTP `GET` operations but not HTTP `POST` operations. To gain this type of capability, you need to use the full-fledged `LWP` module. Before looking at `POST` operations, however, you will first examine how `GET` requests are performed with the `LWP` module. Let's explore this by creating a simple Perl script that will allow you to enter a ZIP code as an argument and will then take the ZIP code and submit it to Weather.com in order to find the temperature at that ZIP code. Listing 6-1 shows the code for this application.

Listing 6-1. *Getting the Temperature from Weather.com*

```
use LWP;

my $request;
my $response;
my $query=$ARGV[0];

my $url="http://www.weather.com/outlook/health/allergies/local/". ($query);

$request=LWP::UserAgent->new();
$response=$request->get($url);
my $content= $response->content;
die unless $response->is_success;

if($content=~/CLASS=obsTempTextA>(\d+)&deg;F/){
    print "It is currently $1 degrees Fahrenheit at $query";
}
```

The script begins by taking the argument that was supplied by the user (in other words, the ZIP code to query) and appending it to a prespecified URL stem. Next, an instance of the LWP::UserAgent object is created and the object's get method is used to request the completed URL (stem + query ZIP code).

The content of the HTML document is then stored in the variable $content, and a die unless statement is executed to prevent further processing if the get request was not successfully completed. If the request was successful, a regular expression is used to parse the current temperature of that ZIP code.

To develop this regular expression, the page source of a representative HTML document was viewed and enough text was taken from around the temperature reading to make it unique. Making your regex unique is important in a situation such as this to ensure that it picks up only the item of interest and not some other value. The temperature is then printed to output and should look something like the following output:

```
It is currently 32 degrees Fahrenheit at 10595
```

Tip When examining the page source for the purposes of creating the regular expression that will be doing the extraction, a viewer or editor with "find" capabilities can be a real time-saver. Ask the editor to find the output text for you. Depending on the length and content of the output, you may get more than one match, but checking a few possible matches is still much quicker than manually inspecting the entire page source.

Not all Web sites use URLs to pass in query parameters, however; and, as with LWP::Simple, HTTP GET requests are thus able to query only a fraction of the data sources available on the Web. Many sites, especially those that require multiple fields, will instead require information to be posted in the form of key-value pairs.

The server will use these key-value pair values to query its database appropriately and then return the results via an HTML document. The LWP modules also allow POST requests to be performed. To illustrate this, the script in Listing 6-2 will query the Pubmed database, a collection of biomedical research articles, and return the titles of the articles that appear on the first results page.

Listing 6-2. *Querying the Pubmed Database*

```
use LWP;

my $request;
my $response;
my $query;
my $i=0;
$query=join(" ", @ARGV);

my $url="http://www.ncbi.nlm.nih.gov/entrez/query.fcgi";

$request=LWP::UserAgent->new();
$response=$request->post($url,['db'=>"pubmed", 'term'=>$query]);
my $results= $response->content;
die unless $response->is_success;
while($results=~/<td colspan="2">(.*?)</g){
    print "$1 \n";
}
```

This script takes the query term(s) that the user is interested in using as arguments. Since it is likely that a multiterm query may be desired, the join method is initially used to process the argument list and create a properly formed query string. Since the URL of the database is unlikely to change, the value is hard-coded into the variable $url. An instance of the UserAgent object is then created, and an HTTP POST request is made. Within the POST request, the URL of the Web page is first specified followed by the key-value pairs in brackets. The script then proceeds to run in the same manner as one utilizing a GET request.

If the results are returned successfully, they are processed with a regular expression designed to extract the title of the articles, which are printed to output. As of the time of this writing, some sample output for a query of "HIV" is as follows:

Aspartic Proteases of Plasmodium falciparum as the Target of HIV-1
Protease Inhibitors.
Levels of L-Selectin (CD62L) on Human Leukocytes in Disseminated Cryptococcosis
With and Without Associated HIV-1 Infection.
HIV-1 Drug Resistance: Degree of Underestimation by a Cross-Sectional versus
a Longitudinal Testing Approach.
The Presence of Anti-Tat Antibodies Is Predictive of Long-Term Nonprogression
to AIDS or Severe Immunodeficiency: Findings in a Cohort of HIV-1 Seroconverters.
Schistosomiasis and HIV-1 Infection in Rural Zimbabwe: Implications of Coinfection
for Excretion of Eggs.

FINDING KEY-VALUE PAIRS IN PAGE SOURCES

The best way to find the key-value pairs required by a given Web page is to examine the page source.
In general, key-value pairs are two types: either fields designed to accept direct user input or fields
where the user is expected to make a selection from a variety of options. HTML markup for input fields
generally looks similar to the following:

```
<input name="key" size="45" type="TEXT" value="">
```

Here the key name can be found in the name field, and the corresponding value pair (user-entered
text) will become assigned to value when the user submits the form for processing. For option input
fields, the markup generally looks like the following:

```
<select name="key">
  <option selected value="Option 1">Option 1</option>
  <option value="Option 2">Option 2</option>
  <option value="Option 3">Option 3</option>
  <option value="Option 4">Option 4</option>
</select>
```

In this case, the key name is still specified by the name field, but the appropriate values are specified by the value values enclosed in each <option> tag. The markup responsible for option input
fields can often be found nested within a pair of <form> tags.

Using HTML::TreeBuilder

So far, you have examined the basic structure of HTML documents as well as how to use the LWP::Simple and LWP modules to access HTML documents from the Web. You also saw how to use regular expressions to perform basic data extraction tasks, such as extracting predetermined values from a recurrent data source. While such extractions are not without use, sometimes a little more flexibility may be desired, such as working with multiple HTML documents that may not share formatting conventions. In these cases, regular expression–based extraction tends to fail, and a more powerful alternative becomes necessary.

The module HTML::TreeBuilder, written by Gisle Aas and Sean M. Burke, is a parser that is specially designed to handle HTML, including some forms of implicit tag closings. Employing a parsing module such as this can help to grant your data extraction routines much more flexibility and robustness.

As you saw in previous chapters, it is possible to take a series of nested elements (such as math equations involving parentheses) and create a parse tree that shows the respective levels and orders of differing tokens and nontokens that can be used to create the text string of interest. The same holds true for HTML documents, in that a hierarchy of tagged elements can be created. Because of the common occurrence of badly formed HTML, this is exactly what HTML::TreeBuilder is designed to do (even though it is not always a trivial task). It creates a parse tree of a given HTML document; this tree can aid in identifying the document's constituent components and hence make data extraction tasks easier.

Note This module is not a stand-alone Perl module but rather part of the HTML::Tree distribution. For the following examples to work on your machine, it is important that you install the entire Tree distribution, since the HTML::TreeBuilder module will use several other modules in that distribution, such as the HTML::Element class.

To get an idea of how the basic TreeBuilder functionality works and what a sample parse tree looks like, let's recall a segment of HTML used in an earlier example and use it in the Perl script shown in Listing 6-3.

Listing 6-3: HTML::TreeBuilder *Basics*

```
$html=q{
   <h1>Apress Weblinks</h1>
   <dl>
   <dt><a href="http://www.apress.com/">Apress Website</a></dt>
   <dd>Apress sells high quality computer books</dd>
   <dt><a href="http://www.apress.com/about.index.html/">About Apress</a></dt>
   <dd>You can learn about Apress at this link</dd>
   <dt>
     <a href="http://www.apress.com/author/authorDisplay.html?aID=37">
       Chris Frenz's Apress Books
     </a>
   </dt>
   <dd>See all the books written by Chris Frenz here</dd>
   </dl>
   };

use HTML::TreeBuilder;

my $tree=HTML::TreeBuilder->new,

$tree->parse($html);
$tree->eof;
$tree->dump;
$tree->delete;
```

This script will first assign a segment of markup to the variable $html and then will create an instance of the HTML::TreeBuilder object. The parse method of the object is then called, as opposed to the parse_file method, since the input is only a string of markup rather than a complete HTML file.

After the parse method is called, you need to call the eof method to let the parser know that the $html string is complete. Next, you call the dump method, which is actually not a native TreeBuilder method but is inherited from the HTML::Element class (see the previous note on the dependency of the module). The dump method is used to print the tree to output. The default is standard out, but a file handle can be supplied as an argument.

Finally, it is good practice to delete your parse tree after processing in order to free memory resources, since large parse trees can actually consume substantial amounts of system memory. The parse tree outputted by the previous script should resemble the following:

```
<html> @0 (IMPLICIT)
  <head> @0.0 (IMPLICIT)
  <body> @0.1 (IMPLICIT)
    <h1> @0.1.0
      "Apress Weblinks"
    <dl> @0.1.1
      <dt> @0.1.1.0
        <a href="http://www.apress.com/"> @0.1.1.0.0
          "Apress Website"
      <dd> @0.1.1.1
        "Apress sells high quality computer books"
      <dt> @0.1.1.2
        <a href="http://www.apress.com/about.index.html/"> @0.1.1.2.0
          "About Apress"
      <dd> @0.1.1.3
        "You can learn about Apress at this link"
      <dt> @0.1.1.4
        <a href="http://www.apress.com/author/authorDisplay.html?aID=37">
@0.1.1.4.0
          "Chris Frenz's Apress Books"
      <dd> @0.1.1.5
        "See all the books written by Chris Frenz here"
```

Note In the previous output results, the @0... numbers at the ends of lines demonstrate the hierarchy of nodes. The main parent node is @0, and its direct child nodes are given the notation @0.0–@0.1, in the order in which they appear. This process then repeats itself for the children of these @0.0/@0.1 nodes, yielding a hierarchal notation of @0.1.1 or @0.1.2, for example, and so on.

Controlling TreeBuilder Parser Attributes

The TreeBuilder parser function is not entirely preset; by modifying certain attributes of the parser, you can alter the manner in which the parser generates the parse tree. Table 6-1 lists these attributes. However, it is normally advisable to change the default values of these attributes only in specialized circumstances, since the default values are supposed to be optimized to behave like a real-world browser.

Table 6-1. *TreeBuilder Parser Attributes*

Attribute	Role	Default
implicit_tags	When set to true, the parser will try to infer where implicit tags are present.	true
implicit_body_p_tag	When set to true, text elements occurring after a <body> tag will be assumed to have an implicit <p> tag.	false
ignore_unknown	When set to true, tags not recognized by the parser will be included in the parse tree.	false
ignore_text	If set to true, the textual elements contained within tagged elements will not be displayed.	false
ignore_ignorable_whitespace	If set to true, this prevents the parser from creating nodes of ignorable whitespace.	true
no_space	Compacts contiguous whitespace in nontext areas to a single space when set to 0. If set to 1, compacting does not occur.	0
p strict	If set to false, it will not close a <p> element until a new <p> element is encountered. If set to true, it will close the current <p> element whenever a nontextual element is encountered.	false
warn	When set to true, any syntax errors encountered during parsing will be output.	false

The code shown in Listing 6-4 demonstrates how to change these attributes, should your application require it.

Listing 6-4. *Parsing with Adjusted Attributes*

```
$html=q{
   <h1>Apress Weblinks</h1>
   <dl>
   <dt><a href="http://www.apress.com/">Apress Website</a></dt>
   <dd>Apress sells high quality computer books</dd>
   <dt><a href="http://www.apress.com/about.index.html/">About Apress</a></dt>
   <dd>You can learn about Apress at this link</dd>
   <dt>
     <a href="http://www.apress.com/author/authorDisplay.html?aID=37">
     Chris Frenz's Apress Books
     </a>
   </dt>
   <dd>See all the books written by Chris Frenz here</dd>
   </dl>
   };

use HTML::TreeBuilder;
```

```
my $tree=HTML::TreeBuilder->new;
$tree->ignore_text(True);
$tree->parse($html);
$tree->eof;
$tree->dump;
$tree->delete;
```

As you can see, this script is the same as the one shown in Listing 6-3, with the only difference being that the ignore_text attribute has been set to true. You can specify other attribute values in the same manner. If the script in Listing 6-4 is executed, the altered behavior of the parser becomes quite obvious when you examine the output:

```
<html> @0 (IMPLICIT)
  <head> @0.0 (IMPLICIT)
  <body> @0.1 (IMPLICIT)
    <h1> @0.1.0
    <dl> @0.1.1
      <dt> @0.1.1.0
        <a href="http://www.apress.com/"> @0.1.1.0.0
      <dd> @0.1.1.1
      <dt> @0.1.1.2
        <a href="http://www.apress.com/about.index.html/"> @0.1.1.2.0
      <dd> @0.1.1.3
      <dt> @0.1.1.4
        <a href="http://www.apress.com/author/authorDisplay.html?aID=37">
@0.1.1.4.0
      <dd> @0.1.1.5
```

Notice that the textual portions of the HTML markup are no longer printed.

Searching Through the Parse Tree

The HTML::Element class provides several methods for searching through the parse tree and returning nodes on the tree that meet the specified criteria. Table 6-2 summarizes the methods, which are explained in more depth in the following sections.

Table 6-2. *Tree Searching Methods*

Method	Use
find_by_tag_name	Returns all parse tree nodes that contain a tag of the named type(s)
find_by_attribute	Returns all parse tree nodes that possess a given key-value pair
look_down	Returns all child nodes that meet specified criteria
look_up	Returns all parental nodes that meet the specified criteria

find_by_tag_name

This method returns all parse tree nodes that contain a tag of the named type, such as an <h2> or <h3> tag. For example, a script could use this method to access the Apress home page and extract all the items enclosed in <p> tags. Listing 6-5 shows the code for this routine.

Listing 6-5. *Using the* find_by_tag_name *Method*

```
use LWP::Simple;
use HTML::TreeBuilder;

$html=get("http://www.apress.com");

my $tree=HTML::TreeBuilder->new;
$tree->parse($html);
$tree->eof;
@pnodes=$tree->find_by_tag_name('p');


foreach node(@pnodes){
    $node->dump;

}

$tree->delete;
```

■**Note** If pnodes is a scalar variable rather than an array, the contents of only the first set of paragraph tags will be returned.

find_by_attribute

This method functions in the same way as the previously described find_by_tag_name method, only it searches using an attribute-value pair rather than using a tag type. The syntax for using this method is as follows:

```
@pnodes=$tree->find_by_attribute("align", "left");
```

With the supplied arguments, this line of code seeks out all tags with an align attribute set to a value of left. In other words, all of the left-aligned elements would be returned.

look_down

This method searches through all of a node's children, including child nodes of child nodes, and returns any nodes that meet the specified criteria. If you want to parse all the nodes of the tree, you can use the root node as a starting point. As an illustration of this method, the script in Listing 6-6 will download Apress's home page and show all the recently posted blog entries.

Listing 6-6. *Using the* look_down *Method*

```
use LWP::Simple;
use HTML::TreeBuilder;

$html=get("http://www.apress.com");

my $tree=HTML::TreeBuilder->new;
$tree->parse($html);
$tree->eof;
@pnodes=$tree->look_down(_tag=>'a',
 href=>qr{http://blogs\.apress\.com/archives/\d+\.html});

# Creates HTML file output will be written to
open(OFile, ">Blogout.html");



foreach $node(@pnodes){
    $url=$node->attr('href');
    $text=$node{_content}[0];
    print OFile "<h1><a href=\"$url\">$text</a></h1> \n";
}
$tree->delete;
```

A careful examination of the arguments supplied in the look_down method will reveal that this can be a significantly more powerful type of search than the aforementioned find methods. The look_down method allows both a tag type and an attribute-value pair to be specified. It is also worth noting that a regular expression can be used to specify an attribute value, which in this case is a regular expression designed to match links to blog entries only. This ability to match both tag types and attribute-value pairs allows for very precise content extraction. Once the tags containing the blog links are extracted, a representative dump of the @pnodes array would look like the following:

```
<a href="http://blogs.apress.com/archives/000463.html">
@0.1.1.0.1.0.1.1.0.0.1.5.0.4.2.1.0.0
  "VoIP Limits in the Future"
<a href="http://blogs.apress.com/archives/000462.html">
@0.1.1.0.1.0.1.1.0.0.1.5.0.4.2.1.1.0
  "IBM Continues Bolstering Open Source Commitment"
<a href="http://blogs.apress.com/archives/000461.html">
@0.1.1.0.1.0.1.1.0.0.1.5.0.4.2.1.2.0
  "What's the future of Java? J2EE/ J2ME / ??"
<a href="http://blogs.apress.com/archives/000460.html">
@0.1.1.0.1.0.1.1.0.0.1.5.0.4.2.1.3.0
  "Music"
<a href="http://blogs.apress.com/archives/000459.html">
@0.1.1.0.1.0.1.1.0.0.1.5.0.4.2.1.4.0
  "GPL FUDs itself"
```

This dump reveals the information you were seeking; however, it is not in a format that makes accessing the blog content easy. Thus, you can add code to process the content of the extracted nodes. The attr method is the simplest way to access the URLs, since the href attribute can be specified to target these items. You can access the link text by referencing the 0 element of the current $pnodes _content hash. Once this information is extracted, it is then written out to an HTML file. If you fire up your browser and view a representative output file (the exact output will change with time), it should look something like Figure 6-9.

■**Tip** The extraction of Web addresses from anchor tags is actually a valuable method of garnering more information. For example, you could make HTTP GET requests to each of the previous extracted links and retrieve every blog entry, thereby creating a full-fledged Apress blog reader. More important, cycles of link extraction followed by GET requests are the basis for spidering applications, though they are a basis only and there is a lot more to consider. Writing considerate spiders means following a number of guidelines, as described next. A useful reference on authoring spiders is *Spidering Hacks* (O'Reilly, 2003) by Kevin Hemenway and Tara Calishain.

SQL Down Under Podcast

Apress Ebooks now available!

Java turns 10 years old...

Introduction to the Spring Framework...

Taking advantage of PEAR

Figure 6-9. *The output of the blog reader*

look_up

The syntax and usage of the look_up method is almost identical to that of look_down, the one difference being that look_up is designed to start with a child node and work its way up through all the parent nodes of that child node.

Understanding the Fair Use of Information Extraction Scripts

By running any of the examples in this script, it becomes evident that you can utilize Perl code to rapidly process HTML, allowing for a large amount of data retrieval and processing in a short period of time. When writing your scripts, it is important to remember that servers have limited amounts of bandwidth and other users will want to access those same resources. Thus, the number of requests that your script makes in any given period of time should be limited by using a function such as sleep.

Furthermore, just because information is available for the taking on the Web, it does not mean one should take it. Content on the Web is often copyrighted material, and the owner of the material may not be willing to grant duplication rights to others. Therefore, when extracting information from the Web, be mindful of the sources you are extracting from and their wishes as to what construes acceptable use of their content.

■Tip Many Web sites have a robots.txt file that can be used to specify parts of the Web site that the owners do not want to have spidered.

Summary

This chapter covered the basic structures that comprise HTML documents, as well as the proper syntax for specifying different types of hypertext markups. The chapter then discussed the LWP modules and how you can utilize them to access information directly from the Web. Lastly, the chapter discussed the HTML::Treebuilder parsing module and how it is able to parse HTML documents into a hierarchal tree of nodes. I also discussed methods of searching these nodes for the purposes of information extraction.

In the next chapter, you will examine another markup standard, Extensible Markup Language (XML). The ability to parse XML-based documents is rapidly growing in importance, since XML is steadily gaining ground toward becoming the de facto standard for data exchange. Chapter 7 will discuss the basic structures and syntaxes of XML as well the XML::Parser module.

CHAPTER 7

■ ■ ■

Parsing XML Documents with XML::LibXML and XML::SAX

In Chapter 6, I presented the concept of a markup language when discussing HTML. Like HTML, Extensible Markup Language (XML) is also a form of markup language; therefore, there will be some similarities between the two document types and how they are parsed. XML documents, however, have a much greater degree of flexibility than HTML documents, since XML can be considered as a markup language that was designed to create other markup languages. XML was not designed to be rendered in a Web browser, but was designed with the idea that XML-based documents should have the ability to represent any type of data-containing document, be it a simple text file divided into one or more hierarchal sections or a complex series of mathematical expressions or even chemical structures. For example, Listing 7-1 shows an excerpt of a CML file (chemical XML markup) that represents the biological molecule of ATP.

Listing 7-1. *CML Example*

```
<molecule convention="MDLMol" id="atp" title="ATP">
   <date day="22" month="11" year="1995"> </date>
   <atomArray>
      <atom id="a1">
         <string builtin="elementType">N</string>
         <float builtin="x2">5.5603</float>
         <float builtin="y2">1.2607</float>
      </atom>
      <atom id="a2">
         <string builtin="elementType">C</string>
         <float builtin="x2">4.2005</float>
         <float builtin="y2">2.1415</float>
      </atom>
```

```
    .
    .
    .
    .

  </atomArray>
    .
    .
    .

  <bondArray>
    .
    .
    .

    <bond id="b33">
        <string builtin="atomRef">a12</string>
        <string builtin="atomRef">a13</string>
        <string builtin="order">1</string>
    </bond>
  </bondArray>
</molecule>
```

Tip If you want to download the full file that Listing 7-1 comes from, you will find a repository of CML structures available at `http://www.xml-cml.org/` under the CML Examples section of the Web site. Once on the examples page, click the *drug discovery* link and scroll down the list of compounds to find the `atp.xml` file.

Within this XML excerpt, you can see that the file contains a listing of atoms (`<atomArray>`) that make up the chemical structure and a set of two-dimensional coordinates (x and y) for each atom. The file specification also lists the chemical bonds (`<bondArray>`) that show the different connections between the atoms. If you use a program such as JChemPaint (available on SourceForge) to open this file, the program will generate the chemical structure shown in Figure 7-1.

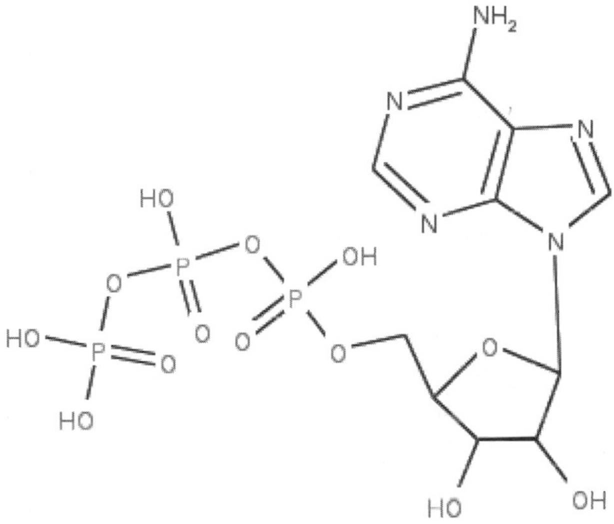

Figure 7-1. *Chemical structure rendered from a chemical XML file*

While this example may not be most pertinent to everyday XML parsing tasks, it illustrates that XML has two key advantages: an almost unprecedented level of flexibility and a foundation based on an open standard. Furthermore, XML documents have a well-defined hierarchical structure that greatly simplifies parsing tasks.

In many ways, XML can actually be simpler to parse than HTML, since rather than containing presentation markup and data-related markup in the same document, XML relies on external stylesheets for formatting documents and concentrates on just the data. Therefore, you can format the contents of a single XML document in multiple ways simply by applying different stylesheets to the document. As this chapter delves further into XML document structure, it will also become evident that the structure of XML documents is actually more strictly structured than HTML, and elements that make parsing difficult, such as implicit tag closings, are not allowed in well-formed XML documents.

Understanding the Nature and Structure of XML Documents

The CML example displayed in Listing 7-1 provided a feel for how XML markup looks, and this section will further clarify the structure of XML documents by systematically explaining the basic structure and layout of well-formed XML. As you examine the different elements of XML structure, you will learn how to construct a simple XML document.

■Note This chapter provides only enough of an introduction to XML to enable those who are unfamiliar with XML to understand the parsing of XML documents. For those seriously considering using XML as a file format for their applications, it is advisable to consult a more thorough introduction. One recommended resource for those who are unfamiliar with XML is *Learning XML* (O'Reilly, 2001) by Erik T. Ray.

The Document Prolog

The *document prolog* does not contain any of the "document data" per se but is instead used to present data to the parser that will aid in the parsing and structure checking of the document. The first item that makes up the document prolog is the XML declaration, which serves the purpose of telling any application that opens the file that the file is written in XML markup as opposed to some other markup language. The XML declaration will always be the first line of any XML document and in its simplest form will look like the following line of markup:

```
<?xml?>
```

You can expand the XML declaration line, however, to include the declaration of three optional properties that may facilitate the processing of the document by an XML parser. The first of these properties is the version property, which specifies the version of the XML standard to which the document syntax adheres. The second possible property is encoding, which announces the character encoding used in the document and is thus often used in conjunction with documents written using an encoding other than XML's default encoding of UTF-8. The final property is the standalone property. This property tells the parser whether the document is an independent entity or whether another source, such as a document type definition (DTD), should be consulted during processing.

DTDs and XML schemas are used to define the acceptable elements of an XML document and how those elements can be laid out within an XML document. The parser can consequently perform comparisons between DTD or schema definitions and determine whether the XML document adheres to the standards. An example XML declaration with these three optional properties is as follows:

```
<?xml version="1.0" encoding="US=ASCII" standalone="no"?>
```

It is important to notice that all the property names are lowercase and that property values must be placed in quotes (either single or double quotes are acceptable).

The Document Type Declaration

You can specify an optional document type declaration section after the XML declaration section. This can serve important purposes, with the first being that if a DTD is required to validate the document, this is the section where the DTD must be declared. For example, if your parser required access to a DTD found locally at /usr/people/MyUserName/MyDTD.dtd, you could access the DTD with the following markup line:

```
<!DOCTYPE rootelement SYSTEM "/usr/people/MyUserName/MyDTD.dtd">
```

In this example, rootelement represents the markup element that serves as the highest hierarchal position in the document (in other words, it signifies the start and finish of the document). It is likewise possible to use a document type declaration to refer to a remote DTD by simply replacing the local path with a URI, as in the following example:

```
<!DOCTYPE rootelement SYSTEM "http://www.example.com/MyDTD.dtd">
```

The other main purpose of the document type declaration section is to declare *entities*. You can think of entities as named attributes that have a piece of data attached to them, allowing the entity name to serve as a placeholder for the given piece of data within the contents of the XML document. The following is an example document that uses entities:

```
<!DOCTYPE books SYSTEM "http://www.example.com/MyDTD.dtd"
[
    <ENTITY name "Christopher M. Frenz">
]>
<books>
    <book>
        <title>Pro Perl Parsing</title>
        <author>&name</author>
        <publisher>Apress</publisher>
        <year>2005</year>
    </book>
    <book>
        <title>Visual Basic and Visual Basic .NET for Scientists and Engineers</title>
        <author>&name</author>
        <publisher>Apress</publisher>
        <year>2002</year>
    </book>
</books>
```

■**Tip** This XML file will be used in an upcoming data extraction example, so you may want to fire up your favorite text editor now and create an XML document with the same content.

Entities

In this particular case, the document lists books by the same author; therefore, rather than having to explicitly write out the author's name multiple times, you instead declare a name entity and use it as a placeholder for "Christopher M. Frenz" in the document body. Entities like this are also useful if information that appears throughout the document must be changed, since the information needs to be updated only in the entity declaration rather than at every instance in the document.

Entity declarations also have the ability to declare entities that are external to the document in much the same way as an external DTD can be called upon. Thus, it is possible to use entities to glue several external data sources together into a single document. The following is an example:

```
<!DOCTYPE document SYSTEM "http://www.example.com/MyDTD.dtd"
[
    <ENTITY paragraph1 SYSTEM "http://www.example.com/paragraph1.xml">
    <ENTITY paragraph2 SYSTEM "http://www.example.com/paragraph2.xml">
]>
<document>
    <p>&paragraph1</p>
    <p>&paragraph2</p>
</document>
```

Elements and the Document Body

For individuals looking to extract data from XML documents, the document body is the portion of an XML document that is of the most interest; this is the portion of the document in which the document data is stored. As you saw in the previous description of document type declarations, each XML document begins with the occurrence of a root element.

You can find all of the document's data between the start and end tags of the root element, and in most instances data found within an XML document will be further subdivided by differing child elements of the root element. In fact, each child element could potentially be further subdivided by its own set of child elements, and so on, allowing for XML documents to take on a treelike structural hierarchy, which can be a great help during parsing tasks.

As an example, let's again consider the document body of the XML document that listed books written by Christopher Frenz:

```
<books>
   <book>
      <title>Pro Perl Parsing</title>
      <author>Christopher Frenz</author>
      <publisher>Apress</publisher>
      <year>2005</year>
   </book>
   <book>
      <title>Visual Basic and Visual Basic .NET for Scientists and Engineers</title>
      <author>Christopher Frenz</author>
      <publisher>Apress</publisher>
      <year>2002</ycar>
   </book>
</books>
```

A close look at the XML document body reveals that the root element of the document is the <books> element, and the <books> element contains child elements called <book>, which are used to store the individual information of each book listed as a child of <books>. The <book> element in turn has its own child elements, which can then be used to store more information, such as the book title and author.

The simplest way Perl offers to create a hierarchal tree of these elements is to employ the XML::Simple module in conjunction with the Data::Dumper module. You can accomplish this with the segment of Perl code shown in Listing 7-2.

Listing 7-2. *Using* XML::Simple *to Display an XML Element Tree*

```
#!/usr/bin/perl

use XML::Simple;
use Data::Dumper;

$tree=XMLin("MyXML.xml");

print Dumper($tree);
```

The XML::Simple module operates by creating a hash that contains the different XML elements and their corresponding value pairs. The Dumper module is then utilized to output the entire contents of this hash, which should look as follows:

```
$VAR1 = {
  'book' => [
    {
      'author' => 'Christopher Frenz',
      'title' => 'Pro Perl Parsing',
      'publisher' => 'Apress',
      'year' => '2005'
    },
    {
      'author' => 'Christopher Frenz',
      'title' => 'Visual Basic and Visual Basic .NET for Scientists and
Engineers',
      'publisher' => 'Apress',
      'year' => '2002'
    }
  ]
};
```

As with HTML, it is also possible to assign attributes to different elements by placing a key-value pair within the corresponding element tag. It is possible for a given element to have as many attributes as needed as long as no two attributes within the tag have the same name. As an example, let's assume you added an attribute to the <book> tags that listed the category each book should be classified under. The resultant XML document would now resemble the following:

```
<book category="opensource">
.
.
</book>
<book category="visualbasic">
.
.
</book>
```

Attribute values can sometimes be useful for parsing tasks, because when a document element uses a known attribute value, adding this attribute-value pair to your search criteria can often significantly narrow the search.

More XML Element Syntax

XML element syntax has some notable requirements that are important to consider when both creating XML documents and parsing XML documents, many of which will cause XML-based documents to parse differently from how those familiar with HTML parsing might expect. For starters, XML tags are case-sensitive; so, in an XML document <h1> would be a different tag from <H1>. An HTML parser would consider both tags as an acceptable level-one heading and would parse and render elements enclosed in each of those tags in the same manner.

A second difference is that, unlike HTML, XML does not permit implicit tag closing. All XML elements require that both a start and end tag be specified, which from a parsing perspective is a great thing since it eliminates any potential ambiguities about where a given element ends and a new element begins. This can allow data extraction to be more easily performed from XML documents using techniques such as regular expressions, since given elements can often be readily extracted by performing a nongreedy search for the contents that occur between the start and end tags for a given element. However, except for the simplest of cases, using an XML parser is recommended over regex-based extraction. For example, let's consider the following Perl script, which is designed to extract the titles from the earlier document containing the listing of books:

```
#!usr/bin/perl

$data = join '',· <>; # get all the lines into $data
while($data =~/<title>(.*?)<\/title>/gcs){
    print $1, "\n";
}
```

Passing the name of the XML file to this script as an argument and executing the contents of this script should yield the following output:

```
Pro Perl Parsing
Visual Basic and Visual Basic .NET for Scientists and Engineers
```

■**Tip** You can get away with regular expression–based extractions like this in the simplest cases, and for such cases this may be advantageous because of the speed at which regular expressions operate at as compared to parsers (although many XML parsers are quite fast). However, the regular expression–based approach is not foolproof and thus if robustness is more important than speed, using a parser is probably a better option.

When working with XML documents and XML parsers, it also important to keep in mind that XML treats whitespace differently than how HTML treats it. In an HTML document, sequential whitespaces are generally just condensed by the parser into a single whitespace. XML parsers, on the other hand, do not opt to ignore sequential whitespace but rather preserve all occurrences of whitespace within a given element.

XML Elements and Document Flexibility

The preceding section makes it quite clear that XML is in many ways more rigidly structured than HTML and less forgiving of syntactic misnomers found within a document. So, how is XML so much more flexible than an HTML document? The answer is that XML does not have predefined markup elements that the document author is forced to work within the confines of. Rather, XML is truly a set of standardized markup rules for creating other markup types. This is the reason that all HTML documents will have common elements such as `<title>`, `<h1>`, or `<p>`, but a CML file can have `<atom>` and `<bond>` elements, which are completely different from the `<book>` elements used in the example file.

It is this ability to create documents with not only customized elements but also customized hierarchies that allows XML to be adapted to almost any application type, whether it's a word processing document (such as an OpenOffice.org document) or a complex scientific structure. This is also the reason that XML documents are often parsed in conjunction with schemas or DTDs, since both schemas and DTDs contain application-specific criteria for the content and structure of a given XML document type. Even if a document is perfectly formed XML, this does not necessarily mean it is in the proper format for an application designed to work with the CML specification; instead, the document schema or DTD can be used to check for CML compliance.

To test this, let's go to the examples section of the CML Web site and download any file that is marked up in the CML format. Next let's go to the DTD/schema section of the Web site and download the CML DTD file (`cml1_0_1.dtd`). At this point, you can open the CML file in a text editor and append the following to the top of the file (if not already present):

```
<!DOCTYPE molecule SYSTEM "cml1_0_1.dtd">
```

This line will alert the parser to the existence of the DTD file and thus allow the parser to use the DTD as a part of its data evaluation criteria. Listing 7-3 shows the code for running a validating parser using the `XML::LibXML:Parser` module.

Listing 7-3. *Validating an XML File with a DTD*

```perl
#!/usr/bin/perl

use XML::LibXML;

my $parser=XML::LibXML->new;
$parser->validation(1); # turns on validation - off by default
$parser->parse_file("atp.xml");
```

If this validation script is executed, it generates the following error message:

```
atp.xml:3: element date: validity error : No declaration for attribute day
of element date
  <date day="22" month="11" year="1995">
                  ^
atp.xml:3: element date: validity error : No declaration for attribute month
of element date
  <date day="22" month="11" year="1995">
                  ^
atp.xml:3: element date: validity error : No declaration for attribute year
of element date
  <date day="22" month="11" year="1995">
                  ^
atp.xml:4: element date: validity error : No declaration for element date
  </date>
          ^
 at 7-2.pl line 7
```

The reason for this error message is that the atp.xml file contains a data element that is not found in the DTD. Therefore, the parser picks this element up as something that does not conform to the CML standard and outputs the error message shown. If you open the atp.xml file in a text editor and delete the <date> element, every element of the atp.xml will validate, and no messages will be printed to STDOUT.

The XML::LibXML modules are currently in the process of adding support for schema-based validation through the XML::LibXML::RelaxNG module, but the module is still a work in progress and not quite robust enough at this stage. Thus, to introduce schema-based validation, I'll use the XML::Validator::Schema module instead. Listing 7-4 shows the code to validate the previous example via the XML::Validator::Schema module.

Listing 7-4. *Validating an XML File with an XML Schema*

```perl
#!/usr/bin/perl

use XML::SAX::ParserFactory;
use XML::Validator::Schema;

$validator = XML::Validator::Schema->new(file => 'cml1_0_1.xsd');
$parser = XML::SAX::ParserFactory->parser(Handler => $validator);

eval { $parser->parse_uri('atp.xml') };
die "Validation Failed: $@" if $@;
```

This validator module does not possess its own parser, so it must rely on an external SAX parser (see the "Parsing with XML::SAX::ParserFactory" section of this chapter for more information). The module author recommends using the XML::SAX::ParserFactory module. The XML::Validator::Schema module works by creating a SAX filter, from the schema, which is then passed to the parser module. The parser module then parses the XML according to the rules in the filter and determines whether the XML document is in compliance with the filter rules.

Introducing Web Services

Before delving deeper into the parsing of XML files, it is well worth taking some time to first examine one of the most common circumstances in which XML files may be encountered. As the previous section highlighted, XML is a highly flexible file format, yet it possesses a strictly defined structure that makes it readily parsable. These properties mean that XML is also an ideal file format for program-to-program communication. Program-to-program communication is not a new phenomenon and has been conducted for a long time now using Remote Procedure Call (RPC) techniques. However, past efforts at program-to-program communication often proved to be tedious, since complex formatting conversions were often required. Today, program-to-program communication is generally accomplished via XML-RPC methods or SOAP (see the next sections).

XML greatly helped overcome the barriers associated with older forms of program-to-program communication by providing a standardized yet flexible means of data exchange. Unlike many past file formats, XML data is readily convertible to diverse presentation formats through the use of XML stylesheet transformations, making XML an ideal application-to-application "go-between" medium.

This has spawned a new type of program-to-program communication mechanism known as *Web services*. In addition to being an ideal medium for interprogram communication, XML and the Web service protocols built around XML allow Web service–based communication to run in a completely platform-independent manner. A Perl client could as easily interact with a Java- or .NET-based Web service as it could with a Web service written in Perl, regardless of the underlying operating systems on which the applications were deployed.

Tip I will not cover XML stylesheet transformations, since this is beyond the scope of a parsing book. Those interested in learning more about the topic should refer to the XML::LibXSLT Perl module on CPAN.

XML-RPC

XML-RPC is a method of remote procedure calling that utilizes HTTP to transmit data and uses XML as the format for data exchange. For example, consider the XML data that is transmitted when an XML-RPC request is made to server that returns the current time:

```
<?xml version="1.0"?>
<methodCall>
    <methodName>currentTime.getCurrentTime</methodName>
    <params>

    </params>
</methodCall>
```

The root element of the XML-RPC procedure call is the <methodCall> element, and the actual name of the method being called on the server is found enclosed in the <methodName> tags. In this particular case, no parameters are required to be passed in the procedure call, but if there were some arguments required by the procedure, they would be passed in the <params> element of the document.

RPC::XML

Now that you understand what an XML-RPC call actually looks like, it is time to see how you can make such a call from a Perl script. One of the more robust modules for XML-RPC functionality is the RPC::XML module by Randy J. Ray. You can utilize this module to access the current time procedure mentioned previously by using the segment of Perl code in Listing 7-5.

Listing 7-5. *Using* RPC::XML

```
#!/usr/bin/perl

use RPC::XML;
use RPC::XML::Client;

$MyClient=RPC::XML::Client->new('http://time.xmlrpc.com/RPC2');

$Response=$MyClient->send_request('currentTime.getCurrentTime');

print $Response->value;
```

Executing this script will result in the current time in Unix format being returned and printed to STDOUT.

Tip If you want to experiment with other XML-RPC–enabled Web services, you can find a listing of publicly available services at http://www.xmlrpc.com/directory/1568/services.

Simple Object Access Protocol (SOAP)

SOAP is a protocol that was designed to replace RPC as a means of fostering interprogram communication. The major advantage to using SOAP is that it does not require your application to use an architecture such as DCOM or CORBA for information to be exchanged but instead allows the transfer of information over common Internet protocols such as HTTP.

SOAP transmits information in an XML document format that contains the <Envelope> root element, which identifies the document as a SOAP message, and a <Body> element, which contains the information relating to either the method call or the method response. Additionally, SOAP messages can contain an optional <Header> element and an optional <Fault> element, which will transmit any error encountered during message processing. Thus, the structure of a generic SOAP message looks like the following:

```
<?xml?>
<s:Envelope
xmlns:s="http://www.w3.org/2001/12/soap-envelope"
s:encodingStyle="http://www.w3.org/2001/12/soap-encoding">
<s:Header>
   .
   .
   .
```

```
</s:Header>
<s:Body>

  .

  .

  .

  <s:Fault>

  .

  .

  .

  </s:Fault>
</s:Body>
</s:Envelope>
```

Over the course of the typical Web service usage cycle, a client will send such a SOAP message to the server that hosts the Web service. The server will then execute the method specified in the message <Body>, using any specified arguments. The server will then package the results into the <Body> of a similar message and return the message to the client, where the results can be parsed out of the message.

SOAP::Lite

Within Perl, you can employ the SOAP::Lite module to create Web service clients. You can also use the module in conjunction with CGI to create Web service servers. In this section, you will learn how to write a client application that will contact a Web service that converts temperatures from Celsius to Fahrenheit and then outputs the results. Although this process of generating XML-based SOAP messages for data exchange and then parsing the results out of such messages may seem like a daunting task, the SOAP::Lite module actually makes the process quite straightforward for the average Perl programmer, since most of these operations are automatically performed under the hood and do not require any work on the part of the developer.

To develop this application, you first need a Web service for your script to interact with. The particular Web service that is going to be used in the upcoming example code is available from http://www.soaplite.com, the official Web site of the SOAP::Lite module and the home to several sample Web services. Listing 7-6 shows the Web service client that will be implemented.

Listing 7-6. *Accessing Web Services with* SOAP::Lite

```perl
#!/usr/bin/perl

use SOAP::Lite;

$uri='http://www.soaplite.com/Temperatures';
$proxy='http://services.soaplite.com/temper.cgi';

my $WebServ=SOAP::Lite->uri($uri)->proxy($proxy);

my $result= $WebServ->call("c2f",56)->result
    or die "Failed to connect to server";

print "The temperature in Fahrenheit is " . $result;
```

■**Note** For those interested in seeing the server-side code that powers this Web service, the authors of the Web service have listed the code at http://guide.soaplite.com/temper.cgi_.

When creating a SOAP client with SOAP::Lite, you must keep in mind two important parameters. The first is the URI of the Web service, and the second is the proxy address. The URI is a unique identifier for the Web service method of interest. URIs often look like Web addresses, and in some cases the URI may be the same as the Web address, but the URI is a separate entity from the Web address and may be completely different.

The proxy specifies the address to which all the Web service requests are made. Once you have obtained these values, you can use them to create uri and proxy objects, respectively. After you have created these objects, you can utilize the call method to make a request to the Web service method of interest (in this case, c2f) and pass any arguments required by the method (for example, 56).

When the Web service returns an XML message containing the response, the SOAP::Lite module extracts the relevant portions of the SOAP message (that is, the temperature found in the message body) and returns it via the result object. If the previous script is executed, the output should resemble the following:

```
The temperature in Fahrenheit is 132.8
```

Parsing with XML::LibXML

As you can see from the previous example, the SOAP::Lite module makes extracting results from SOAP responses seamless and requires little action on your part. SOAP messages adhere to a predefined schema, and as such you can tune the parser integrated into the XML::Lite module to consistently extract the proper values from the SOAP messages.

As you saw earlier, however, XML files can contain innumerable combinations of elements and element hierarchies. This raises the question of how you can accomplish such information extraction without having to resort to writing an entirely customized parser. The answer is that you can use a generic XML parser, such as that made available through XML::LibXML, to parse the XML document into its constituent parts and then search these parts for the elements of interest. Currently, two major ways of approaching the parsing of XML exist: a SAX-based approach and a DOM-based approach. I will explain this terminology in full in the next sections, beginning with the DOM-based approach to parsing.

Using DOM to Parse XML

The principle behind Document Object Model (DOM) parsing is one that will be familiar to you, since creating parse trees has been a frequently recurring theme throughout this entire book. The basic idea behind DOM is that the parser will map the XML document into a treelike structure and then enable the application to traverse the tree for the purposes of accessing and editing the tree's content and structure. While it may be feasible to use XML::Simple and a loop structure to traverse simple XML document structures, the DOM tree is hierarchal in nature and thus allows greater control over element access. Before you begin to explore how to use XML::LibXML as a DOM parser, let's first take a moment to recall the atp.xml example file used earlier:

```
<molecule convention="MDLMol" id="atp" title="ATP">
   <date day="22" month="11" year="1995"> </date>
   <atomArray>
      <atom id="a1">
         <string builtin="elementType">N</string>
         <float builtin="x2">5.5603</float>
         <float builtin="y2">1.2607</float>
      </atom>
      <atom id="a2">
         <string builtin="elementType">C</string>
         <float builtin="x2">4.2005</float>
         <float builtin="y2">2.1415</float>
      </atom>
      .
      .
      .
</molecule>
```

Now let's assume you were hired by a pharmaceutical company to write an application that will extract the elemental composition of chemical compounds like this. In other words, the company wants to know what percentage of the elements are oxygen (O), what percentage are carbon (C), and so on, and the task needs to be accomplished via a DOM-based parser. Listing 7-7 shows the result of this assignment.

Listing 7-7. *Parsing XML via DOM*

```perl
#!/usr/bin/perl

use XML::LibXML;

#Constructs the DOM tree
my $parser=XML::LibXML->new;
my $domtree=$parser->parse_file("atp.xml");

#Outputs appropriate elements to @atoms
my @atoms=$domtree->getElementsByTagName("string");

my $i=0;
my $element;
;
my %Counts=(C=>0,
            N=>0,
            O=>0,
            P=>0
            );

#Iterates through @atoms to count element types (e.g. C,O,etc.)
foreach my $atom (@atoms){
    if ($atom->firstChild->data =~ /([CNOP])/){
        $Counts{$1}++;
    }
}

print "ATP is \n";
print $Counts{C}/$i*100 . "% Carbon \n";
print $Counts{N}/$i*100 . "% Nitrogen \n";
print $Counts{O}/$i*100 . "% Oxygen \n";
print $Counts{P}/$i*100 . "% Phosphorous \n";
```

Within this example, the parser object is initially utilized to process the XML document and create the DOM tree. Once this DOM tree has been created, it is possible for the application to search through the different nodes of the tree and try to find those nodes that interest you.

Looking back at the `atp.xml` file, you can see that atom types can be found within XML `<string>` elements. Thus, the script needs to traverse the parse tree and output all the nodes that contain `<string>` elements so they can be further processed. You can accomplish this via the `getElementsByTagName` method, which will output all such nodes to `@atoms`.

Next, the script declares a hash with several keys that will serve as counters and then proceeds to process the `@atoms` array looking for the atomic symbols (C, N, O, P) that are being counted. This process is facilitated by using the `firstChild` method to extract the textual data found in the `<string>` node present within each array position. The percentages of each element are then calculated, and the results are printed to output. The results should appear as follows:

```
ATP is
32.258064516129% Carbon
16.1290322580645% Nitrogen
41.9354838709677% Oxygen
9.67741935483871% Phosphorous
```

■Tip In the previous example, note how regular expressions were combined with the XML parser to enhance the functionality of the application. The ability to combine parsing and extraction techniques presented in this book is an important concept to keep in mind. It is entirely possible, for example, to extract paragraphs of text from an XML document and then parse the extracted paragraphs with `Parse::RecDescent` or the like in order to really fine-tune the functionality of your application and extend its processing capabilities.

Parsing with XML::SAX::ParserFactory

In the previous section, I discussed DOM-based parsing methods, which provide the ability to individually access the contents of each element with the created DOM tree. While such fine-grained control is often extremely useful, it is not without drawbacks.

The XML documents parsed in this chapter are not very large documents. A DOM-based parser has no problem generating a parse tree for them and then holding the parse tree in memory so that its nodes can be searched or modified. With large XML documents, however, this can become problematic because, in order for DOM to function, the system running the DOM parser must have enough memory to retain the parse tree.

For very large XML documents, this can either be an impossibility or lead to incredibly slow parse and utilization times. This is where Simple API for XML (SAX)–based parsers can come in handy. SAX-based parsers do not generate parse trees by default (although their output can sometimes be used to reconstruct one) but rather generate a series of parsing events. In this context, a parsing event is defined as the start or end of an XML tag. Consider the following short segment of XML:

```
<?xml?>
<p>
   Document data
</p>
```

If this segment of XML were parsed by a SAX-based parser, several events would be generated. Table 7-1 summarizes these events.

Table 7-1. *SAX Parsing Events Generated for the XML Segment*

Event	Reason for Event
Start document	`<?xml?>` tag
Start element p	`<p>`
Characters	"Document data"
End element p	`</p>`
End document	No remaining elements

Once the events have been generated, specialized handlers are called that execute a specified action in response to the raising of the event. You can program these handlers to do simple things such as write out the XML that triggered the event or perform some other customized action. As silly as it may at first sound, writing out the XML that triggered the event is not a useless handler when you consider that SAX parsers allow filters to be readily applied to the XML documents being parsed. As an example, let's recall a modified version of the sample XML document that lists the books authored by Christopher Frenz:

```
<books>

   <book>
      <title>Visual Basic and Visual Basic .NET for Scientists and Engineers</title>
      <author>Christopher Frenz</author>
      <publisher>Apress</publisher>
      <year>2002</year>
   </book>
```

```
    <book>
        <title>Pro Perl Parsing</title>
        <author>Christopher Frenz</author>
        <publisher>Apress</publisher>
        <year>2005</year>
    </book>
</books>
```

This example file contains only two books in order to keep within the allotted space constraints, but the principle that is going to be applied would work for much larger data sets as well. The document is going to be parsed by a SAX parser and a filter will be applied to sort all the books by their titles. This sorted list will then be written to a second XML file. Listing 7-8 shows the code that accomplishes this.

Listing 7-8. *Parsing XML with SAX*

```perl
#!/usr/bin/perl

use XML::SAX::ParserFactory;
use XML::Handler::YAWriter;
use XML::Filter::Sort;

my $handler = new XML::Handler::YAWriter(AsFile=>'sorted.xml');
my $filter = new XML::Filter::Sort(
    Record => 'book',
    Keys => 'title',
    Handler => $handler,
);
my $parser = XML::SAX::ParserFactory->parser(Handler => $filter);

$parser->parse_uri('MyXML.xml');
```

Within this example, you first create a $handler object that is set to write out XML markup to the file sorted.xml. This $handler is then assigned to serve as the handler for the XML::Filter::Sort module. The filter will then order all the <book> elements by their title. After the sorting is complete, you can utilize the handler to write out the sorted elements. If this script were executed on the example file, it would yield an output similar to the following:

```
<?xml version="1.0" encoding="UTF-8"?><books>
   <book>
      <title>Pro Perl Parsing</title>
      <author>Christopher Frenz</author>
      <publisher>Apress</publisher>
      <year>2005</year>
   </book>
   <book>
      <title>Visual Basic and Visual Basic .NET for Scientists and Engineers</title>
      <author>Christopher Frenz</author>
      <publisher>Apress</publisher>
      <year>2002</year>
   </book>

</books>
```

As you can see, the order of the documents has been reversed. This example illustrates the key advantage of SAX-based parsers in that they can be more efficient than DOM-based parsers, since the generation and traversal of a parse tree is not required. The major downside to SAX-based parsers, however, is that they can be extremely difficult to debug.

Summary

This chapter covered the structure and syntax of XML documents and how you can use XML's open standard to create customized XML elements and syntaxes. Next the chapter discussed how this flexibility works to make XML an ideal medium for exchanging information between programs.

In recent years, the chief method of exchanging information between programs has been Web services. Web services are able to exchange information using SOAP, which allows you to pass XML messages over HTTP. The chapter also introduced the SOAP::Lite module as a way for you to access Web services and extract information from the messages that are returned.

Lastly, the chapter covered the two possible methods used for parsing XML documents: the DOM and SAX approaches. The DOM approach to parsing constructs a parse tree from the elements found in the XML document, and document data can then be checked via the traversal of the parse tree. The SAX-based approach, on the other hand, does not involve the construction of a parse tree but rather operates by generating a list of parser events.

At this point in the book, most of the major parsing-oriented modules have already been covered, and anyone who has read this book up until this point should have an idea of how to parse HTML and XML, as well as how to use the Yapp and RecDescent modules. Despite these modules being able to cover most parsing needs, it does not mean CPAN is not rife with other modules that carry out smaller and less specialized parsing tasks. In the next chapter, I will cover how to use several of these smaller but still highly useful parsing modules.

CHAPTER 8

■■■

Introducing Miscellaneous Parsing Modules

By this point in the book, I have covered the most widely used and the most powerful parsing modules available on CPAN. These include powerful parser generators such as RecDescent and Yapp, which allow you to create parsers capable of handling almost any task, as well as specialized parsing modules designed to parse HTML and XML documents. The main benefit of these specialized parsers is that they save development time, since their implementation generally does not require you to create a grammar, unlike RecDescent or Yapp. A specialized parser may also be more efficient, since the parsing logic can often be optimized.

In this chapter, you will examine several more parsing modules, each of which enables specialized parsing tasks to be performed. These modules are grouped into a single chapter and covered only briefly, since, despite performing tasks that may be useful in certain instances, they do not have the widespread applicability of HTML or XML parsers. This chapter's coverage will begin with the module Text::Balanced.

Using Text::Balanced

Text::Balanced is a module authored by Damian Conway that can be used to extract balanced, delimited strings, such as elements of text that appear in quotes or between a set of parentheses. The module comes with a variety of different extraction methods that all function in pretty much the same manner, but each is designed to extract slightly different things. Table 8-1 summarizes these methods.

Table 8-1. Text::Balanced *Extraction Methods*

Method	Use
extract_delimited	Returns the substring delimited by two occurrences of a user-defined delimiter
extract_bracketed	Returns the substring delimited by (), {}, [], and <>
extract_quoted	Returns the substring delimited by ""
extract_tagged	Returns the substring delimited by XML tags
extract_codeblock	Returns the substring that corresponds to bracketed Perl code
extract_variable	Returns a Perl variable and/or variable expression
extract_multiple	Returns substrings that result from the sequential application of one or more extract methods or regular expressions

Using extract_delimited

You can use this method to extract text that occurs between the first two instances of a user-specified delimiter and is thus helpful when you want to extract text found between an atypical set of delimiters, such as #. Listing 8-1 illustrates how this process works.

Listing 8-1. *Using the* extract_delimited *Method*

```
#!usr/bin/perl

use Text::Balanced qw(extract_delimited);

$text=q{#abc#12345};
$delim='#';

($extracted,$remainder)=extract_delimited($text,$delim);

print "Extracted= " . $extracted . "\n";
print "Remainder= " . $remainder;
```

First, you define a text variable that contains the text to be parsed. Next, you must specify the delimiter of interest, which in this case is assigned to a variable named $delim. Although this example does not show it, it is also possible to define a text prefix that extract_delimited will disregard before checking for the existence of the first delimiter. The default for this prefix is whitespace, but if another prefix is desired, it can be passed to the extraction method as a third parameter.

When the extract_delimited method is called, it returns an array that contains the extracted text, followed by the remaining unextracted text and any matched prefix. In the previous case, you are interested only in the extracted and remaining text, so these values are assigned to the $extracted and $remainder variables, which are then printed to output to verify that the module extracted the proper information. When this script is executed, the output is as follows:

```
Extracted= #abc#
Remainder= 12345
```

When using this module, it is important to consider that the various extraction methods operate only on the current position of a string. Consider the following input string:

```
$text=q{z#abc#12345}
```

The module would not extract anything unless z was specified as a prefix. This is because the current position in the string would be at z and not #. This presents somewhat of a problem, because prefixes might not always be known in advance. However, there is a simple workaround for this issue—you can use the index() function to find the first instance of the delimiter and then extract a substring, which begins at the delimiter with the substr() function. Listing 8-2 shows the code to accomplish this.

Listing 8-2. Using the extract_delimited *Method with Regular Expressions*

```perl
#!usr/bin/perl

use Text::Balanced qw(extract_delimited);

$text=q{12345#abc#12345};
$delim='#';

 $pos=index($text,$delim);
$string=substr($text,$pos);
($extracted,$remainder)=extract_delimited($string,$delim);

print "Extracted= " . $extracted . "\n";
print "Remainder= " . $remainder;
```

The results will be the same as the previous example.

Using extract_bracketed

This method operates in the same manner as the previous method, except the delimiters are limited to (), {}, [], and <>; in addition, for the delimiters to be considered balanced, you must have opposing delimiters on each side of the extracted text. It is this ability to extract balanced delimiters that is the main advantage of this method over the previous, since balancing enables the proper handling of nested delimiters. For instance, consider the code in Listing 8-3.

Listing 8-3. *Using the* extract_bracketed *Method*

```
use Text::Balanced qw(extract_bracketed);

$text=q{((efg)hi)jk};
$delim='()';

($extracted,$remainder)=extract_bracketed($text,$delim);

print "Extracted= " . $extracted . "\n";
print "Remainder= " . $remainder;
```

When executing this code, the extract method will properly return the following:

```
Extracted= ((efg)hi)
Remainder= jk
```

As a comparison, the following is what extract_delimited would have produced:

```
Extracted= ((
Remainder= efg)hi)jk
```

■Tip If you specify delimiters for this method, the unspecified bracket delimiters will be ignored. If you do not specify delimiters, the method will default to using the full set of bracket delimiters, which includes (), {}, [], and <>.

Using extract_codeblock

This method operates in much the same way as extract_bracketed, except it is designed to return balanced code blocks rather than just balanced brackets. For instance, you can extract a set of nested for loops with the code in Listing 8-4.

Listing 8-4. *Using the* extract_codeblock *Method* #!/usr/bin/perl

```perl
use Text::Balanced qw(extract_codeblock);

($text=<<'MYCODE');
    # code
    for($i=0;$i<=5;$i++){
        for($j=0;$j<=10;$j++){
          # more code
        }
    }
    # more code
MYCODE

$delim='{}';

#substring capturing used to
#get code that leads into code block
if($text=~/(for\s*?\(.*?\))/sg){
    $for=$1;
    ($extracted,$remainder)=extract_codeblock($text,$delim);

    print "Extracted= " . $for . $extracted . "\n";
}
```

Tip Within the line ($text=<<'MYCODE');, the MYCODE part must be enclosed in single quotes to prevent Perl from trying to interpolate the values of $i and $j within the code segment. The single quotes ensure that the code segment is instead treated as a normal string.

In this segment of code, a regular expression searches for the start of the outer loop and the code matching the expression stored in the variable $for. The extract_codeblock method then extracts the code contained within the block defined by the outer loop. Finally, a print statement concatenates $for with the extracted code block and outputs the entire nested loop:

```
Extracted=
    for($i=0;$i<=5;$i++){
        for($j=0;$j<=10;$j++){
            # more code
        }
    }
```

Using extract_quotelike

You can use this method to extract delimited text that is contained between any set of valid Perl "quote-like" operators (see Table 8-2).

Table 8-2. *Perl Quote-like Operators*

Operator	Meaning
' '	Literal
" "	Literal
` `	Command
/ /	Pattern match
q{ }	Literal
qq{ }	Literal
qx{ }	Command
qw{ }	Word list
m{ }	Pattern match
qr{ }	Pattern
s{ }	Substitution
tr{ }	Transliteration

Unlike `extract_bracketed`, this method does not allow you to specify a quote delimiter of interest. This method takes only two arguments—the text to be processed and the optional prefix argument. The usage of this method is identical to `extract_delimited`; see Listing 8-5.

Listing 8-5. *Using* `extract_quotelike`

```
#!usr/bin/perl

use Text::Balanced qw(extract_quotelike);
```

```
($text=<<'MYCODE');
    qw{abcd}
MYCODE

($extracted,$remainder)=extract_quotelike($text);

print "Extracted= " . $extracted . "\n";
```

■**Caution** Just like the `extract_delimited` method, `extract_quotelike` will operate only on the current position of the string. To circumvent this, you can use the same technique described in Listing 8-2.

The output for the previous script should resemble the following:

```
Extracted= qw{abcd}
```

Using extract_variable

You can use this method to extract Perl variables and variable expressions from a seg-ment of Perl code. These variables can be of any type that Perl accepts, including scalars, arrays, and hashes, and the module is even able to successfully extract any variable argu-ments specifying positions within an array or hash. Listing 8-6 shows an example.

Listing 8-6. *Using the* extract_variable *Method*

```
use Text::Balanced qw(extract_variable);

($text=<<'MYCODE');
    $myvar[$i][$j]=500;
    # more code
MYCODE

($extracted)=extract_variable($text);

print "Extracted= " . $extracted . "\n";
```

This outputs the following:

```
Extracted= $myvar[$i][$j]
```

Using extract_multiple

This method allows you to sequentially extract elements of delimited text and return them via an array. For example, to extract multiple variables from a segment of Perl code, you can use the script in Listing 8-7.

Listing 8-7. *Using the* extract_multiple *Method*

```
#!/usr/bin/perl

use Text::Balanced qw(extract_multiple);
use Text::Balanced qw(extract_variable);

($text=<<'MYCODE');
    $myvar[$i][$j];
    $myvar2;
    # more code
MYCODE

@extracted=extract_multiple($text,[sub{extract_variable($_[0])}]);
for($i=0;$i<=$#extracted;$i++){
   print $extracted[$i];
}
```

Here is the output:

```
;$myvar[$i][$j];
    $myvar2;
    # more code

    $myvar2
```

It is also possible to ask for multiple types of extractions. For example, if you wanted to extract variables and code blocks, you can use the following code:

```
@extracted=extract_multiple($text,[sub{extract_variable($_[0])},
                                    sub{extract_codeblock($_[0])}]);
```

By default, if no extraction subroutines are specified, the module will automatically extract variables, code blocks, and quotes.

■**Tip** If you encounter any problems while using `Text::Balanced`, accessing `$@->{error}` will yield an error message indicating why the extraction failed. Accessing `$pos->{pos}` will yield the position in the string that caused the failure.

Using Date::Parse

This module can be highly useful when writing an application that has to process dates and time, since it can read in a string that comprises a valid date/time format and parse the string into its constituent elements, such as the month, day, hour, minute, and so on. The module was written by Graham Barr, and the current version is 2.27.

Two main methods are associated with this module. The first is `str2time`, which will take a valid date/time string and return a Unix time value. If the operation is unsuccessful, a value of `undefined` is returned. Listing 8-8 shows how to use `str2time`.

Listing 8-8. *Using the* `str2time` *Method*

```
use Date::Parse;

$date='19 Nov 2005 03:18:55 -0500';
$unixtime=str2time($date);
print $unixtime;
```

The method that is more useful from a parsing perspective, however, is `strptime`. This method will parse the date string into an array of values, which correspond to seconds, minutes, hours, day, month, year, and time zone. You can invoke this method as shown in Listing 8-9.

Listing 8-9. *Using the* `strptime` *Method*

```
use Date::Parse;

$date='19 Nov 2005 03:18:55 -0500';
($sec,$min,$hr,$day,$month,$year,$zone)=strptime($date);
print "seconds=" . $sec . "\n" . "minutes=" . $min . "\n" . "hours=" . $hr .
   "\n" . "day=" . $day . "\n" . "month=" . $month. "\n" . "year=" .
   $year . "\n" ."zone=" . $zone;
```

Executing this script should yield the following output:

```
seconds=55
minutes=18
hours=03
day=19
month=10
year=105
zone=-18000
```

Note When evaluating the $year output from the Parse::Date module, keep in mind that values begin with the year 1900. Thus, in the previous example, the year is 2005, which is the result of 105 + 1900.

As you can see, strptime was able to successfully parse the date string and assign values to each of the respective variables. If an element is not present in the date string, the corresponding variable is set to zero. Thus, if you removed the seconds from the date string and reran the script, your output would instead begin with the following:

```
seconds=0
minutes=18
```

Note Date::Parse is part of a larger set of modules referred to as TimeDate. Thus, when searching CPAN to download the module's makefile, look at the TimeDate module's page.

Tip The TimeDate module set also contains the Date::Format module, which allows you to reverse the process and use either a Unix time or a listing of variables to output date/time strings. You can use these two modules in tandem to perform formatting conversions. As an alternative, the POSIX module has the strftime() function, which can also be used for formatting conversions.

Using XML::RSS::Parser

Really Simple Syndication (RSS) is an XML format for distributing news and other syndicated content. Many individuals like to be kept informed of new content that has been posted to Web sites or updates on news stories via RSS. This is facilitated by programs called *aggregators*, which accept various RSS feeds and present the information to the user.

XML::RSS::Parser is a Perl module, authored by Timothy Appnel, that facilitates the extraction of information from RSS feeds by helping to parse the various markup tags present. Figure 8-1 shows an example of an RSS feed file taken from http://www.apress.com/rss/whatsnew.xml, which demonstrates these markup tags.

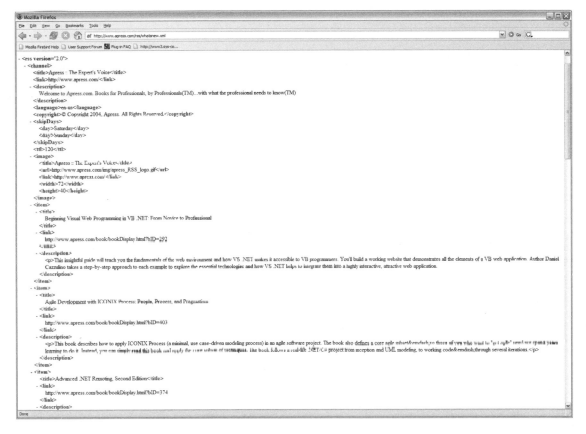

Figure 8-1. *An example RSS file*

Note This module depends on the XML::Parser module, so make sure it is installed as well, prior to using the XML::RSS::Parser module. If you use the CPAN module for installation, you can have it install dependencies automatically. You can check the documentation for the CPAN module with perldoc CPAN.

Before examining an example of how this parser works, it is a good idea to make sure you have the LWP::UserAgent module installed as well, since you will use this module to access the RSS feed file from the Web. Alternatively, if you want to test the functionality of the parser locally, you can manually download the RSS file from the Web address provided and set the $rssfile variable equal to the name of the file, including the path. Listing 8-10 shows the code for a simple RSS reader.

Listing 8-10. *Extracting Information from an RSS Feed*

```perl
#!/usr/bin/perl -w

use strict;
use XML::RSS::Parser;
use LWP::Simple;

my $rssfile='whatsnew.xml';
my $url = 'http://www.apress.com/rss/whatsnew.xml';
getstore($url,$rssfile);

my $parser = new XML::RSS::Parser;
my $feed = $parser->parsefile($rssfile);

my $title = XML::RSS::Parser->ns_qualify('title',$feed->rss_namespace_uri);
print "item count: ".$feed->item_count()."\n\n";
foreach my $i ( $feed->items ) {
        map { print $_->name.": ".$_->value."\n" } $i->children;
        print "\n";
}
```

■**Tip** If you require a brief overview of how LWP works, please refer to Chapter 6. This chapter covers LWP as a means of obtaining HTML documents from the Web.

Within this script, a simple Perl-based RSS feed reader is created. The LWP::Simple module accesses the RSS feed from the Web and makes it available to the RSS::Parser module.

The parser portion of this script operates by first creating a new parser object and then using the parsefile method to parse the RSS file and create an RSS::Parser::Feed object. The item_count method of this feed object can then be accessed to tell you how many items are in the RSS feed. Next, the items method of the Feed object can be invoked, which returns an array that references all the item objects in the RSS feed. This allows you to print the contents of each item, so the contents of the RSS feed can be read.

While the results obtained from this script will vary somewhat depending on what content Apress currently has in its XML file, a truncated sample output should look like the following:

```
item count: 14

title: Beginning Visual Web Programming in VB .NET: From Novice to Professional
link: http://www.apress.com/book/bookDisplay.html?bID=292
description: <p>This insightful guide will teach you the fundamentals of the web
environment and how VS .NET makes it accessible to VB programmers. You'll build a
working website that demonstrates all the elements of a VB web application. Author
Daniel Cazzulino takes a step-by-step approach to each example to explore the
essential technologies and how VS .NET helps to integrate them into a highly
interactive, attractive web application.

title: Agile Development with ICONIX Process: People, Process, and Pragmatism
link: http://www.apress.com/book/bookDisplay.html?bID=403
description: <p>This book describes how to apply ICONIX Process (a minimal, use
case-driven modeling process) in an agile software project. The book also defines a
core agile subset&emdash;so those of you who want to "get agile" need not spend
years learning to do it. Instead, you can simply read this book and apply the core
subset of techniques. The book follows a real-life .NET/C# project from inception
and UML modeling, to working code&emdash;through several iterations.</p>
```

Using Math::Expression

This module is authored by Hakan Ardo and can create parse trees for mathematical equations, including ones that incorporate functions such as $\log(x)$. The usage of this module is quite straightforward; see Listing 8-11.

Listing 8-11. *Working with Mathematical Expressions*

```
use Data::Dumper;
use Math::Expression;

$parser=new Math::Expression;
$tree=$parser->Parse("a-b*6+sin(x)/f-3");

print Dumper($tree);
```

Initially, this creates a `Math::Expression` parser object. You can then use this object to generate a parse tree by passing a mathematical expression to its `Parse` method. Finally, you can print the parse tree by using the `Dumper` functionality. The parse tree for the previous equation should appear as follows:

```
$VAR1 = {
          'left' => {
                     'left' => {
                                'left' => {
                                           'oper' => 'var',
                                           'name' => 'a'
                                          },
                                'right' => {
                                            'left' => {
                                                       'oper' => 'var',
                                                       'name' => 'b'
                                                      },
                                            'right' => {
                                                        'oper' => 'const',
                                                        'val' => '6'
                                                       },
                                            'oper' => '*'
                                           },
                                'oper' => '-'
                               },
                     'right' => {
                                 'left' => {
                                            'right' => {
                                                        'oper' => 'var',
                                                        'name' => 'x'
                                                       },
                                            'oper' => 'func',
                                            'fname' => 'sin'
                                           },
                                 'right' => {
                                             'oper' => 'var',
                                             'name' => 'f'
                                            },
                                 'oper' => '/'
                                },
                     'oper' => '+'
                    },
```

```
            'right' => {
                          'oper' => 'const',
                          'val' => '3'
                     },
            'oper' => '-'
          };
```

An examination of the parse tree reveals that the parse tree hierarchy matches the order of operations that you would expect for an algebraic expression. The operations that have the highest precedence are listed in the parse tree in the area farthest to the right, with operations of decreasing precedence listed going toward the left. Within the parse tree, the terms left and right are precedence declarations, which control the order in which the parser would evaluate the tokens that comprise the expression. You can find more information about precedence declarations and their operation in Chapter 4.

Summary

This chapter examined several different parsing modules that may be of occasional use to Perl programmers. The Text::Balanced module is a highly useful module to consider when you encounter structures involving nested delimiters, since its balancing capability ensures that the extracted text lies between the appropriate opening and closing delimiters.

You saw how the diverse formats that time and date information can be stored in often presents a programming challenge, since writing a parser that can handle all of these different formats is a tedious task. Luckily, the Date::Parse module can handle these situations for you and extract the time and date information.

Another module examined, XML::RSS:Parser, enables you to take an RSS feed and extract items of interest from it, which is an ability that will likely grow in importance as RSS feeds increase in prominence. Finally, you examined the Math::Expresssion parsing module, which can generate parse trees of mathematical equations.

The next chapter will draw on elements of parsing that have been covered throughout the book and will apply this parsing knowledge to a diverse range of parsing tasks. Chapter 9 will present a series of cookbook-style solutions that will benefit all Perl programmers.

CHAPTER 9

■ ■ ■

Finding Solutions to Miscellaneous Parsing Problems

Up until this point, I have covered a diversity of parsing tasks, ranging from using regular expressions for data extraction to using a DOM-based parser for constructing a parse tree of an XML document. Yet, despite this breadth of coverage, I have not discussed some areas in which the parsing techniques presented in this book can be valuable. This chapter covers some of those areas by demonstrating alternative uses of parsers.

■**Note** Although I have not previously covered the types of problems addressed in this chapter, I have covered many of the modules and methods employed to develop these solutions. Therefore, understanding of material that appeared in previous chapters will be beneficial when reading this chapter.

Parsing Command-Line Arguments

You can execute Perl scripts at the command line by typing a command whose syntax resembles the following:

```
Perl MyScriptName.pl MyArguments
```

Within this syntax, `MyArguments` is used to pass arguments, such as the name of a file to be processed, to the Perl script. These arguments are made available to the script via the @ARGV array in the order in which they appear in the `MyArguments` list.

Now that I have established how arguments are passed to a script, I will digress from talking about Perl scripts for a moment and instead cover an average Unix/Linux utility, such as `tar`. For example, if you want to install a new application, you are likely to find that at some point you need to use the tar utility to extract the setup package; the command to do so might look something like the following:

```
tar xvf MyFiles.tar
```

In this example, MyFiles.tar contains the files to extract, and xvf are flags passed to the utility to control its behavior. As a means of facilitating user control over the script, such command-line arguments can be extremely advantageous; therefore, it is desirable to develop a way for a Perl script to process flags that could be used to control program function. As a means of implementing such functionality, consider the example code in Listing 9-1.

Listing 9-1. *Processing Argument Flags*

```perl
#!/usr/bin/perl

use Parse::RecDescent;

$grammar=q{
            startrule:   Commands(s) eof
            Commands:    '-i ' input|'-it ' intype|'-o ' output|'-ot ' outtype
            input:       /\S*/ {$::ConfigHash{I}=$item[1]}
            intype:      'text' {$::ConfigHash{IT}=$item[1]}
                        |'XML' {$::ConfigHash{IT}=$item[1]}
                        |'HTML' {$::ConfigHash{IT}=$item[1]}
            output:      /\S*/ {$::ConfigHash{O}=$item[1]}
            outtype:     'text' {$::ConfigHash{OT}=$item[1]}
                        |'XML' {$::ConfigHash{OT}=$item[1]}
                        |'HTML' {$::ConfigHash{OT}=$item[1]}
            eof:     /^\Z/
            };

my $parser=new Parse::RecDescent($grammar)
   or die("Parser Generation Failed");

$list=join(" ", @ARGV);

$parser->startrule($list);
if (scalar keys %ConfigHash < 4) { die "Missing Arguments" }
print "Input file name is $::ConfigHash{I} \n";
print "The input file is a $::ConfigHash{IT} file \n";
print "Output file name is $::ConfigHash{O} \n";
print "The output file is a $::ConfigHash{OT} file \n";
```

■**Note** The various GetOpt modules provide some similar functionality, but you can achieve a greater level of customization and functionality by implementing Parse::RecDescent.

This script utilizes the Parse::RecDescent module (see Chapter 5) and begins by specifying a grammar that will be used to generate the recursive-descent parser. The grammar listing proceeds to lay out the flag argument format that the parser will use, which in this case is as follows:

```
-i filename -it file type -o filename -ot file type
```

Examining the start rule shows that the Commands subrule is allowed to match one or more times, and it is notable that the elements that comprise the right side of the Commands subrule are separated by using alternation. This allows the flags to be placed in any order and even allows flags to be left out. Within the grammar you will notice that several productions use a %ConfigHash variable. Upon an appropriate match, these productions will populate %ConfigHash appropriately for each flag. This allows your flag arguments to be parsed for proper format checking while still providing a means of gathering together all the arguments. Once the grammar is declared, a new parser object is created that will use this grammar as a part of the generation process.

Once the parser object is created, the elements of the @ARGV array are concatenated into a single string using the join function, which can then be passed to the parser object for processing. The parser object will then generate an argument listing and store it within the %ConfigHash variable. The elements' values stored in this hash are then printed to output but could just as easily be used to instead signal the execution of certain subroutines that may be specific to a given file type or to signal that a certain file should be opened or created.

Here's an example run:

```
Perl ArgumentScript.pl -i input.txt -it text -o output.txt -ot text
```

Here are the results:

```
Input file name is input.txt
The input file is a text file
Output file name is output.txt
The output file is a text file
```

Parsing Configuration Files

The utility of this section is much in line with the previous section in that custom settings or choices that affect execution can also be passed to a script via a configuration file. If you have more than a few parameters to set, a configuration file is actually a better alternative than using flags, since it can be both hard to remember all the necessary flags and tedious to type them.

Configuration files can come in a variety of formats, but it is becoming more common to see configuration files adopting an XML file format. Thus, I will show how to program an example that is able to extract some settings information from a small segment of XML markup. To do this, you will take advantage of the XML::Simple module, which was introduced in Chapter 7, when I showed how to use it to create a parse tree of an XML file. In this upcoming example, you will learn how to extract specific elements from the parse tree for use within a Perl script. Listing 9-2 shows the code you can utilize to accomplish this.

Listing 9-2. *Parsing an XML Configuration File with* XML::Simple

```perl
#!/usr/bin/perl

use XML::Simple;

($Config=<<'CONFIGINFO');
    <config Name="MyCustomConfig" Program="MyScript.pl">
        <settings> Setting A </settings>
        <settings> Setting B </settings>
    </config>
CONFIGINFO

my $Settings = XMLin($Config);

print "Name=$Settings->{Name} \n";
print "First Setting=$Settings->{settings}->[0]";
```

Within this script, the sample configuration file data is stored in the $Config variable, which is then parsed via the XMLin method. A reference to the parsed data structure is stored in the $Settings variable. Once the parsed structure has been created, the script executes two print statements, which illustrate how data can be accessed for each of the two possible ways that configuration data could be listed. The first print statement demonstrates how to access data that is stored as a parameter within an XML tag. The second print statement illustrates how data that is found between a set of tags can be accessed. The output for this script should resemble the following:

```
Name=MyCustomConfig
First Setting= Setting A
```

■**Tip** Another great module for parsing configuration files is the `AppConfig` module by Andy Wardley. This module is not XML-specific and allows you to develop configuration files that are quite robust.

Refining Searches

Much of the content of this book has dealt with extracting or evaluating information from relevant resources. Of course, this assumes you have a way of first obtaining those relevant resources, which is not always an easy task. Although search engines such as Google have undoubtedly simplified the process of locating information on the Web, and the continued development of databases has simplified other aspects of information retrieval, returned search results are still often far from perfect. This is especially true for locating information that cannot be easily expressed as a keyword, which is the strategy of choice for most major search engine providers.

An example of this from the biological sciences is the location of protein mutation data. A mutation in a protein is generally characterized as a letter representing the amino acid that is normal, followed by a number that specifies the position in the sequence where the amino acid can be found, followed by another letter that represents the amino acid to which the normal one was mutated. Creating a "keyword" to query for a single specific mutant may therefore not be that difficult, but trying to gather data on all mutations found in a given protein can be quite a chore if you use a keyword approach. However, you can readily express this mutation using a regular expression such as the following:

```
[ARNDCEQGHILKMFPSTWYV]\d+[ARNDCEQGHILKMFPSTWYV]
```

Thus, it would be helpful to develop a way of using Perl's pattern matching capabilities to locate such patterns within returned search results. As it turns out, this is possible using some of the skills you have learned in previous chapters. To demonstrate how this works, I will show the source code for the Perl RegExps for Pubmed (PREP) program, which was authored to perform that type of search refinement task. Listing 9-3 shows the code for the program.

Listing 9-3. *Source Code to the PREP Program*

```perl
#!/usr/bin/perl

# PREP (Perl RegExps for Pubmed) is a script that allows you to use
# Perl regexs when searching Pubmed records, providing the ability to search
# records for textual patterns as well as keywords

# Copyright 2005 - Christopher M. Frenz
# This script is free software; it may be used, copied, redistributed, and/or
# modified under the terms laid forth in the Perl Artistic License

# Please cite this script in any publication in which literature cited within the
# publication was located using the PREP.pl script.

# Usage: perl PREPv1-0.pl PubmedQueryTerms

# Usage of this script requires the LWP and XML::LibXML modules are installed
use LWP;
use XML::LibXML; #Version 1.58 used for development and testing

# Change the variable below to set the text pattern that Perl
# will seek to match in the returned results
my $regex='[ARNDCEQGHILKMFPSTWYV]\d+[ARNDCEQGHILKMFPSTWYV]';

my $request;
my $response;
my $query;

# Concatenates arguments passed to script to form Pubmed query
$query=join(" ", @ARGV);

# Creates the URL to search Pubmed
my $baseurl="http://www.ncbi.nlm.nih.gov/entrez/eutils/esearch.fcgi?";
my $url=$baseurl . "db=Pubmed&retmax=1&usehistory=y&term=" . $query;


# Searches Pubmed and Returns the number of results
```

```perl
# as well as the session information needed for results retrieval
$request=LWP::UserAgent->new();
$response=$request->get($url);
my $results= $response->content;
die unless $response->is_success;
print "PubMed Search Results \n";
$results=~/<Count>(\d+)<\/Count>/;
    my $NumAbstracts=$1;
$results=~/<QueryKey>(\d+)<\/QueryKey>/;
    my $QueryKey=$1;
$results=~/<WebEnv>(.*?)<\/WebEnv>/;
    my $WebEnv=$1;
print "$NumAbstracts are Available \n";
print "Query Key= $QueryKey \n";
print "WebEnv- $WebEnv \n";

# Opens a file for output
open(OFile, ">PREPout.html");

my $parser=XML::LibXML->new;

my $retmax=500; #Number of records to be retrieved per request-Max 500
my $retstart=0; #Record number to start retrieval from

# Creates the URL needed to retrieve results
$baseurl="http://www.ncbi.nlm.nih.gov/entrez/eutils/efetch.fcgi?";
my $url2="http://www.ncbi.nlm.nih.gov/entrez/query.fcgi?
cmd=Retrieve&db=pubmed&dopt=Abstract&list_uids=";

my $Count=0;
# Retrieves results in XML format
for($retstart=0;$retstart<=$NumAbstracts;$retstart+=$retmax){
    print "Processing record # $retstart \n";
    $url=$baseurl .
"rettype=abstract&retmode=xml&retstart=$retstart&retmax-$retmax
&db=Pubmed&query_key=$QueryKey&WebEnv=$WebEnv";

    $response=$request->get($url);
    $results=$response->content;
    die unless $response->is_success;

    # Uses a DOM based XML parser to process returned results
```

```
    my $domtree=$parser->parse_string($results);
    @Records=$domtree->getElementsByTagName("PubmedArticle");
    my $i=0;
    foreach(@Records){
# Extracts element data for regex processing and output formatting
        $titles=$Records[$i]->getElementsByTagName("ArticleTitle");
        $journals=$Records[$i]->getElementsByTagName("MedlineTA");
        $volumes=$Records[$i]->getElementsByTagName("Volume");
        $pgnums=$Records[$i]->getElementsByTagName("MedlinePgn");
        $abstracts=$Records[$i]->getElementsByTagName("AbstractText");
        $IDS=$Records[$i]->getElementsByTagName("PMID");


        # Processes title and abstract for pattern match and if a match occurs
        # data is written to output
        if($titles=~/($regex)/ or $abstracts=~/($regex)/){
            print OFile "<h1>Pattern Match: $1 </h1>\n";
            print OFile "<h3><a href=\"$url2$IDS\">$titles </a></h3> \n";
            print OFile "<p>$journals $volumes, $pgnums </p>\n";
            print OFile "<p>$abstracts </p>\n\nv;
            $Count=$Count+1;
        }
        $i=$i+1;
    }
}
close OFile;
print "$Count records matched the pattern";
```

■Note This script accesses Pubmed's records and query capability through the National Center of Biotechnology's E-Utilities interface. You can find more information about this interface at `http://eutils.ncbi.nlm.nih.gov/entrez/query/static/eutils_help.html`.

As with the script found in Listing 9-1, this script uses argument values, which in this particular case allow a Pubmed query to be passed to the script, which is then concatenated using the `join` function. This query term is then used to construct a URL, as shown in the following code snippet:

```
# Concatenates arguments passed to script to form Pubmed query
```

```
$query=join(" ", @ARGV);
```

```
# Creates the URL to search Pubmed
my $baseurl="http://www.ncbi.nlm.nih.gov/entrez/eutils/esearch.fcgi?";
my $url=$baseurl . "db=Pubmed&retmax=1&usehistory=y&term=" . $query;
```

The important things to note about this URL is that it calls upon the ESearch method to search Pubmed for records that match the query term(s) and that it tells the method to employ the "use history" option. Invoking use history tells the Pubmed server to temporarily store the identification codes of the records that matched the query so that they can be retrieved later. The server is able to identify the specific query request by assigning a query_key variable and a WebEnv variable to the search. Thus, when your search is performed, it is imperative to extract this information from the returned results, which is accomplished in the following code snippet:

```
# Searches Pubmed and Returns the number of results
# as well as the session information needed for results retrieval
$request=LWP::UserAgent->new();
$response=$request->get($url);
my $results= $response->content;
die unless $response->is_success;
print "PubMed Search Results \n";
$results=~/<Count>(\d+)<\/Count>/;
    my $NumAbstracts=$1;
$results=~/<QueryKey>(\d+)<\/QueryKey>/;
    my $QueryKey=$1;
$results=~/<WebEnv>(.*?)<\/WebEnv>/;
    my $WebEnv=$1;
print "$NumAbstracts are Available \n";
print "Query Key= $QueryKey \n";
print "WebEnv= $WebEnv \n";
```

In addition to the query key, the code snippet also extracts the total number of records that matched the query, which will be used later to ensure that all the records are retrieved and screened for the presence of the text pattern of interest.

Once you have all the required session information, it is possible to begin retrieving the matching records. You can retrieve returned records in groups of up to 500 by setting the $retmax variable. The $retstart variable specifies the record that the server should begin with and should remain set to its initial value of zero (the first record). Also, an output file is opened so that upon processing the returned records, those that match the text pattern of interest can be written to it for later examination by the user. Last, you need to once again specify the URL that will be used for retrieving the records that matched your initial query. This functionality takes place in the following snippet of code:

```
# Opens a file for output
open(OFile, ">PREPout.html");

my $parser=XML::LibXML->new;

my $retmax=500; #Number of records to be retrieved per request-Max 500
my $retstart=0; #Record number to start retrieval from

# Creates the URL needed to retrieve results
$baseurl="http://www.ncbi.nlm.nih.gov/entrez/eutils/efetch.fcgi?";
my $url2="http://www.ncbi.nlm.nih.gov/entrez/query.fcgi?
cmd=Retrieve&db=pubmed&dopt=Abstract&list_uids=";
```

The base URL created in this snippet is actually not a complete URL. You need to append several other parameters to it, including the session information and the values of $retmax and $retstart. To keep retrieving additional blocks of 500 records, $retstart will be incremented by $retmax, and a new set of records will be retrieved until all the records (as specified by $NumAbstracts) have been retrieved. For example:

```
# Retrieves results in XML format
for($retstart=0;$retstart<=$NumAbstracts;$retstart+=$retmax){
    print "Processing record # $retstart \n";
    $url=$baseurl .
"rettype=abstract&retmode=xml&retstart=$retstart&retmax=$retmax
&db=Pubmed&query_key=$QueryKey&WebEnv=$WebEnv";

    $response=$request->get($url);
    $results=$response->content;
    die unless $response->is_success;
```

The results of these record retrievals are returned in XML format and will be processed using the parsing capabilities of the module XML::LibXML. Next, all the returned records (as indicated by the XML tag <PubmedArticle>) and their child elements are located in the parse tree and stored in the @records array. Data contained in individual child elements of the records can then be extracted, as demonstrated in the following bit of code:

```
# Uses a DOM-based XML parser to process returned results
    my $domtree=$parser->parse_string($results);
    @Records=$domtree->getElementsByTagName("PubmedArticle");
```

```
    my $i=0;
    foreach(@Records){
# Extracts element data for regex processing and output formatting
        $titles=$Records[$i]->getElementsByTagName("ArticleTitle");
        $journals=$Records[$i]->getElementsByTagName("MedlineTA");
        $volumes=$Records[$i]->getElementsByTagName("Volume");
        $pgnums=$Records[$i]->getElementsByTagName("MedlinePgn");
        $abstracts=$Records[$i]->getElementsByTagName("AbstractText");
        $IDS=$Records[$i]->getElementsByTagName("PMID");
```

Within this snippet of code, it is important to note that elements such as the titles of articles and the abstract texts are not extracted directly from the main parse tree but rather on a record-by-record basis. This is because Pubmed often has records that are missing one or more fields, and a direct extraction would produce a set of arrays whose elements and indexes will become out of sync. Processing the records one at a time avoids this problem.

Once the child node data is extracted, the $titles and $abstracts variables are then checked for the presence of the text pattern(s) of interest; if a match occurs, the article information is written to a HTML file. For example:

```
# Processes title and abstract for pattern match and if a match occurs
        # data is written to output
        if($titles=~/($regex)/ or $abstracts=~/($regex)/){
            print OFile "<h1>Pattern Match: $1 </h1>\n";
            print OFile "<h3><a href=\"$url2$IDS\">$titles </a></h3> \n";
            print OFile "<p>$journals $volumes, $pgnums </p>\n";
            print OFile "<p>$abstracts </p>\n\n";
            $Count=$Count+1;
        }
        $i=$i+1;
    }
}
close OFile;
print "$Count records matched the pattern";
```

Just checking the abstracts and titles can eliminate false matches, such as matching an author name or journal volume number mistakenly. If this script is executed, the output should resemble the sample shown in Figure 9-1.

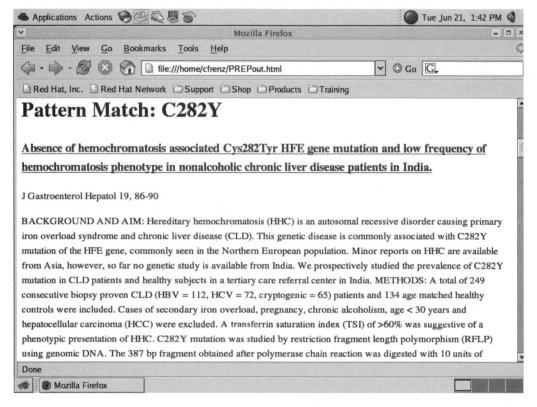

Figure 9-1. *A sample output file generated by the PREP script*

Formatting Output

This section of the chapter actually has nothing to do with parsing in particular, but formatting output can be a useful skill to have if you generate reports. It is likely that any script you write that involves a parser or performs data extraction will be used to generate output for the person who chose to run the script. As I say in many examples throughout this book, you can handle simple output with one or more `print` or `printf` statements, but this is not a convenient way to deal with more complex output formats.

One option that you saw in the PREP example and in the blog link extraction example from Chapter 6 is that you can have your program generate HTML markup as output and rely on the browser rendering to handle some of the formatting tasks. However, outputting HTML is not appropriate for every application; sometimes generating a text file is a better option. For these cases, Perl allows the declaration of formats. The simplest way to understand the formatting of Perl data is to actually look at an example, so consider the code shown in Listing 9-4.

Listing 9-4. *Using Format Declarations to Generate Aesthetically Pleasing Reports*

```
#!/usr/bin/perl

format OFILE_TOP=
        A report of My Formatted Data
        Date: @||||||||||||||||||||||||
                        $Date
Column1      Column2      Column3      Column 4

_____
.
format OFILE=
@<<<            @>>>        @||||||    @<<<<<<<<
$var1,         $var2,      $var3,     $var4
.

# specifying STDOUT is not necessary it is
# stated to demonstrate where a file handle would go
open(STDOUT, ">formattedout.txt");

$Date='June 3, 2005';
foreach my $i(0..9){
  $var1=rand()*5;
  $var2=rand()*-7;
  $var3=rand();
  $var4=rand()*3;
  write OFILE;
}
```

Within this segment of code, two format declarations have been set up to work with the output specified by a file handle. In cases where a file handle is not provided, the format declaration will be applied to STDOUT. The first format declaration listed is called a *header declaration*, which is indicated by having the flag _TOP appended to the end of the file handle name. Header format specifications are executed once when the write method is called and are generally used to output formatted titles and headings under which the actual data later be output.

The actual header declaration portrays several different types of output that can be written to the file. Some lines in the declaration consist entirely of text, which will be output verbatim to the target file when the write method is called. Another line contains an @symbol followed by multiple pipe (|) symbols. The at (@) symbol specifies a field, and the number of pipe symbols is indicative of the length of the field. Field lengths can be specified using a pipe for centered justification, a left bracket (<) for left justification, or a right bracket (>) for right justification of the variable that will be written into the field space. In the line immediately below the field-containing line, you will notice the presence of the variable $Date. This variable will be written into the field space when the write method is invoked.

After the header format is declared, a second format declaration is provided that will be responsible for outputting the remainder of the report's body. In the case of this example, it specifies several fields that will allow values to be written below each column heading that was specified in the header declaration. This example uses different types of justification for each of the fields in order to give readers a feel for how the different types of justification influence the actual output. After the fields are declared, the variables that should be printed to each field are listed. Unlike the header declaration, this type of declaration can be used multiple times, and thus this allows every variable generated to be written to the appropriate column. The output for this script should resemble the following:

```
            A report of My Formatted Data
            Date:        June 3, 2005
    Column1     Column2      Column3      Column 4

    4.60          -2.3      0.08013      1.823547
    0.23          -2.1      0.38513      1.017059
    0.55          -5.1      0.95690      1.973327
    0.15          -2.9      0.42584      1.007171
    0.01          -4.9      0.28881      1.657287
    4.88          -5.5      0.39239      0.214691
    1.26          -3.4      0.55834      2.966491
    1.79          -2.0      0.75808      2.501403
    4.38          -3.0      0.74224      0.918640
    1.75          -5.8      0.53149      1.286041
```

Summary

In this chapter, you learned some useful applications of parsers that did not directly integrate themselves well into any of the previous chapters. The chapter covered how you can allow users to have greater control over the operation of Perl programs by parsing command-line arguments and by parsing configuration files. The chapter also demonstrated how you can use some of the parsing knowledge in this book to refine results returned by a search engine. Last, the chapter discussed the issue of output formatting in order to allow readers to programmatically create professional-looking reports from the data their parsers extract.

In the final chapter of the book, you will examine the topic of data mining, which will allow the analysis of extracted data in the hopes of uncovering trends within the data. You can use the discovery of such trends either for learning more about the system in question or for predicting results. In other words, Chapter 10 will demonstrate ways you can put your data to work for you.

CHAPTER 10

■ ■ ■

Performing Text and Data Mining

Up until this point, one of the major themes of this book has been using parsers or regular expressions for extracting relevant textual information. As you can see from the examples in this book, such extractions can often be highly useful for staying informed about a certain topic or obtaining a needed piece of information. However, modern computer systems are powerful enough to allow you to go beyond simple text extraction and actually utilize various extracted pieces of information to try to locate correlations between data sources or in some other way analyze data to find a greater overriding meaning to extracted data. In other words, extracted data can often be analyzed in aggregate to yield information that would not be apparent to anyone examining single pieces of information alone. This process of searching for associations and trends within sets of data is known as *data mining*, and performing data mining on data extracted from document text (as you have been doing with various parsing routines) is referred to as *text mining*.

Data mining is actually becoming an increasingly important task in many fields. For example, health informatics professionals often use data mining to provide correlations between a set of risk factors and a disease of interest or to determine the best treatment course for an individual based on how other similar cases responded to the various treatments. Further, businesses often use data mining as part of their processes for recommending items of interest to consumers or for deciding whether to extend credit to a given individual. The sciences also are beginning to use data and text mining heavily and are beginning to uncover new research findings by examining the outcomes of many previously published studies in aggregate. Data mining and other forms of knowledge discovery are becoming increasingly relevant areas of research and development as the amount of readily available information continues to increase. Data mining helps make such huge knowledge bases manageable, and parsing can often play a crucial role as a part of a larger data mining framework.

The goal of this chapter is not to provide a comprehensive look at performing data mining tasks in Perl, since such a subject could easily fill a large book on its own, but rather to demonstrate the basic ideas behind data mining and give a perspective of what you can do with the extracted information. This chapter will provide an overview of the different types of data mining tasks and will point out various resources you can use to further explore the topic of data mining.

USEFUL BOOKS ON DATA MINING

The following books cover most of the mining algorithms mentioned in this chapter as well as a number of additional algorithms:

- *Data Mining: Introductory and Advanced Topics* (Prentice Hall, 2003) by Margaret H. Dunham

- *Data Mining Concepts and Techniques* (Morgan Kaufmann, 2000) by Jiawei Han and Micheline Kamber

---

Introducing Data Mining Basics

The goal of all data mining tasks is to develop a model that can provide an accurate representation of the data of interest. For example, if you were performing data mining for a hospital, you may be asked to see if any correlations are present between patients admitted for coronary heart disease and their blood pressure, weight, and height. If you were instead employed by a bank, you may be asked to determine if an individual is a credit risk based on the bank's past experience with customers of a similar income, FICO score, and type of employment. In other words, by looking at a large aggregate data set of hospital records or bank records, you can hope to in some way establish how certain factors relate to a given outcome (for example, getting heart disease or defaulting on a loan).

You can generally use such correlations between variables and outcomes to accomplish one of two things. The first is to mine for correlations in order to gain information that is descriptive. *Descriptive* mining seeks to explicitly define the relationships between one or more variables and a particular outcome, in the hopes of learning more about the data being modeled. The second type of task that data mining is routinely used for is *predictive* modeling. Rather than just seeking to learn about the relationships present within a data set, predictive modeling seeks to use data collected in the past to predict the outcomes of future events.

The methodologies that accomplish both descriptive and predictive data mining tasks are highly diverse and can range from basic statistical measures such as linear regression to sophisticated machine learning algorithms. Data mining is still a field that is in its infancy, and in many cases the best way to approach a specific type of data mining problem has not been established. However, you can divide the various approaches to descriptive and predictive modeling into some general classifications. I will summarize the approaches briefly in the upcoming sections on descriptive modeling and predictive modeling, and in many cases you will notice that CPAN is noticeably lacking modules capable of performing certain tasks. Given Perl's top-of-the-line text processing capabilities, adding data mining capabilities to Perl's repertoire would likely be a valuable addition, however, and will probably be an area for which modules become increasingly developed for on CPAN.

■**Tip** Although you can apply the techniques discussed in this chapter to data obtained through document parsing, the techniques themselves are applicable to all types of data regardless of the source. In other words, the utility of this chapter extends beyond applications that rely solely on parsers.

Introducing Descriptive Modeling

The job of descriptive modeling is to determine the types of relationships or patterns that are present within a data set in order to study how various factors interact to produce an outcome. As shown in Table 10-1, several common types of descriptive mining approaches exist; I will describe each in more depth in the sections following the table.

Table 10-1. *Descriptive Data Modeling Approaches*

Approach	Function
Clustering	Divides data into groups that are not predefined
Summarization	Groups data into subsets based on descriptions
Association rules	Identifies the rules that govern the relationships found between elements of data
Sequence discovery	Identifies time-based patterns in data sets

Clustering

The purpose of *clustering* is to group elements of a data set based on similarities. In clustering, these groups are not predefined but are instead derived from similarities present in a set of predefined attributes. For example, if you were asked to sort a pile of beads based on their color, you would be performing a clustering operation. You would not necessarily know prior to seeing the beads that you would need piles for blue, green, and red; however, once you saw the beads, the similarities and difference present between the beads would become apparent and allow you to sort the beads. At the most basic level, clustering often works by calculating either the similarity or the distance measure (how different two things are) of some form and by ensuring that all elements of a given cluster have a higher degree of similarity or a lesser degree of distance than elements not found in the cluster. Various algorithms are available to accomplish this task, including the K-means algorithm and Kohonen Self-Organizing Maps.

■**Note** For more information on the K-means algorithm, refer to `http://www-2.cs.cmu.edu/~awm/tutorials/kmeans.html`. For further information on Kohonen Self-Organizing Maps, refer to `http://davis.wpi.edu/~matt/courses/soms/` or *Fundamentals of Neural Networks* (Prentice Hall, 1994) by Laurene V. Fausett.

Summarization

Summarization is basically a method of succinctly representing the contents of the data set or a segment of the data set. Any process that returns information that is representative of the contents of the database can be considered summarization, but summarization is often used in conjunction with numeric elements of a data set, in which a representative value is derived by calculating the mean and standard deviation of the numeric element. The ability to numerically summarize such data is often highly useful because the calculation of descriptive statistics allows for the comparison of one or more sets of data. For example, if you were hired to determine the efficacy of a pharmaceutical treatment for blood pressure, you could evaluate the performance of the drug by comparing the mean blood pressures plus or minus the standard deviation of those who took the treatment and those who did not. As another example, you could use the temperature lookup program from Chapter 6 to determine the temperature for two locations in the United States over a period of time and then use such descriptive statistics to compare the average temperatures in each locale.

When calculating basic statistics in Perl, a useful module to consider is the `Statistics::Descriptive` module by Colin Kuskie. For instance, you could use the module to calculate the mean blood pressure for a group of individuals by utilizing the code in Listing 10-1.

Listing 10-1. *Using* `Statistics::Descriptive`

```
#!/usr/bin/perl

use Statistics::Descriptive;

#declares a new instance of the statistics object
my $stats=Statistics::Descriptive::Full->new();

#passes data values to the statistics object
$stats->add_data(110,125,147,131,119);
```

```
#retrieves mean and standard deviation
$mean=$stats->mean();
$SD=$stats->standard_deviation();

printf("The average blood pressure is %.2f +/- %.2f",$mean,$SD);
```

This segment of code functions by first declaring a new instance of the statistics object ($stats) and then passing a list of numeric values to the object. The mean() method and the standard_deviation() method are then called to return the appropriate statistical values, and the results are printed to STDOUT. The results obtained from executing this script are as follows:

```
The average blood pressure is 126.40 +/- 13.89
```

■Tip You can use numerous other methods to return statistical quantities such as the median, range, mode, variance, and so on. The methods are employed in the same manner as demonstrated previously; you can find the method names in the module's documentation page.

Association Rules

The *association rules* method seeks to determine relationships between elements of data, with the most common example being merchants trying to discover what products are often purchased together. For example, is it true that milk is frequently purchased in conjunction with cookies? If so, an association would exist between the purchase of milk and the purchase of cookies. However, the use of association rules can extend beyond consumer associations and can also include things such as searching for associations between a disease and a list of potential risk factors. In this case, you could parse out the occurrence of certain risk factors from patient data files as well as any diseases they develop and try to use association rules to determine if any risk factors or combination of risk factors are frequently observed before the occurrence of a certain disease state.

CPAN has limited modules available for association rule mining, but one module, Dan Frankowski's Data::Mining::AssociationRules module, can create association rules for a set of transactions such as the purchase of groceries by different individuals. Before you examine the function of the module, however, you need to create an appropriately formatted input file for use with the module. This file will contain the transaction data that is going to be mined for associations. The file should contain two columns: the first containing the transaction ID and the second containing an item ID. Enter the code in Listing 10-2 into a text editor, and save the file as Data.txt.

Listing 10-2. *The* Data.txt *File*

```
123 Milk
579 Eggs
646 Bread
123 Cookies
646 Milk
123 Bread
579 Meat
579 Bread
```

■**Note** The transaction IDs do not need to be grouped together if the same ones appear multiple times.

Now that you have a file that contains a set of transaction information, you can use the Data::Mining::AssociationRules module to create a set of association rules for these transactions. You can accomplish this with the code in Listing 10-3.

Listing 10-3. *Using* Data::Mining::AssociationRules

```perl
#!/usr/bin/perl

use Data::Mining::AssociationRules;

my %TransactionMap;
my $File="Data.txt";
my $Support=1;
my $OFilePrefix="Data";

read_transaction_file(\%transaction_map, $File);

generate_frequent_sets(\%transaction_map, $OFilePrefix, $Support);

generate_rules($OFilePrefix, $Support);
```

This script functions by first using the read_transaction_file() method to create a transaction map based on the listing of transactions contained within a file. In the case of this example, this transaction file is the Data.txt file provided in Listing 10-2. After the transaction map is created, the generate_frequent_sets() method is called, which generates sets of items based on the number of items within a transaction. These sets are automatically output to a series of files, where each file corresponds to the set number.

For example, the file executing this script will generate the files Data-support-1-1set.txt, Data-support-1-2set.txt, and Data-support-1-3set.txt, where the *-1set.txt file lists all one-item transactions, the *-2set.txt file lists all two-item transactions, and the *-3set.txt file lists all three-set transactions. As an example, the following shows the Data-support-1-3set.txt file:

```
1 Bread Cookies Milk
1 Bread Eggs Meat
```

The calculation of these sets is a requirement for the generate_rules() method to function. You can apply the generate_rules() method to generate an output file that contains a list of association rules. Executing this method will generate a file named Data-support-1-conf-0-rules.txt, whose content is as follows:

```
1 0.333 1 1 2 Bread => Meat
1 1.000 1 1 2 Meat => Bread
1 0.333 1 1 2 Bread => Eggs
1 1.000 1 1 2 Eggs => Bread
1 0.333 1 2 3 Bread => Eggs Meat
1 1.000 1 2 3 Eggs => Bread Meat
1 1.000 2 1 3 Bread Eggs => Meat
1 1.000 1 2 3 Meat => Bread Eggs
1 1.000 2 1 3 Bread Meat => Eggs
1 1.000 2 1 3 Eggs Meat => Bread
1 1.000 1 1 2 Cookies => Milk
1 0.500 1 1 2 Milk => Cookies
1 1.000 1 1 2 Eggs => Meat
1 1.000 1 1 2 Meat => Eggs
1 0.333 1 2 3 Bread => Cookies Milk
1 1.000 1 2 3 Cookies => Bread Milk
1 1.000 2 1 3 Bread Cookies => Milk
1 0.500 1 2 3 Milk => Bread Cookies
1 0.500 2 1 3 Bread Milk => Cookies
1 1.000 2 1 3 Cookies Milk => Bread
1 0.333 1 1 2 Bread => Cookies
1 1.000 1 1 2 Cookies => Bread
2 0.667 1 1 2 Bread => Milk
2 1.000 1 1 2 Milk => Bread
```

The output presented here is listed in the order of support count, confidence, left set size, right set size, frequent set size, and then the association rule, in the form *left set => right set*. The *support count* is the number of transactions in which a given item set appears, and the *confidence* refers to the probability of the rule's right side occurring when presented with the left side. The *set size* variables refer to the number of items listed on the left side of the rule, the right side of the rule, and the total number of items in the rule, respectively.

■**Note** For more information on association rules, it is worth looking at `http://www.cs.wpi.edu/~ruiz/KDDRG/association_rule_mining.html`.

Sequence Discovery

The remaining type of descriptive modeling is *sequence discovery*, which is concerned with finding patterns in times at which events occur. For the most part, sequence discovery attempts to establish an order in which a group of events could be expected to proceed. For example, if you consider the case of people wanting to learn Perl, you may find a common sequence pattern that says most people will first buy a book on Perl programming and then will download an updated Perl compiler. Establishing such sequences is often important for businesses in that they can use the information to better target their sales efforts. Thus, perhaps if a sequence analysis established that most consumers bought a game within one week of buying a gaming console, video game companies could appropriately target their sales practices to maximize game selling. Sequence discovery processes share much in common with mining association rules; however, sequence mining is specific to time-based patterns, whereas association rule mining is not restricted in such a way.

Introducing Predictive Modeling

Unlike descriptive modeling, predictive modeling does not seek to just describe what is already present in the data set. Rather, it tries to either predict some form of future state based on the data or predict a value that is associated with the data set but not present within the data set. For example, banks often want to know if an individual is likely to default on a loan (future state), and scientists often want to predict hard-to-measure properties of a system (associated values) without having to explicitly measure the quantity. As with descriptive mining, you can use various approaches to predictive modeling, as shown in Table 10-2.

Table 10-2. *Predictive Data Modeling Approaches*

Approach	Function
Classification	Sorts data into predefined classes
Regression	Fits data to a function that can be used to predict values
Time series analysis	Seeks to predict how values change over time
Prediction*	Seeks to predict future outcomes from current states

* Note: The term prediction *describes both a type of data modeling and a method of modeling.*

Classification

Classification is the process of sorting data into classes of predefined attributes. In other words, classification algorithms try to determine how similar a given data element is to the class criteria and predict to which class the element most appropriately belongs. Classification is generally performed by means of supervised learning algorithms. That is, the machine learning algorithm is trained using a training set for which the appropriate classes are known. In this manner, the algorithm is able to attempt a classification and check to see if the classification was made appropriately. Depending on the result of the classification, the algorithm can then adjust its parameters to improve its classification accuracy. Supervised learning approaches often involve the use of neural networks or naïve Bayes algorithms. For more information on the basics of neural networks, refer to the code listings in the upcoming "Prediction" section.

■Tip One Perl module that can perform the classification of text documents is the AI::Categorizer module by Ken Williams. The demo.pl script that illustrates the functionality of the module is worth looking at, since it demonstrates the magnitude often associated with data mining tasks. The script trains and validates a document classifier based on a body of almost 11,000 text files. The module is available on CPAN; you can view the demo.pl script at http://search.cpan.org/src/KWILLIAMS/AI-Categorizer-0.07/ eg/demo.pl.

Regression

Regression is the process of taking a set of data and trying to fit the data to a function. If the function is a good fit for the data, the function can in theory then be used to make future predictions, because new data can be entered into this function and the output can be considered representative of what the actual outcome will be. Regression is useful when dealing with extracted numeric data for which you think there may an association present between two or more value types. In other words, these are situations where the value of data of type *x* is believed to influence the value of data of type *y*. Various types of regression analysis are possible, including linear regression, logistic regression, and polynomial regression. The Perl module `Statistics::Regression` by Ivan Tubert-Brohman allows you to perform multivariate linear regression. In other words, it allows you to fit data to an equation of the following form:

$$y = \theta_1 x_1 + \theta_2 x_2 + \ldots + \theta_{n-1} x_{n-1} + \theta_n x_n$$

Within this equation, *y* is representative of the numeric output that should be achieved by the equation when *x* values are input. The regression process itself will be used to determine the values of θ. Each *x* value is representative of some numeric element of data that is believed to contribute to the outcome value *y*. For example, consider the *x* and *y* data values in Table 10-3.

Table 10-3. x *and* y *Values for Regression Example*

x	y
0.5	4.0
1.0	12.0
2.0	38.0
8.0	129.0

To generate a function that can generate value *y* from input *x*, use the Perl code in Listing 10-4.

Listing 10-4. *Using the* Statistics::Regression *Module*

```perl
#!/usr/bin/perl

use Statistics::Regression;

my $reg = Statistics::Regression->new(
    2, "Example",
    ["intercept", "slope"]
  );
```

```
# Setting the value of x1 to 1.0 will
# allow for the calculation of a Y intercept
$reg->include( 4.0, [1.0, 0.5] );
$reg->include( 12.0, [1.0, 1.0] );
$reg->include( 38.0, [1.0, 2.0] );
$reg->include( 129.0, [1.0, 8.0] );

# Print the result
$reg->print();
```

The data in Table 10-3 contains only one series of x values; thus, the data lends itself well to fitting it to an equation of the following form:

$$y = \theta_b + \theta_m x$$

Here, θ_m is the slope, and θ_b is the intercept. Therefore, when you create an instance of the Regression object, you have to specify that you will be determining two θ values. Also, name the regression *Example*, and name the first θ value *intercept* and the second one *slope*. Once the object is created, you have to pass the x and y values to the object, which is accomplished by using the include method. Within this method's argument list, the first value corresponds to the value of y, and the bracketed values correspond to the x values. The value of the equation's intercept need not be dependant on any value of x and should always be constant; therefore, in all calls to the include method, the intercept value of x is always set to 1. When dealing with the slope term's contribution to the final value of y, the value of x is important; so, for the slope-related values of x, the numbers from Table 10-3 are used. Once all the data is passed to the Regression object, the object's print method can be called to show the calculated θ values. The output generated by this script should resemble the following:

```
****************************************************************
Regression 'Example'
****************************************************************
Theta[0='intercept']=     -1.5907
Theta[1='slope']=     16.4663
R^2= 0.994, N= 4
****************************************************************
```

Thus, the equation that models the data would be in the following form:

$$y = -1.5907 + 16.4663x$$

The trend line in Figure 10-1 represents a plot of the function $y=-1.5907+16.4663x$. The points represent the data values upon which the regression was performed to generate the linear function.

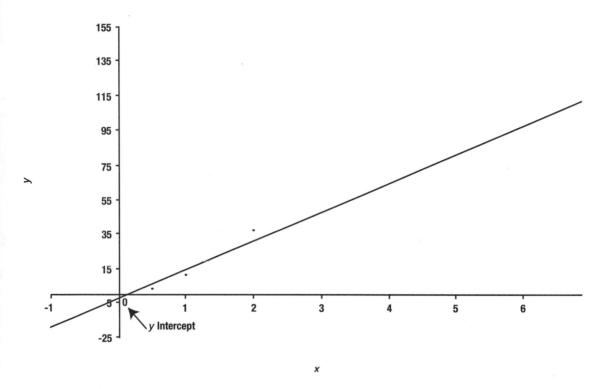

Figure 10-1. *A plot of the function* y=-1.5907+16.4663x

Time Series Analysis

Time series analysis seeks to establish how a given value varies over the course of time in the hopes of being able to predict what the value will be at some future point in time. For example, it is well known that within the northern hemisphere of the earth, the amount of daylight gradually increases between December and June, and after June gradually decreases again until December passes. Having uncovered such a trend, it can be easily predicted that the daylight hours in November will likely be shorter than those in May. Within the business world, time series analysis is often used as a means of trying to determine when various commodities should be bought and/or sold.

Prediction

Prediction is a general term for any method that can be used to predict future outcomes based on current data values. While there are a variety of predictive algorithms that can be implemented, many of the most common approaches to prediction involve using machine learning. Therefore, I will introduce machine learning in this section in the form of a feed-forward neural network that trains itself to solve the XOR problem. Machine learning techniques such as this are used in a manner somewhat similar to regression, in that they are generally used to approximate a function that produces a given output for a given input sequence. The distinction is that techniques such as regression work well for generating functions where the relationship between variables are straightforward, such as the linear relationship demonstrated in the previous example. Neural networks and other machine learning techniques are more appropriate for dealing with complex variable relationships in which multiple factors interact to produce a given output in ways that are not easy to model using more traditional mathematical approaches.

Neural networks are analogous to biological neural networks in that they consist of many simple information-processing units that operate in parallel. Within both biological and artificial neural networks, information processing occurs within many simple units referred to as *neurons*. Signals can be passed between neurons through a series of weighted connections. Neural networks are able to "learn" by adjusting the strengths of these connections until they can approximate a function that accurately computes the proper output for a given input pattern.

This typical architecture contains three layers: an input layer, a hidden layer, and an output layer (see Figure 10-2). The input layer is used to transfer the array of input values into the neural network. The input layer data is then multiplied by a weight matrix (w_{ij}) and passed into the hidden layer neurons. Every possible interconnection possesses its own weight; therefore, the weight matrix has $n \times m$ dimensions, where n is the number of input layer neurons, and m is the number of hidden layer neurons. It is the presence of the hidden layer neurons that allows the network to form internal representations of how the differing elements of a complex pattern work together to produce a given output.

A similar weight matrix (w_{jk}) connects the hidden layer neurons to the output neuron(s). A bias is also added to each neuron in the hidden and output layers, which scales a neuron's input values before they pass through the neuron's transfer function. The transfer function, or *activation function* as it is referred to in some books, is a mathematical function that takes the sum of all the neuron's weighted inputs and uses the value to calculate the neuron's output. Typically, neural networks will use a bipolar sigmoid as a hidden layer transfer function that is scaled to output values between -1 and 1. The equation for this type of sigmoid is as follows

$$f(X) = \frac{2}{1 + \exp(-X)} - 1$$

where X is the neuron's scaled input. The sigmoid of the output neuron can be scaled to yield a range of output values that is appropriate for the given application.

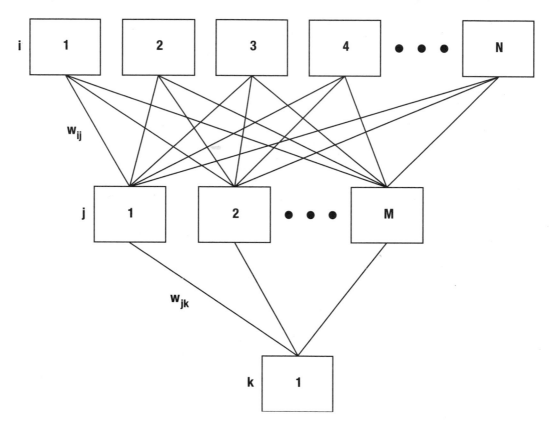

Figure 10-2. *A representative feed-forward neural network architecture*

As a demonstration, I will show how to program a feed-forward neural network with a two-four-one architecture (two input neurons, four hidden neurons, and one output neuron). Listing 10-5 shows the code for this neural network and the back-propagation training algorithm.

Listing 10-5. *A Basic Feed-Forward Neural Network That Learns with Back-Propagation of Error*

```perl
#!/usr/bin/perl -w

use strict;

use constant alpha=>0.2; # the learning rate
use constant mu=>0.6; #The momentum constant
use constant N=>2;
use constant M=>4;

our(@hbias,@hbiasold,@dhbias);
our(@hweight,@hweightold,@dhweight);
our($obias,$obiasold,$dobias);
our(@oweight,@oweightold,@doweight);
our(@hin,@hout);
our($oin,$oout);
our($odelta,$hdelta);
our(@X,@X1,@targval);

sub trans {
    my($val)=@_;
    my $trans;
    $trans-(2/(1+(exp(-$val))))-1;
    return $trans;
}

sub dtrans {
    my($val)=@_;
    my $dtrans;
    $dtrans=(1/2)*(1+trans($val))*(1-trans($val));
    return $dtrans;
}

sub init {
    my($i,$j);
    for($i=0;$i<=(N)-1;$i++) {
        for($j=0;$j<=(M)-1;$j++) {
            $hweight[$i][$j]=(rand)-0.5;
        }
    }
```

```perl
    @hweightold=@hweight;
    for($j=0;$j<=(M)-1;$j++) {
        $hbias[$j]=(rand)-0.5;
        $oweight[$j]=(rand)-0.5;
    }
    @hbiasold=@hbias;
    @oweightold=@oweight;
    $obias=(rand)-0.5;
    $obiasold=$obias;
}

sub hiddeninput {
    my($i,$j);
    my $sum;
    for($j=0;$j<=(M)-1;$j++) {
        $sum=0;
        for($i=0;$i<=(N)-1;$i++) {
            $sum=$sum+($X[$i]*$hweight[$i][$j]);
        }
        $hin[$j]=$hbias[$j]+$sum;
    }
}

sub hiddentransfer {
    my $j;
    for($j=0;$j<=(M)-1;$j++) {
        $hout[$j]=(trans($hin[$j]));
    }
}

sub outputinput {
    my $sum=0;
    my $j;
    for($j=0;$j<=(M)-1;$j++) {
        $sum=$sum+($hout[$j]*$oweight[$j]);
    }
    $oin=$obias+$sum;
}

sub outputtransfer {
    $oout=trans($oin);
}
```

```perl
sub updateout {
    my($i)=@_;
    my $j;
    $odelta=(dtrans($oin))*($targval[$i]-$oout);
    for($j=0;$j<=(M)-1;$j++) {
        $doweight[$j]=(alpha*($odelta)*$hout[$j])+
                        (mu*($oweight[$j]-$oweightold[$j]));
        $oweightold[$j]=$oweight[$j];
        $oweight[$j]=$oweight[$j]+$doweight[$j];
    }
    $dobias=((alpha)*($odelta))+((mu)*(($obias)-($obiasold)));
    $obiasold=$obias;
    $obias=$obias+$dobias;
}

sub updatehidden {
    my($i,$j,$k);
    my $deltatemp;
    for($j=0;$j<=(M)-1;$j++) {
        $hdelta=$odelta*$oweight[$j]*dtrans($hin[$j]);
        for($i=0;$i<=(N)-1;$i++) {
            $dhweight[$i][$j]=(alpha*$hdelta*$X[$i])+
                            (mu*($hweight[$i][$j]-$hweightold[$i][$j]));
            $hweightold[$i][$j]=$hweight[$i][$j];
            $hweight[$i][$j]=$hweight[$i][$j]+$dhweight[$i][$j];
        }
        $dhbias[$j]=(alpha*$hdelta)+(mu*($hbias[$j]-$hbiasold[$j]));
        $hbiasold[$j]=$hbias[$j];
        $hbias[$j]=$hbias[$j]+$dhbias[$j];
    }
}


@X1=([1,1],[-1,1],[1,-1],[-1,-1]); # input values
@targval=(-1,1,1,-1);
init();
my($i,$j);
my @outvals;
for($j=0;$j<1000;$j++) {
    for($i=0;$i<=3;$i++) {
        $X[0]=$X1[$i][0];
        $X[1]=$X1[$i][1];
```

```
        hiddeninput();
        hiddentransfer();
        outputinput();
        outputtransfer();
        $outvals[$i]=$oout;
        updateout($i);
        updatehidden();
    }
print $outvals[0]," ",$outvals[1]," ",$outvals[2]," ",$outvals[3],"\n";
}
```

Before you can use any neural network, you must first lay out the architecture of the network by specifying the number of neurons your network will contain in each layer and establishing the various connections and biases that are present between neurons in each layer. You can accomplish this via the following initialization subroutine:

```
sub init {
    my($i,$j);
    srand;
    for($i=0;$i<=(N)-1;$i++) {
        for($j=0;$j<=(M)-1;$j++) {
            $hweight[$i][$j]=(rand)-0.5;
        }
    }
    @hweightold=@hweight;
    for($j=0;$j<=(M)-1;$j++) {
        $hbias[$j]=(rand)-0.5;
        $oweight[$j]=(rand)-0.5;
    }
    @hbiasold=@hbias;
    @oweightold=@oweight;
    $obias=(rand)-0.5;
    $obiasold=$obias;
}
```

You can use this initialization routine to generate a network with n input neurons, m hidden layer neurons, and a single output neuron. The initialization routine also sets starting values for the weights and biases of each connection. Prior to training the neural network, it is not feasible to know the proper values for each weight and bias; therefore, they are randomly initialized to a value between -0.5 and 0.5. Variables prefixed with an h are for the connections between the input and hidden layers, and those prefixed with an o are for the connections present between the hidden and output layers. The variables that have a suffix of *old* will be used as part of the training process and are initialized to values equivalent to those used for the respective weights and biases. This is a necessary step because the training algorithm requires that you keep track of the current set of weights and biases as well as one previous set.

At this point, you have the architecture of the neural network laid out and the strength of the interconnections initialized, but you still lack a means of transferring data between layers. So, you need to establish a means of transferring the input data from the input neurons to the hidden layer neurons. When coding the procedure to do this, it is important to consider that each hidden layer neuron is connected to every input neuron and that each individual hidden layer neuron will receive the sum of the weighted input neuron values. Applying the bias of this hidden layer neuron then scales this summation. Thus, for each individual neuron, the process should proceed according to the following formula:

$$hin_j = hbias_j + \sum_{i=0}^{n-1} X_i w_{ij}$$

Here, X_i represents the input neuron values, and w_{ij} represents the weight connecting the input neuron to the hidden layer neuron. You can find the code responsible for this functionality in the following hiddeninput subroutine:

```
sub hiddeninput {
    my($i,$j);
    my $sum;
    for($j=0;$j<=(M)-1;$j++) {
        $sum=0;
        for($i=0;$i<=(N)-1;$i++) {
            $sum=$sum+($X[$i]*$hweight[$i][$j]);
        }
        $hin[$j]=$hbias[$j]+$sum;
    }
}
```

Once the hidden layer neuron input values have been determined, it is time for each hidden layer neuron to process its input by passing the value through its transfer function. You can find the code responsible for this functionality in the following hiddentransfer subroutine and trans subroutine:

```
sub hiddentransfer {
    my $j;
    for($j=0;$j<=(M)-1;$j++) {
        $hout[$j]=(trans($hin[$j]));
    }
}
sub trans {
    my($val)=@_;
    my $trans;
    $trans=(2/(1+(exp(-$val))))-1;
    return $trans;
}
```

The hiddentransfer subroutine ensures that the scaled input of each hidden layer neuron is processed, while the trans function encodes the actual bipolar sigmoid. The hout values yielded by this code are the values that need to now be passed over the next layer of weighted connections to the output neuron. This process is almost identical to the process you used to transfer values from the input neurons to the hidden layer neurons, only these connections have a unique set of weights, and the output neuron has a unique bias. Thus, you can accomplish this data transfer with the code in the following outputinput subroutine:

```
sub outputinput {
    my $sum=0;
    my $j;
    for($j=0;$j<=(M)-1;$j++) {
        $sum=$sum+($hout[$j]*$oweight[$j]);
    }
    $oin=$obias+$sum;
}
```

As with the hidden layer neurons, the output neuron also possesses a transfer function. When considering a transfer function for your output neuron, it is important to consider the range of output values over which you want your network to make predictions, and you should scale the bipolar sigmoid accordingly. Alternately, you may also find that some networks will employ a more linear function as a transfer function to encompass a more unrestricted range of possible output values. Since you are just going to train the network to approximate the XOR, you can stick with the same bipolar sigmoid used previously and just consider a -1 as false and a 1 as true. Since you are choosing to use the same transfer function, the only code you need to add is code that will pass your output neuron's scaled input into this transfer function, as demonstrated in the following outputtransfer subroutine:

```
sub outputtransfer {
    $oout=trans($oin);
}
```

At this point, the architecture of the neural network is laid out, but it still lacks the capability to learn. You need to develop a method of adjusting the weights and biases so that over time the neural network will be able to accurately predict disease based on input variables. The way you accomplish this is through a process known as *back-propagation* of error, which utilizes a gradient-descent algorithm that seeks to minimize the error of the values that are outputted from the neural network.

The first step in this process is to take output computed by the neural network for a given pattern and compare it to a corresponding target value. Target values are known outcomes for given patterns, and they are used as part of the training process so that the network can learn what patterns can be associated with what output values. An error information term (*delta*) is then calculated by multiplying the difference between these two terms by the derivative of the activation function.

$$\delta = \frac{1}{2}(1 + trans(oin))(1 - trans(oin) * (t \arg val - oout))$$

This error term is then used to compute a weight adjustment term as well as a bias adjustment term. The computation of these terms, however, also requires two additional terms to be taken into account. One term is the learning rate (*alpha*), which works to control how big a weight/bias adjustment step can be made in a single training iteration. The smaller the value of alpha, the longer a network will take to train. However, if alpha is too large, the network may never reach a reasonable solution to the problem, since the large step size will keep making the network step over the set weights and biases where the error is minimized.

The second value is that of mu, or the momentum term. Momentum is an addition to the weight adjustment equation, which enables the weight change to occur in a direction that is dictated not only by the current gradient step but also by the previous one. This generally has the advantage of improving training time by allowing the network to find a reasonable solution in fewer training iterations. The weight and bias update equations, including the momentum terms, are as follows:

$$w_{jk}(t+1) = w_{jk}(t) + \alpha\delta * hout + \mu(w_{jk}(t) - w_{jk}(t-1))$$

$$bias_k(t+1) = bias_k(t) + \alpha\delta + \mu(bias_k(t) - bias_k(t-1))$$

Here, *t* represents the current set of weights/biases, *t-1* the previous set, and *t+1* the new set being calculated. To employ these methods within the program code, call the updatehidden subroutine:

```
sub updatehidden {
    my($i,$j,$k);
    my $deltatemp;
    for($j=0;$j<=(M)-1;$j++) {
        $hdelta=$odelta*$oweight[$j]*dtrans($hin[$j]);
        for($i=0;$i<=(N)-1;$i++) {
            $dhweight[$i][$j]=(alpha*$hdelta*$X[$i])+
                            (mu*($hweight[$i][$j]-$hweightold[$i][$j]));
            $hweightold[$i][$j]=$hweight[$i][$j];
            $hweight[$i][$j]=$hweight[$i][$j]+$dhweight[$i][$j];
        }
        $dhbias[$j]=(alpha*$hdelta)+(mu*($hbias[$j]-$hbiasold[$j]));
        $hbiasold[$j]=$hbias[$j];
        $hbias[$j]=$hbias[$j]+$dhbias[$j];
    }
}
```

This subroutine takes care of back-propagating the error to the interconnections present between the output and hidden layer neurons, but you still need a procedure to do the same for the interconnections between the hidden layer and the input neurons. The procedure for updating the weights is similar to that used for the weights of the connections between the output and hidden layers, with the difference being that there are no target values you can use to calculate the error of each neuron. Instead, you can calculate the error term of each hidden layer neuron using the value of odelta multiplied by the weight of the connection between the current hidden layer neuron and the output neuron. This allows you to distribute the error of the output unit back to all units within the hidden layer. From this point onward, the procedure is the same as previously; you can find the code to accomplish in the updateout subroutine:

```
sub updateout {
    my($i)=@_;
    my $j;
    $odelta=(dtrans($oin))*($targval[$i]-$oout);
    for($j=0;$j<=(M)-1;$j++) {
        $doweight[$j]=(alpha*($odelta)*$hout[$j])+
                    (mu*($oweight[$j]-$oweightold[$j]));
        $oweightold[$j]=$oweight[$j];
        $oweight[$j]=$oweight[$j]+$doweight[$j];
    }
```

```
        $dobias=((alpha)*($odelta))+((mu)*(($obias)-($obiasold)));
        $obiasold=$obias;
        $obias=$obias+$dobias;
}
```

At this stage, you have specified all the functionality behind the neural network and training algorithm. All that remains is for the remaining portion of the script to call the previous subroutines in the proper sequence. The following segment of code handles this:

```
@X1=([1,1],[-1,1],[1,-1],[-1,-1]); # input values
@targval=(-1,1,1,-1);
init();
my($i,$j);
my @outvals;
for($j-0;$j<1000;$j++) {
    for($i=0;$i<=3;$i++) {
        $X[0]=$X1[$i][0];
        $X[1]=$X1[$i][1];
        hiddeninput();
        hiddentransfer();
        outputinput();
        outputtransfer();
        $outvals[$i]=$oout;
        updateout($i);
        updatehidden();
    }
print STDOUT $outvals[0]," ",$outvals[1]," ",$outvals[2]," ",$outvals[3],"\n";
}
```

First, you call the previously coded init subroutine to lay out the architecture of the neural network as well as randomly initialize the weights and biases of the network. Next, you come to a nested loop structure in which the outer loop controls the maximal number of training iterations. The inner loop is what controls the actual training process. A training set input pattern is transferred from the X1 array to the input neurons. These input neuron values are then used to calculate the input into each hidden layer neuron via the hiddeninput subroutine. The hiddentransfer function then calculates the outputs of the hidden layer neurons, and the outputinput subroutine utilizes these values to determine the value that will be input into the output neuron. The outputtransfer subroutine then calculates the value output from the neural network.

Of course, given random initialization of weights and biases, the initial output value is likely far from the actual target value. Thus, you will call the updateout and updatehidden subroutine to update the weights and biases between the output and hidden layer and between the hidden layer and input layer, respectively. At this point, the next training pattern is transferred to the input neurons from X1, and the process is repeated. Once all four training patterns have been used, the first training iteration (or *epoch*) is complete, and the next epoch can begin. Training will continue until the value of $j reaches its specified cutoff. After each training iteration, the output values for each pattern are printed to STDOUT. As you can see, with successive training iteration the prediction begins to asymptotically approach the target values.

In a more real-world scenario (that is, more complex input patterns), it is possible that the first training attempt fails to ever reasonably approximate the output values for the given input patterns. Thus, the training process will often involve the adjustment of several parameters. The first two parameters you could consider adjusting are the learning rate and the momentum term. Since these values control the degree of weight adjustment with each training step, an inappropriate value could cause the training algorithm to either be unable to converge upon a solution in the number of iterations specified or be unable to converge at all.

The second parameter you could consider adjusting is the number of training epochs, since it is possible that the number of iterations allotted was insufficient for the network to converge upon a solution.

The remaining parameter you could consider adjusting is the number of hidden layer neurons, since the more hidden layer neurons within the network, the more sophisticated the internal representations of the network can become, allowing for more complex patterns to be mastered. However, you want to avoid using more input neurons than needed, since having too many input neurons helps to promote a condition known as *overtraining*.

Overtraining is problematic because an overtrained neural network will generally be able to output highly accurate values for the training set input patterns, but it loses the ability to predict novel patterns. In other words, the network is able to create accurate predictions only for training set patterns. Losing the ability to deal with novel patterns greatly diminishes the usefulness of neural networks since this ability is considered one of the principal strengths of neural networks.

Luckily, you can easily test for overtraining by using a set of validation data. Validation data is similar to training data in that you are aware of what the output should be for each input pattern in the set. However, the members of the validation set should not be repeats of patterns contained in the training set. A validation set is basically a set of known unknowns, in that the patterns are novel to the neural network but you know what the answers should be so you can accurately assess the performance of the network. The validation set can then be input into the neural network and the predicted results compared to the expected results. If the results match to within a predetermined degree of accuracy (for example, 90 percent), you can consider the neural network properly trained and use it to make predictions for true unknowns (that is, patterns that neither you nor the neural network have seen before). However, if the network fails to predict the validation set to within the specified degree of accuracy, you can assume that the network has been overtrained and discard it. You can then train and validate a new network and can repeat the process until you achieve a network that successfully passes validation.

Tip Production-scale neural networks will likely also involve more sophisticated training and initialization methods, since completely random initialization and the generic back-propagation algorithm can require copious amounts of time and data to train all but the simplest of neural networks. For those interested in learning more about neural networks and more modern network implementations, the following resources are recommended: *Neural Networks for Pattern Recognition* (Oxford University Press, 1995) by Christopher M. Bishop; *Fundamentals of Neural Networks* (Prentice Hall, 1994) by Laurene V. Fausett; *Neural Smithing: Supervised Learning in Feedforward Artificial Neural Networks* (MIT Press, 1999) by Russell D. Reed and Robert J. Marks II.

Summary

Within this chapter, I gave you an overview of data mining and the various types of descriptive and predictive data modeling tasks in order to give you some perspective as to how you can put parsed or extracted data to work for you. I also covered several Perl modules that you may find beneficial when programming data mining routines. However, it is notable that the field of data mining is still in a developmental stage, and many areas of data mining exist for which applicable Perl utilities have not yet been developed. Finally, the chapter briefly introduced machine learning via a feed-forward neural network that was trained to solve the XOR problem. Although the XOR example is a far cry from a modern data mining neural network, the example illustrates the basic principles of machine learning.

This chapter concludes the *Pro Perl Parsing* book, but I hope you view it not as an ending but rather as a step toward gaining the skills necessary to successfully navigate the momentous volumes of data being generated in this information age. Happy hacking.

Index